The Pastor-Congregation Duet

❧ Gary Harder ❧

Audry, special friend -
I hope you enjoy
the book

Gary Harder

 FriesenPress

Suite 300 - 990 Fort St
Victoria, BC, V8V 3K2
Canada

www.friesenpress.com

ISBN

978-1-5255-3020-3 (Hardcover)
978-1-5255-3021-0 (Paperback)
978-1-5255-3022-7 (eBook)

1. RELIGION, CHRISTIANITY, MENNONITE

Distributed to the trade by The Ingram Book Company

The Pastor-Congregation Duet

TABLE OF CONTENTS

Foreword

by Carol Penner

I first heard about Gary Harder forty years ago. One of my good friends was doing a pastoral internship at his congregation in Edmonton. I didn't meet Gary then but heard what a great mentor he was. I saw my friend's calling to ministry confirmed and clarified because of the time spent under his supervision.

A few years later I was in doctoral studies along with his wife, Lydia. From her I heard about their partnership in life, and I could see his unwavering support for her development as a scholar.

When I became a minister and crossed paths personally with Gary, I started to value him as a wise colleague. At conferences and meetings, I noticed how carefully people listened when Gary talked. He was not a talkative person, but when he spoke there was attention and respect in the room.

Gary's first book, *Dancing through Thistles in Bare Feet*, was everything I expected, a distillation of insights from long and fruitful years of ministry. Since first reading it, I've returned numerous times, photocopying chapters to share with colleagues and students. I was thrilled to hear that Gary was writing a new book and honoured to be asked to write a foreword.

The Pastor-Congregation Duet resonated with me deeply and had me nodding along. While the book is rooted in the particularities of Gary's ministry in specific locations, the descriptions of the mundane and exhilarating parts of ministry rang true for me, as they will for anyone who has worked in church ministry. The book is permeated with Gary's deep love for God and the congregations he served, and with their love for him. At the same time, Gary doesn't take himself too seriously. His self-deprecatory humour seasons every chapter.

Reading this book feels like sitting down for a heart-to-heart talk with a good friend as he shares about his lifelong calling. Anyone with a love for the church will enjoy this book. Sunday school teachers and worship leaders will find Gary's use of the Bible insightful. I was glad he included a selection of sermons and readings and prayers that he wrote over the years, because worship is central to ministry. These examples give us an insight into Gary's approach through the way he uses Scripture to reach his congregation.

Another thing that stands out is how often Gary talks about listening carefully to his congregation. It is one of his strongest gifts. I remember turning to Gary for advice about managing a challenging supervisory situation. He listened attentively, asking a few clarifying questions to help me get to the heart of my discomfort. He commiserated with me and shared a few wise words. Mostly he helped by allowing me to tell the story, then assuring me that I was exactly the right person to be in that role. In this book you will find many examples of how listening to people and affirming them are an important part of caregiving.

As a professor, I teach students who are just beginning the journey toward church ministry. They will read books that teach and explore specific skills. By contrast, Gary's book, written at the end of a professional pastoral ministry, has a retrospective feel: "What was this all about?" "What stands out?" It too will be valuable assigned reading for my students, because it shows how a calling to ministry is lived out across the years in one pastor's life. It is a faithful story that doesn't edit out the hard bits. We hear how the work is a calling and how much Gary loved it, even as it sometimes broke his heart.

This is a book about ministry that has me humming along. I am glad you are reading it.

Carol Penner

Acknowledgements and Permissions

Writing a book is in one sense a solitary, lonely enterprise, sitting at a typewriter trying to find words to express what is in the writer's head and heart. But so many of the words in this book, often told in story form, brought images of people and communities to mind; people and communities I care very deeply about. Loneliness evaporated. A deep sense of gratitude accompanied me throughout the writing. Gratitude to God for my calling to be a pastor. Gratitude to all the churches that invited me to be their pastor. Gratitude to the countless people who opened their lives to me in deep ways. Gratitude to the many colleagues, from a number of denominational traditions, who engaged me in robust dialogue.

I have been deeply shaped by the schools I have graduated from: Canadian Mennonite Bible College, Goshen College, Associated Mennonite Biblical Seminaries (Master of Divinity) and St. Stephen's College (Doctor of Ministry). Each of them contributed rather profoundly to my pastoral journey.

More particularly, I owe thanks to those who contributed directly to the writing of this book. I start with family. My wife, Lydia, not only supported and encouraged me during the times when words were extremely hard to come by, but so often helped reshape an impasse into a new direction. My children, Mark, Kendall, and Kristen, brought reality and insight into life issues and faith issues over many years of lively debates in the family circle.

Thanks also to Hugo and Doreen Neufeld, who read some of these chapters, and offered helpful suggestions. Likewise, Doreen

Martens read parts of the manuscript and helped reshape them. A very special thanks to Maureen Epp, who was my editor and did an amazing job polishing my quirky writing style.

This book includes many stories. The nature of story-telling is that the story-teller shapes the narrative out of memory – a memory that may be flawed. The people about whom the story is told may have a different memory of its unfolding. I beg forbearance if my telling cannot always be factually verified. And I thank those people who gave permission for their stories to be told.

The centre of these stories are the congregations I served. I have a deep appreciation and love for each of them. I recognize their vulnerability in this story-telling. They too may wish to challenge my memory.

Thank you also to the following publishers who first of all published the articles I included in my "Intervals" and then gave permission for them to be included in this book.

"Congregational Singing as a Pastor Sees It," in Bernie Neufeld, editor, *Music in Worship: A Mennonite Perspective* (Scottdale, PA, and Waterloo, ON: Herald Press/MennoMedia, 1998).

"The Morning after a Sign," *The Mennonite*, Dec. 18, 1984.

"A Life Too Brief: A Memorial Meditation for Adam Daniel Shantz," *Vision: A Journal for Church and Theology* 4, no. 1 (Spring 2003).

Unless otherwise noted, all passages quoted from the Bible are taken from the NSRV (New Revised Standard Version).

PRELUDE

I am now one of them. A retired pastor, that is. Most other workers just retire from their jobs and stay in their community (unless they relocate to warmer climes, of course). And if they are church people, they stay in their home church. Retired pastors have more of a problem. In fact, they are the problem. If they stay in the church where they were pastor, they may interfere with how the congregation bonds with the new pastor. If they go elsewhere, they tend to leave ghosts behind anyway. Sometimes the congregation over-idealizes them, overlooking the old flaws that used to be so annoying and not seeing the new wrinkles and age deterioration that now beset them. Others who felt differently can now dredge up all the old annoyances and inadequacies of their finally departed pastor, and with these litanies poison the process of hiring a new pastor.

And so I really am a problem. And I have a problem. Actually, we have a problem. My wife, Lydia, and I share this space. At this stage in life, fully retired and aging (not always gracefully), we particularly need spiritual nurture, and we especially need a caring congregation and community. What are we supposed to do? Do we stay with our "old" congregation, where our hearts are, and risk messing things up there? Or do we look for a new congregation and try to grow new hearts there?

The church also faces a problem when a pastor retires. The church and the pastor have been in an intense partnership. If the pastor was well loved, the church may struggle to let go of that relationship and what it valued about that pastor while trying to embrace a future with a new leader. If the ending of that ministry was not a happy one, there will be many emotional dynamics to process before the church is ready to move into the next pastoral relationship.

I have been a pastor now for over fifty years – make that a fully retired pastor as of several years ago. I began my pastoral ministry in July 1965 as a far-too-young and inexperienced twenty-three-year-old, and eased into full retirement in February 2015. No more big responsibilities. No more meetings. No more crisis calls in the middle of the night. No more overloaded schedules. No more dealing with difficult people. No more waking up Sunday morning realizing the prepared sermon is probably a dud.

More free time. More golfing (this dream is still far from reality). More sleeping in (but try as I might, I can't turn off my inner alarm clock). More time for travel (if only we could agree on the destination and mode). More leisure time for reading, for daytime coffee with friends, for watching the Toronto Blue Jays, for gardening, for …

But am I still a pastor? Does God's calling to be a pastor end suddenly with retirement? Is that part of who I am (was?), so deeply ingrained in my identity, now excised? I ponder these things as I look back on a calling I have loved and a retirement I am enjoying. I do serve as a guest preacher occasionally – mostly in other churches. I have officiated at several weddings within the last year. I continue to mentor several younger pastors. There are workshops coming up in other churches. Lydia and I have stated that we are ready to take on assignments as long as there is no longer-term responsibility connected to them. But these one-off engagements do not help answer the question: How do I define myself now that I am retired?

I have been a pastor for most of my lifetime. I know that my personal identity has been profoundly shaped by my vocation and my calling. But I have always insisted, at least to myself, that being a pastor is not the centre of who I am, and is not the sole dimension of my identity. I am who I am apart from the vocational hat that I wear. I have said, at least to myself, that I could lay aside the pastoral side of my identity and still have a solid core left. I have said that being me, being a husband and father and grandfather and family man, being a people person, an outdoors lover, a bumbling athlete and sports enthusiast, a follower of Jesus, are all dearer to my heart than what I do for a living.

That should make my retirement easier, shouldn't it? But the reality is that I have loved my vocation. I have deeply valued my calling. Not all the time, of course. There certainly have been situations, experiences, crises, difficult people, challenges, and even routines that have stolen my joy and my sleep and have filled my soul with dread.

And yet I fully embraced my calling – yes, calling. Being a pastor was always more than a job. As slow as I was to hear this call, as startled as I was to have my other plans for my life abruptly changed, I retired knowing that nothing else could have given me the joy and satisfaction that I experienced being a pastor. I know that there is now a big hole in my being and in my life, one that can't be filled with hobbies and trivial pursuits.

I did not rush to retirement feeling burnt out, disillusioned, resentful, exhausted, or even relieved. It simply felt as if God was inviting me to a new phase of life. God in fact invited Lydia and me to ease into retirement by opening the possibility of working together as part-time interim pastors for two years in each of three separate congregations. And again, we thoroughly enjoyed this work and came to love these congregations, as challenging as these assignments were.

Mostly I enter full retirement now with a deep sense of gratitude for my calling. And with this comes a reflective mode. What was it that sustained me, gave me joy through some of the very deep challenges of my ministry? How did these fifty years go by so quickly?

The heart of what kept me going and gave me such joy, I think, was what I am calling the "congregation-pastor duet."

This duet is a very complex one, with the music ever changing. I had so much to learn about the dynamics and moods and challenges of that singing. In the end, it still comes down to each partner trusting the other to stay in harmony, even when they hit sour notes along the way, and even when they argue over which key to sing in. If you don't trust your partner you can't harmonize with them, and the song will end. And so, the title of this book: *The Pastor-Congregation Duet*.

I write these stories and reflections hoping that pastors, church leaders, and congregational lay members alike will be prompted to enter their own reflections on what makes for a healthy relationship between congregation and pastor. Ministry always takes place among people, whether this happens within the congregation, or among the general public, or just through private and personal encounters. Surely the effectiveness of any ministry, and even the health of any congregation, is impacted by the kind of relationship between leaders (in this case pastors) and the congregation.

And since I am now a lay person in my congregation (some would challenge whether a long-term pastor can ever be "just an ordinary lay person"), I can look at that relationship a bit more from the perspective of someone within the congregation who is not a leader. With this book I want to do the following:

1. Consider what was life-giving, sustaining, enjoyable in my pastoral journey. I am aware that not all my colleagues end their ministries on an upbeat note, and I can certainly understand the many reasons for a litany of lament for some endings. I will tell stories of my own turmoil and discouragement and brokenness, but even then, I was surprised that so often these experiences turned into reconciliations and healing that re-energized my ministry. But not always. Some messes stay messy. And yet I do feel positive. I do feel blessed. I do celebrate a calling

I embraced. And so I want to explore what was so life-sustaining about it.

2. Reflect on and share stories about how I wrestled to understand pastoral leadership, and how I envision a healthy relationship between pastor and congregation. It was easier for me to understand and gain skill in fulfilling the specific tasks and responsibilities that were part of a pastor's mandate. But the bigger picture is pastoral leadership, a very complex notion to come to terms with, especially as our society, including the church, moved through dramatically changing world views. What congregations want and expect by way of leadership has changed significantly as society has moved from a pre-modern mindset to a modernity world view, and now to a post-modern way of looking at our context. Through this book I try to reflect on my own struggles with and growing understanding of what it means to be a pastoral leader.

3. Include, at key intervals, either a sermon I have preached or an article I have written. These interludes are chosen to illustrate what I have written in the sections in which they are placed. They provide a contextual setting for my pastoral journey. They reflect something of the relationship between congregation and pastor, which is the primary focus of this book. These interludes are part of the music created in the holy space of pastoral ministry.

The heart of any ministry is the relationship between pastor and congregation. This relationship is complicated by an Anabaptist understanding of church. The congregation is a priesthood of all believers, all of whom are invited to participate in building the church and working for God's Kingdom – that is, every member of the church is also a leader in one way or another. The pastor is not the big boss. But the church still needs overall leadership. For a congregation to thrive, the relationship between pastoral leadership and lay leadership needs a lot of attention and constant renewal. At its best, that relationship is like a growing covenant of mutuality, a relationship of deep respect, love, and accountability.

It is the pastor-congregation duet that exudes spiritual health or spiritual malaise in the community. The key to the health and well-being of both congregation and pastor is the integrity and harmony of their relationship – their joint music making. I believe it was the nature of the relationships I had with each of the congregations I served as pastor that sustained my enthusiasm for my calling – especially through times of conflict and challenge and discouragement.

My musical comfort zone is the Western classical tradition. I listen mostly to the music of the classical masters – especially Bach and Mozart and Schütz and Brahms. But I am intrigued by jazz, especially its improvisational nature. Most summers that I served at Toronto United Mennonite Church, we acknowledged the rather famous Beaches International Jazz Festival that took place in our area of the city. We would invite local jazz musicians to lead our music and tried to include more spontaneity in how the worship service developed. A few times I even tried to improvise in my sermon – using a few basic notes and melodies and seeing where that would lead me. I realized again that this is totally outside of my comfort zone.

The thing is, improvisation is key to pastoral ministry. There is something "jazzy" about being a pastor. As much as I like structure and routine and planning, the unexpected is almost the norm. People in crisis don't check a pastor's calendar before calling. Over the years I needed to learn to relax, and even to welcome, the improvisational nature of my calling. Now in retirement I can consider and explore the opportunities these improvisations provided for a fulfilling ministry. I cringe a bit at some of the sour notes I hit. I delight in the times when it seemed that God inspired the music making.

This book is partly a memoir. But I hope it will be read as more than that: my wish is that it will convey the music and the rhythms of a healthy pastor-congregational duet.

I feel incredibly grateful and blessed!

PART ONE
THE CONGREGATION AS DUET PARTNER

I begin my reflections on the pastor-congregation duet by exploring my experience in each church that invited me to be its pastor. Central to a healthy ministry and a healthy church is an honest, reciprocal, and supportive relationship between pastor and congregation. This kind of relationship creates a safe space for working through difficult issues, for meeting conflict in direct ways, and for challenging each other to grow toward God's future for all of us.

The reality is that congregation and pastor are bound together not only by their covenant of accountability and common faith but also by their common humanness. We are all followers of Jesus who take after the first disciples of Jesus, who so often misunderstood and even denied and betrayed him. Congregation and pastor often fail in following. We get into messy situations, we fail each other, we get angry at each other, we disappoint each other. And yet, by the grace of God, we can renew our covenant relationship, forgive each other, and cherish the gifts we offer each other.

Probably no one can survive for long in a hostile or indifferent work environment. I feel particularly fortunate and immensely grateful for each of the churches that have invited, and embraced, my ministry. Each of them offered me challenges and gifts that brought out the best in me, and extended grace and forgiveness when I fell short of my ministry potential. Each of them offered a ministry setting and atmosphere in which I could grow as a pastor and as a person. Each of them provided themes and steps for my retirement postlude. I do not take for granted how fortunate and blessed I have been by the churches that have welcomed – and sometimes endured – my ministry. Lydia and I both have warm feelings about each of these congregations, and we still have significant friendships in most of them.

I don't think any pastor can thrive, or even survive, in long-term ministry without being replenished by what the congregation offers. The pastor cannot only be in giving mode but must also be open to being in receiving mode. To be always the giver, always the strong one, always invulnerable would lead to an unbalanced and unhealthy relationship, with negative impacts on both pastor and congregation. To be in a receiving mode doesn't mean that we pastors are looking to meet our own deep needs through constant affirmation from the congregation. Rather, it means that we are open to a healthy reciprocal relationship.

At its best, the relationship between congregation and pastor is a covenant-like relationship. That is, it is a reciprocal relationship in which both parties are committed to nurturing and growing their common life together. Each is committed to being faithful to the other. Each helps the other fulfill their calling from God. Each feels pain when there is something broken or damaged or unfulfilled in their relationship. Each must establish the weekly habits that help the other grow and thrive. Together both parties put into place the structures that will nurture their joint ministry. The relationship is intended to be life-giving to both.

Each of the congregations where I have been pastor has enriched my life immensely by the gifts they offered me: the gifts of response, challenge, feedback, partnership, acceptance, and love. In each of them I felt that the congregation and I were partners in ministry, giving and receiving, nurturing and being nurtured, joining together in a covenant duet. As I reflect in this section on my relationship with each of these congregations, I especially want to name some of the gifts that nourished me and deepened my love for my calling to pastoral ministry.

1

Beginnings

Waters Mennonite Church

I was twenty-three years old and barely married when Lydia and I set off in our little Volkswagen "bug," travelling from Winnipeg to northern Ontario in July of 1965. It wasn't actually Waters Mennonite Church in Lively, Ontario (near Sudbury), that had invited me to be their pastor. Rather, the Missions Committee of our denomination, the Conference of Mennonites in Canada, with – I assume – the approval of the congregation, had called me, unseen and un-interviewed, to this ministry.

Here everything for me was new and exciting and terrifying. I was totally inexperienced and untrained. I had graduated from Canadian Mennonite Bible College with two degrees: a Bachelor of Christian Education, and a Diploma of Sacred Music. Neither prepared me to be a pastor.

The congregation itself was different from any church I had experienced. It had been started by several families of Swiss Mennonite background who had moved to that area specifically to do mission work. They weren't pastors, just zealous lay people eager to live out their faith. The church hadn't been able to get enough financial support from its denomination to sustain it during a building project, so it turned to our denominational body for support. By then the church had also drawn some community folk into its fellowship, people from various backgrounds, including non-church as well as from several different denominations and nationalities.

This small group of thirty to forty people was a genuine community church, something else that was new to me. Its members lived in the community, interacted with the community, and opened their doors and hearts to the community.

The church's key leaders were more conservative than was I and had a more evangelical theology. None of this seemed to matter. They simply loved us and embraced us, no matter that they found my preaching too academic and my pastoral care too naive. Maybe my age and inexperience mitigated my amateurism. "Hey," said a middle-aged couple, "why don't you kids come over for dinner after church." I wasn't offended at all that they called me, their pastor, a "kid." We had a fine time together over dinner.

It amazed me how open the people of this church were to inviting me into their lives at surprisingly deep levels. Floundering, inexperienced, and young I might be, but still they invited me to walk with them and pray with them through life situations that seemed overwhelming. And they offered Lydia and me friendship – friendship so deep that we still feel emotionally connected to that community fifty years later.

I did have one gift that Waters Mennonite Church particularly valued: music. This was not a traditional Mennonite congregation with a long heritage of singing hymns in strong four-part harmony. I started a choir. I offered sectional rehearsals so that people could learn their harmonic parts to simple hymns and Christmas carols. I gave conducting lessons to several young people, one of whom now leads a very fine community choir. Perhaps I won my way into their hearts through music. Come to think of it, when we attended the church's fiftieth anniversary celebrations several years ago, the individuals who shared memories of my two years there had more to say about my music gifts than about my preaching – or my pastoral care.

Some things one learns in a shocking and difficult way. We had been at the church only several weeks when it was time for the annual Daily Vacation Bible School that the church offered. Many of the children attending were from the community. I taught a group of close to a dozen adolescents. I felt confident. I had studied Bible and theology at a Bible college.

My lesson that day was on how we understand God. The text was the story of the prodigal son, the story of a loving and forgiving father. I launched out on my lesson: "God is like a father, a loving father-- " A fourteen-year-old girl from the community interrupted me. "Did you say God was like a father?" she asked, rather belligerently, I thought. "Yes," I responded, "God is like a father who --" I got no further. "If God is like a father, I hate him. I hate my father. I hate God."

The rest of that class was a total blur to me. We never did get to the prodigal son. I don't remember how I responded or how I continued the lesson, if I did at all. I had no way then of dealing with that scenario. Vaguely I was aware that something awful must have been perpetrated on that adolescent girl. In hindsight, it is clear to me that she was the victim of abuse by her father. But I had no way of dealing with it appropriately. Nothing in my experience or training had prepared me to hear that outburst. I am probably writing about it now because I still carry some guilt for my inaction at the time.

But sometimes intuition serves when experience isn't there. A Catholic woman from the community had begun attending some of the Bible studies led by a few women from the church. She and her family were still a part of the Catholic church in the community, but not very active. A family member, I think her father, had died, and they asked their priest to conduct the funeral and lead the graveside prayers. But apparently the family was not in the priest's good books. Somewhat reluctantly, he agreed to conduct the funeral in the church, which he performed very routinely, but then he didn't show up at the graveside to say the prayers there. In some distress, the woman asked me to pray and bless her father's return to the earth. I did my very first graveside, very spontaneously, and realized only later how significant this seemingly small thing was to her. And how hurtful it is for a priest or pastor to ignore the needs of a parishioner out of spite.

What do you do when you as a pastor face the prospect of being a midwife? A neighbourhood woman who attended the church had invited me over for coffee, conversation, and a request. She was getting close to the due date of her fifth child. Her husband often worked out of town, and should he be away when she went into labour, she would need a ride to the hospital in Sudbury. And since I lived close by, she asked if she could phone me to be her chauffeur. She also admitted that she usually had a very short labour and didn't always get to the hospital in time. "Are you ready to be a midwife?" she asked me jokingly. "Well," I responded, also in joking mode, "I have assisted in delivering calves on the farm." As it turned out her husband was out of town when she went into labour, she did call me, and I did race the twelve miles to Sudbury as fast as our small Volkswagen would go, praying all the way for the baby to have patience. We arrived just moments before the baby did.

Sudbury was a city built on mining, copper mining its main industry. A huge smokestack in Copper Cliff, a few miles east of the church, spewed innumerable poisons into the air. During a temperature inversion one day in August, our flowers, vegetables, and even the leaves on our trees dried up and died from the acids that seemed to singe even our lungs.

One day the union went on strike. A few people in our church were in management positions in the company, but more were labourers in the union. This strike was a very bitter and conflict-laden one. Some of the management folks (none from the church) were locked into the plant, couldn't get out, and couldn't get food brought in because of the union's blockade. Helicopters were called in to deliver food. Someone started shooting at the helicopters. No one was killed, but the atmosphere was caustic.

This bitter conflict in the community did not get carried over into the church, one of the many things that amazed me about this small congregation. I'm sure there were some tensions. But within the church, people still talked to each other and were decent to each other, no matter which side of the strike they were on. What I did become aware of – a rather shocking insertion of reality – was that within a few weeks of the strike, one family from the community whom I visited had essentially no food left in their fridge. After missing only one two-week paycheck, they no longer had the reserves to buy groceries. Despite having a relatively good mining job and owning their home, they lived on the edge of poverty.

One day, Lydia and I were invited into a rather unique evangelism opportunity. A young couple from the community had attended the church a few times but had recently been visited by a Jehovah's Witness pair doing door-to-door evangelism. The young couple were trying to decide whether to join the Jehovah's Witnesses or the Mennonites, and so they put us both to the test. They arranged a meeting with the six of us at our place. We each shared our perspectives on faith. Truth be told, we argued with each other. We must have had much to argue about because the time was approaching midnight, and it seemed the young couple was still no closer to a decision. At that point, I suggested we conclude the evening anyway, and end our discussion by praying together. The Witness couple said they could not do this: they could not pray together with unbelievers. As it turned out, this is what helped the couple from the community make their decision to become Christians and come to the Mennonite church. They wanted to pray together with us. They asked for baptism and joined the church.

The greatest challenge for me in those two years at Waters Mennonite was to try to grasp what it meant to be a pastoral leader. I understood, from my immersion in Anabaptism, that the pastor is not the big boss doing all the important things in a church. In the past I had reacted to some ministers who were too authoritarian and too controlling. I recognized that being a pastor is more than doing all the preaching and praying, administrating and leading, and visiting of the distressed. In this congregation, in fact, quite a few people could preach and teach and pray and lead a meeting. And everyone visited and cared for people who were distressed. But what then was the role of the pastor?

It was slowly becoming clear to me that being a pastor consisted of more than doing a certain number of tasks and being in charge of everything. The church did look to me for direction. Passively completing tasks as required was not yet leadership. Trying to understand what kind of leadership a church needs from a pastor was a long journey for me, a journey only begun at Waters Mennonite.

In part, I needed to discover what my unique gifts and joys and passions were, and then offer them. I needed to be aware which gifts I lacked and those I had not yet developed. I needed to recognize the things that did not bring me joy, no matter how hard I worked at them. Of course, every pastor, and probably everyone who has a job, will be required to do some things which are on that "I'm not very good at and don't enjoy at all" list.

Apparently one of the things that I was not good at was fishing and hunting, no matter how much I enjoyed being on a lake or in the bush. Fishing and hunting were important in that community. I was sometimes invited to come along. I was spectacularly unsuccessful. Ontario fish must be very discerning, because they just would not bite the hook of an Alberta lad. The youth group gave me a "fisherman's crying towel" as farewell gift.

It was in Sudbury that I first interacted with colleagues from a variety of denominations. The Sudbury Council of Churches held monthly meetings for clergy of all denominations, with no demarcation between more evangelical and more mainline clergy. I always enjoyed the discussions and the friendships that developed. And then they asked me to get involved in something no one else wanted to do. The Council of Churches offered a weekly, half-hour Sunday morning radio program entitled *Praise and Prayer*, which needed a new host. The format consisted of twenty minutes' worth of recorded music and ten minutes of speaking. I had foolishly talked about my love for music. Thus, I was the obvious candidate. During my last six months in the community I hosted this radio program.

There, at Waters Mennonite Church, I became more fully aware that I enjoyed music making, preaching, teaching, working with young people, and making pastoral visits. These parts of my ministry were affirmed. I wasn't so good at administration, at keeping good notes of things. I was afraid of conflict. And I had a passive streak that sometimes kept me from taking initiative when that was needed.

It was becoming clear to me that the relationship between pastor and church is a very intimate and mutual one. On the one hand, the people of Waters Mennonite had many gifts to offer. They did not desperately need a pastor. They were deeply involved in the community. They could quite easily keep the church going on their own. They were a generous, loving, accepting, giving group of people. They embraced me and loved me and affirmed me, despite my youth and inexperience and inadequacies.

But on the other hand, they too needed loving and affirmation and encouragement. They needed to hear and know that despite being a small church, located far from the rest of the Mennonite world and sometimes struggling to stay alive, they were being God's people there in Lively, Ontario, and they were being faithful to their calling.

I was still a long way from understanding what I was called by God to be as a pastoral leader, but I left Waters Mennonite feeling blessed, affirmed, loved, and encouraged to continue my pastoral journey. And still I was hesitant about my calling, not yet fully convinced that this was where God wanted me to be, or where I wanted to be for the long haul. But my experience there was enough to point me toward going to seminary. If I was going to be a pastor I certainly needed more education. And maybe going to seminary would clarify my calling.

I couldn't have begun the journey into my calling in a better place than at Waters Mennonite Church. I was learning the first few notes in a career-long ministry duet. Lydia and I had another reason to sing as we were leaving Sudbury. Our first child, a boy we named Mark, was born two weeks before we left. That congregation still claims him as their own native son.

Recently Waters Mennonite Church invited us to spend a weekend with them to help them process their future. Almost the whole church participated. The enthusiasm was contagious, and our love for that congregation was re-kindled.

Yellow Creek Mennonite Church

I went on to continue my studies, first a year at Goshen College, Indiana, to finish a recognized BA, and then at Associated Mennonite Biblical Seminaries (AMBS) in Elkhart, Indiana. During that time, I was a part-time assistant pastor at Yellow Creek Mennonite Church in Elkhart County. The church was made up of folks of Swiss Mennonite background who majored in hospitality and dinner invitations. They were also experiencing a major shift in their culture and traditions. Until then, all baptized women had worn white prayer caps to church. And Lydia, to fit in, also wore one, though this was new and strange to her. But some of the teenage girls were starting to rebel and challenged this practice, also challenging Lydia for accommodating to it.

A few things were new to us in that context. Many of the churches of the Mennonite Church denomination practised foot-washing before celebrating communion. Men would gather in one area of the church to wash each other's feet, as did women in another area of the church. I rather liked this witness to servanthood and humility. Later, when I suggested this to some of the General Conference Mennonite congregations that I was involved with, they were not very keen on the practice. We did get as far as handwashing.

Also new to me was the practice of offering the "brotherly/ sisterly kiss" to those who were baptized or were joining the church through transfer of membership. These deeply rooted and very meaningful liturgical expressions of community impressed me.

I was further impressed by the congregation's strong four-part hymn singing —usually a cappella. These folks did not want any instruments in church. They wanted only the pure human voice in offering their praises to God. It was during that time that our seminary, by then a joint venture of the Mennonite Church and General Conference denominations, was struggling with deciding whether or not instruments could be used in its worship. Someone had offered to donate funds to buy a small pipe organ for the seminary chapel. This stirred up a huge controversy. What impressed me during this debate was how respectful and honest the dialogue was between our two Mennonite traditions. We held a number of student forums and community meetings. Eventually the pipe organ was brought in, but with rather clear limitations on its use. Those of the Mennonite Church tradition acknowledged that they were in a transition time about the use of instruments in worship, and that the dialogue at the seminary was one the wider denomination was also beginning. Yellow Creek Mennonite Church was also in transition on this issue. Meanwhile, I quite enjoyed the exposure to unaccompanied congregational singing.

The more rural aspect of this church made me feel at home. I was still not urbanized. I enjoyed dinner invitations from farm families who proudly showed us their dairy production, their apple orchards, their farm machinery, their generations-long development of the home farm. We even spent a few days each fall picking apples.

I did not enjoy one typical form of employment in that church community. Quite a few of the men were employed in one of the dozens of trailer factories in the Elkhart area. I too needed a summer job, so a seminary friend and I were hired by a nearby trailer factory to stand in an assembly line and screw a piece of metal moulding into place as each gradually forming trailer moved relentlessly past us. While my friend thrived in this "easy" job, I became depressed. For the first and only time in my life, I couldn't sleep well. I dreaded each new morning. Never again would I want to come close to an assembly line. I had both admiration and sympathy for the men of the church who made a good living doing what I could not.

Overall, my experience at Yellow Creek Mennonite Church was a very positive one. Hospitality and generosity oozed from this church. When I finished my two-year, very part-time role as assistant pastor, Lydia and I were surprised by a goodwill offering the congregation held for us, gifting us with some hundreds of dollars we had not expected. This was a healthy growing and learning environment for us. In the meantime, I had thoroughly enjoyed the rigorous academic studies at seminary. And yet I was still unsettled about my true calling.

Decision Making Time

It was the summer of 1969. I had completed one very satisfying year of seminary, but despite enjoying my studies I still struggled with indecision. Maybe my calling was to make music – I loved conducting choirs. I knew I had to come to terms with my ambivalence. The tipping point came in a rather mystifying way.

That summer, the two Mennonite Bible colleges in Winnipeg (Canadian Mennonite Bible College and Mennonite Brethren

Bible College) were hosting a month-long music school for Mennonite musicians from across Canada. They had invited leading choral and vocal resource people from Germany as guest experts. I knew I had to attend, though rationally this made little sense. I had to cut short a summer ministry placement in Leamington, Ontario. The expense of it all was a bit daunting.

I went anyway. That month was all I could have dreamed of. I loved the intense music making. I even had the privilege of being selected to conduct a choral piece at our closing concert.

And yet, in the car, travelling back to Elkhart, I knew within me that my calling from God was to be a pastor, not a professional musician. It wasn't a rational knowing. But it was totally clear to me. It still feels like a mystery that I could be so satisfied and sated with music for a month, and then know deep within me that God was calling me to be a pastor, not a musician, and that I was fully content with that knowing.

Valleyview Mennonite Church

I was not yet fully content with my preparation for my calling. I had thrived in the academic milieu of the biblical and theological and Anabaptist studies in the seminary world. But I knew this wasn't enough. And I felt that the seminary's practical "work of the church" courses weren't fully meeting my needs. At that time, the seminary specialized more in academics than in preparing potential pastors for the applied side of their work. When the opportunity came to spend a year at Valleyview Mennonite Church in London, Ontario, in supervised clinical pastoral education, I jumped at the chance. This would help me prepare more fully for a life of pastoral ministry. I did not anticipate that this internship would push me into emotional fatigue and even into marriage crisis.

I assumed that the program offered what I most needed – hands-on training in ministry tasks. After all, said the brochure, I would spend time in an impressive variety of ministry settings: a home for troubled adolescents, a recovery program for alcoholics, a nursing home, and significant time in chaplaincy training at the London Psychiatric Hospital, where I would receive a certificate in supervised clinical education. In addition, I would preach, teach, and provide pastoral care at Valleyview church. All under supervision. I was confident I would learn all the skills I needed to be an effective pastor.

What I hadn't understood or anticipated was that my biggest need was not skills development as much as it was emotional development. I wasn't in touch enough with my emotional makeup. My supervisors, both wise and confronting, probed my inner life. They examined my inner emotional passivity. They pointed to my hidden angers. As I wrote in my earlier book, "We happily moved to London for the year – and into crisis. I had no idea that the path to learning pastoral 'skills' would be a train track running through my guts. My supervisors and peers kept probing my emotions, not my abilities."[1] I became emotionally exhausted. Vaguely I realized that my marriage was suffering. I just wasn't emotionally available on a deep enough level. Lydia and I sought much-needed help and discovered new emotional intimacies in the process.

This year-long internship opened me up to a lifelong journey toward greater emotional wholeness, with huge implications for both my marriage and my career. One moment of significant insight in this regard stands out for me – even though this event happened away from my supervisors and peers. We were relaxing after supper when a stranger knocked on the door. He said he was representing an educational company doing research on educational practices. So, being very supportive of education

---

1 *Dancing through Thistles in Bare Feet: A Pastoral Journey* (Scottdale, PA, and Waterloo, ON: Herald Press, 2008), p. 107.

and thus of research on it, we invited him in to hear him out. It turned out he was an encyclopedia salesman. His opening pitch was only a way to get in the door.

And I got angry, very angry. But I also recalled the many ways my supervisors had made me aware of my emotional responses, including the way I processed anger. I now recognized that I tended to either withdraw into sullen silence or risk exploding when I got angry. In fact, I usually denied my anger and buried it. This time, I determined to move outside of my comfort zone. I responded – rather calmly, I thought – by expressing how I felt about the way the salesman had taken us into confidence under false pretenses. "I feel very angry with you for pretending to be a researcher when your real purpose was to sell us an encyclo-pedia. I want you to know that I am feeling angry."

To my amazement, the salesman acknowledged that he often used this pitch, usually successfully. And then he said, "I have never had someone express anger to me in such a direct and non-threatening way. Can I tell you my story and the struggles I'm having with my life?" What followed was a deep pasto-ral encounter as he poured out his story to us – all because I expressed my anger, but apparently in a way that made it safe for him to respond. I pondered that moment for weeks.

I feel immensely grateful for the Valleyview congregation, the clinical pastoral education program, and its supervisors for naming my emotional reticence and challenging me to a greater wholeness of personhood and ministry. I was slowly learning to sing in harmony with both my feelings and my responsibilities. And today I delight in the fact that our son Kendall, two years old then, has been co-pastor together with his wife, Charleen, of that same Valleyview Mennonite Church for the past ten years.

2

First Mennonite Church

Fast-forward to November 1971. My time in London had been invaluable, exactly what I needed. Now I was back in Elkhart to finish the last semester in my seminary program. I was ready to be called to be a pastor somewhere. But no call had come. I was starting to feel uneasy, anxious, and afraid. Would nothing come?

Finally, at what seemed to me the last minute, a letter arrived inviting me to be a candidate for pastor at First Mennonite Church in Edmonton, Alberta – my home province. I was eager to respond. A weekend visit was arranged. A bonus of that trip was a stopover in Winnipeg for some hours, giving me time to visit my brother and family. We Harders are punctual people, and so we carefully allowed plenty of time to get back to the airport. But then an unexpected blizzard hit. The streets grew clogged and icy. We hadn't started for the airport in time. Traffic was almost stopped in its place. In desperation, I jumped out of the car and guided my brother around stuck cars, onto sidewalks, anything to get us moving again. We arrived at the airport in a panic, twenty minutes after my flight was scheduled to leave. But the plane, too, was delayed a bit. I ran to the gate just as the door was closing, got on, and made it to Edmonton. And received an invitation to be pastor of First Mennonite Church. The starting date was February 1, 1972.

We moved to Edmonton with all our earthly goods. They fit into a small Ford car pulling a small two-wheel trailer. Eight years of marriage had produced two children but no furniture

– only books and papers and mostly home-sewn clothes. This made that move much easier than subsequent moves.

First Mennonite Church had many members who were highly educated professionals. These included university professors, high-level administrators, and educators. There were also tradespeople and office workers. The ethos of the congregation placed a very high value on education and professionalism. There was nothing its members couldn't organize and no project they couldn't see through to completion. The congregation had embraced the values of the modernity mindset, which had only recently entered the Mennonite church world. Robert's Rules of Order prevailed in all decision making.

And I thrived in that milieu. I too had embraced modernity in the way I interpreted Scripture and in how I liked to organize my life and my work. In preparation for preaching I did thorough historical-critical biblical work – which sometimes baffled some folks in the congregation. I knew I had to lighten up a bit and learn to communicate better. That, I hoped, would still come.

There was an undercurrent of anxiety in the congregation. The church had released its last pastor, and a residue of unhappiness and dissatisfaction lingered around this. As a result, the congregation was probably overly nice to me to make sure the same thing wouldn't happen again. But this also made it hard to get at the root causes of the conflict with the previous pastor. I don't think I was very helpful in resolving these issues. Part of the reason was that I was still not that comfortable dealing with conflict, and wasn't eager to raise issues that brought conflict into the open.

I was comfortable with conflicting ideas – with intellectual conflict. These were for the most part educated people who easily processed new ideas and new interpretations of difficult biblical passages. But I had much to learn about dealing with more substantive conflict. That would be a career-long journey.

There was one area where the congregation and I were a particularly good match. It needed a choir conductor, and I loved conducting choir. For most of the time that I was at First Mennonite, I was both pastor and choir conductor. It was probably easier for me to express the emotional, artistic, intuitive, and spiritual side of myself openly through music making than in any other way – at least at first. In addition, while candidating at First Mennonite, I had made it clear that I would preach only twice a month. I felt very strongly that the church needed to hear the voice of its lay people in preaching, and lay people needed to be challenged to express their faith publicly. It was easier for church members to accept this if they saw me busy conducting the choir the other two Sundays of the month.

I was gradually becoming more confident in fulfilling some of the tasks of ministry. I received positive feedback for my public ministry in preaching, worship leading, and especially for officiating at weddings. I increasingly enjoyed providing pastoral care. But I wasn't always clear within myself what it meant to be a leader in a church full of leaders.

One day one of the church members, a cousin of mine and a university professor, challenged me on this: "Gary, we are looking for more leadership from you. You are doing your tasks very well. We all affirm you for that and like you. But we don't always get the leadership we need from you. Sometimes you are too quiet and too passive when you could be helping us more to face the future."

This was much more a challenge than it was criticism. My cousin and I had a very good relationship with each other. And as much as I initially felt defensive, I also knew that I needed to take him seriously. What did it mean to be a pastoral leader who offered the congregation more than the expected pastoral tasks, done well? I did tend toward being a bit passive-aggressive in church board meetings. I could be silent when I might offer a helpful voice. And sometimes I spoke too strongly about things that weren't very important. I wasn't finished yet with the inner journey I had begun in London.

A Quick, Painful Lesson in Leadership

My cousin wanted more leadership from me. But my first attempt at leading a significant change in the church did not go very well. I had not yet learned how to process change organizationally.

First Mennonite Church had bought an older Lutheran church building. The sanctuary was long and narrow, and to me it felt as if the people sitting in the back pews were a long way from the pulpit. This didn't seem to reflect the kind of community and peoplehood vision that was core to the Anabaptist vision I was so enamoured with. So, within a few months of arriving in Edmonton I proposed an experiment.

I enthusiastically suggested that we rearrange the sanctuary. Why not move the pulpit to one side of the sanctuary, and arrange the pews in a semicircle around it? That way everyone would be much closer to the pulpit, and we would really feel like a worshipping community. I thought I was quite persuasive in making this proposal to church council. And church council, after some discussion, agreed with me – I thought. Council members assented to a three-month trial of this new arrangement. They may not have considered this idea as brilliant as I did, but neither did they want to offend their brand-new pastor coming straight out of seminary. And they were still carrying the pain of how their relationship with their last pastor had ended.

They moved the worship centre the way I had proposed. I really liked it. I saw the experiment as a great success. Everyone was much closer to the pulpit, and much closer together – a real community at worship.

I didn't hear much response. On the Tuesday after the three-month trial period was over, I came to my office in good spirits

– and experienced a huge shock. The pews were back in their original place. Not a word had been said. There had been no feedback, no discussion, no processing of this experiment. Not only were the pews now back "where they belonged," but they had been screwed down, never to be moved again.

By now it's just a funny story. But then the shock of it all told me that I still had a great deal to learn about how to lead change. I had not processed my plan well – I had persuaded the church council to do it, but not the whole congregation. Most of the church had no idea why I wanted to rearrange the sanctuary. I hadn't communicated my vision.

But the church also was somewhat dysfunctional in how it processed things. I wasn't aware of any discussion at all about where this experiment should go. Both pastor and congregation had much to learn about working together and having healthy dialogue around change.

Yes, for a while after that I was too much of a reluctant leader.

The Challenge of Shifting World Views

A huge challenge for leadership during the early 1970s was how the modernity mindset we were all just beginning to embrace was turning notions of leadership in general, and pastoral leadership in particular, upside down. Neither I nor the congregation of First Mennonite had even begun to sort this out. The very high sense of "office," and with it, the power that our tradition had given to pastors and especially to bishops (*Ältesters*) was being called into question. The modern world view was much more concerned with function than with office. Now the pastor was an employee of the congregation, charged with the duties and tasks of ministry but not always feeling empowered to give leadership. Performance evaluations for pastors were becoming routine, but these were very functional evaluations. How well did the pastor score on the tasks being done? "Give a number between 1 and 10 to indicate how well you think the pastor is doing in each assigned task." How could the pastor improve and do a better job of these tasks? Often, instead of affirming the highly rated tasks, the evaluation committee saw it as their role to challenge the pastor to improve the score on poorly rated tasks.

My ordination, shortly after arriving in Edmonton, reflected this changing ethos. Even ten years earlier, ordination in the Mennonite tradition had been a huge event, attended by church dignitaries from far and wide and celebrated as a major festival. My ordination, in contrast, was a rather small, quiet in-house affair, which suited both me and the congregation quite well. I wasn't even interviewed or processed in any way by the wider church. My mother came from British Columbia for my ordination, as did an uncle of mine, an *Ältester* from Didsbury, Alberta. Our Alberta-Saskatchewan conference pastor officiated the ordination. But I do not recall many other guests. In essence, ordination had now become a licence to perform the official tasks of ministry, conducted more as a routine than as a holy investiture.

It is no wonder that I — and the church — was struggling to understand what pastoral leadership was all about. My cousin was spot-on in naming that.

The other aspect that I didn't yet understand was how to look at the church as a system rather than only as individuals who needed pastoral and spiritual care. And yet I knew that "systems theory" was beginning to be applied to families in trouble, especially when a family member was acting out. We were beginning to look at the family as a whole and not isolate the troublemaker from the larger family system. We were beginning to look at what was dysfunctional and what was healthy in the whole family, and to consider an individual's acting out in that context.

So why not look at the congregation as a system, rather than only as a collection of lay people? Perhaps the pastor could play an important role by helping the congregation to see what was healthy and what was unhealthy in how it functioned as a system. Could this be a form of leadership that went beyond only carrying out various pastoral tasks as diligently as possible? It took some time before I came to this insight.

Leadership Outside the Local Church

Meanwhile, I was happily busy with the work at First Mennonite and with involvements in the wider church. I wasn't conscious of it at the time, but in hindsight, I became aware that I found it easier to exert stronger leadership outside of the local church than within it.

One of these places of leadership was my participation in the Edmonton Council of Churches. I valued this interaction with colleagues from a vast variety of church traditions. I became friends with Catholic and Anglican and United Church clergy. We preached in each other's churches. A Catholic priest who became a good friend very publicly invited me, a Protestant, to participate in the sacrament of Eucharist the morning that I preached in his church. He too was ready to move beyond strict church protocol.

I became involved in two projects with the Edmonton Council of Churches, although one of these seemed to lead nowhere. Some of my colleagues were getting tired of doing weddings. They didn't mind performing wedding ceremonies for couples from their church whom they knew well, but some of these mainline clergy were also being asked to conduct weddings for many couples who seldom darkened the door of any church. They were being asked to do a public service for people they didn't know. They felt a bit overwhelmed, even resentful.

Several of them talked about conducting three or four weddings almost every Saturday. One of them said, "It's like I'm running a marriage machine. I feel relieved when I get the right names at the right wedding. I'm totally stressed out about it. I don't have the time to do marriage preparation or wedding preparation. I feel used. Isn't a marriage licence something the state requires? Shouldn't the state then be responsible for performing the wedding? Why should we clergy do the state's work for it? We will gladly perform a religious wedding ceremony, but let the state do the legal stuff."

The discussion escalated: "Why don't we write a 'brief-petition' to the Alberta government, recommending that we follow the European model of separating church and state and having the state officiate the legal wedding? Then, if a couple requests it, we will offer a religious ceremony. No doubt that would free up many of our Saturdays. And Gary, since your Mennonite tradition has always emphasized the separation of state and church, why don't you write the brief?"

Reluctantly I did so. I received a polite note from the Alberta government, thanking me and the Council of Churches for the submission. But nothing came of it. I assume that the same pastors continued to be burdened with doing three or four weddings each Saturday afternoon, desperately trying to get the right names attached to the right couple. And we Mennonite pastors in Canada are still required to obtain an official state licence in order to officiate weddings.

The other Council of Churches project I was asked to be involved with bore more fruit. The Edmonton Police Force – specifically, the chief of police – approached the council for help with two concerns. One was that many police officers were suffering from burnout and from an assortment of personal and relational issues and stresses. They were finding it difficult to do their job well. The other concern the police chief named was that in his observation, clergy and social workers were often able to go into a tense personal or family situation and de-escalate and calm down the situation. But when police officers entered such a situation, with so much more authority and power than clergy or social workers had, the tension often escalated. He wondered what police officers could learn from clergy about dealing with such situations.

The chief of police told us that the Edmonton Police Force was considering hiring a police chaplain who would help police officers cope with their stress and burnout – and teach them less threatening ways of dealing with tense personal conflicts. Would we help them with this process? Would we work together with him and with the police association to create such a chaplaincy position and hire a chaplain?

An Anglican priest and I were asked by the Council of Churches to represent them in this undertaking. I said yes, even as I struggled to understand what it meant for a pacifist Mennonite to be so deeply involved with the Edmonton police. But my colleagues said they wanted the pacifist tradition represented in developing this chaplaincy program. We met together regularly for over a year – police force leaders and two clergy – and developed a mandate for and eventually hired a chaplain for the Edmonton Police Force. Apparently, this was the first such hiring in Canada. One of the surprises for me was how much I learned to respect and appreciate the man who was then the police chief.

I thoroughly enjoyed these ecumenical involvements and relationships.

Wider Work within the Mennonite Conference

In the 1970s and '80s I was invited to participate in work beyond our congregation, on the North American level. The first invitation was a small writing project. The General Conference Mennonite Church (United States and Canada) had launched a project of producing a series of small booklets on various aspects of worship and the sacraments. I was asked to write the booklet on weddings. I very much enjoyed marriage preparation and wedding planning. I liked to involve the couple in thinking through their wedding service and the vows they would make to each other. This forty-two-page booklet included some theological reflection and several samples of wedding vows, ring exchange wordings, and ways to involve bridal couple's families and the congregation.

There was a humorous aspect to this project. Lydia and I had been invited to write the booklet together, but it happened that at that time she was just too busy to do so. I wrote the booklet, submitted it, and when it was published we were listed as co-authors. This seemed only fair, since many other times she did not get credit for assisting me in my work. *Celebrating Christian Marriage* was published in 1980.[2]

A second invitation from the General Conference Mennonite Church was to join a sub-committee of the Education Committee concerned with higher education and the production of resource books. I mention this mostly so that I can tell a travel story here.

Shortly after a plane tragedy in Cranbrook, British Columbia, when an airplane crashed while trying to avoid a snow plow on the runway, killing forty-two of forty-nine passengers, I was on my way to Newton, Kansas, for meetings. There was a stopover for more passengers in Calgary. The wheels of the plane had just touched down briefly when the pilot gunned the motors and took off again, circled, and then completed the landing. The pilot then told us that on the first try he had spotted a small plane still on the runway.

On the next leg of the flight, shortly after gaining altitude, while we passengers were still a bit nervous, we heard from

---

2   Published jointly by Faith and Life Press (Newton, KS) and Mennonite Publishing House (Scottdale, PA).

the pilot again. In a slow, drawling, almost sepulchral tone, he intoned, "We are sorry, ladies and gentlemen, that there has been a M A L F U N C T I O N ... [long pause] with the coffee machine – we are so sorry that we can't serve you any coffee this morning." My racing heart could return to normal.

I enjoyed this involvement in a committee charged with exploring the publication of potential resources a great deal, and thought that we chose some rather significant books for publication. Then came an invitation to be on the board of Canadian Mennonite Bible College (CMBC; now Canadian Mennonite University), located in Winnipeg. I was thrilled to be a part of the CMBC board for a number of years. CMBC has played such a significant role in my life. Both Lydia and I had graduated from it (1964 and 1965 respectively), as did two of our sons and two of my brothers. There I obtained a good grounding in theology, Bible, and music. I thrived on community life there, finding ways to balance my introversion. I thoroughly enjoyed playing many sports that were mostly recreational, not highly organized and serious. During my time at CMBC, I was the editor of *The Scroll*, our student paper, edited the 1963 yearbook, and served as student council chair one year. Our annual choir tours were wonderful experiences. Many friendships begun there have lasted a lifetime.

My involvement on the CMBC board required several trips to Winnipeg each year for meetings. Later I was asked to be chair of the board, which required yet more meetings in Winnipeg. On one of these flights I was questioned about my loyalties – no, not my conference or church loyalties, but my football loyalties. I was on an early Sunday morning flight to Edmonton so that I could get back in time for the worship service. I settled into my window seat, wondering who, if anyone, would sit next to me. At the last moment – no doubt this wait was planned – a very beautiful woman in a stunning outfit, together with her chaperone, came down the aisle – and sat down right next to me! Wow. I had forgotten that this was Grey Cup Sunday, and that the Winnipeg Blue Bombers were in Edmonton to play the Edmonton Eskimos for the Canadian football league championship. And this beautiful young woman was Miss Grey Cup Winnipeg, flying to Edmonton to contest the title of Miss Grey Cup. We had a lighthearted and fun conversation. In the end, I did promise her that I would cheer for her to win that title, but that I could not cheer for her football team. And in the end, she did not win her title, despite my cheering for her, but the Edmonton Eskimos won the championship.

For me, participation beyond the local church was, in the long run, a huge gift. It gave me a broader perspective on church life and church politics and church-society relations. My involvements in various councils, committees, and boards were highly stimulating, sometimes challenging, and always rewarding. They were a gift to me from the congregation who gave me time to do this work and always gave new energy to my ministry.

Summer Student Ministry

Another vision had been growing in my heart. Because of my earlier, transformative experience of being supervised in a ministry setting in London, I felt a deep inner urge and prompting to explore whether First Mennonite Church could offer a supervised experience in ministry to young students attending a Mennonite Bible college or Bible school. Neither I nor the church was equipped to run a CAPE (Canadian Association of Pastoral Education) program. I did not have the credentials to be a CAPE supervisor. And that program was intended for people already active in pastoral ministry, or at least committed to some area of ministry. Many discussions followed within our church and also with CMBC.

I proposed a program growing out of two motivations. First, this Summer Student Ministry Program would be designed to address a very specific niche in the development of church workers. We would not invite seminary students who were already committed to pastoral ministry as a vocation. Rather, we wanted to select Bible college or Bible school students at an earlier stage of development, at a point where they were open to pastoral ministry and had perhaps experienced a general awareness of God's call to a church vocation, but needed to vigorously test out this calling in a practical, supervised setting. We would specifically invite second- or third-year students from CMBC or one of the Mennonite Bible schools.

The second motivation was to enrich the life of the congregation. The theology students we wanted to recruit would be at a stage of education and personal development where they would tend to be at a "sharp personal cutting edge." They would be ready to offer new ideas and insights, ready to try new things. They might be at a place in their own development where they were beginning to synthesize and put together their theological ideas, their personal faith, and their enthusiasm for bringing about change. The congregation would be enormously enriched by the ministry of these students. First Mennonite in fact felt a sense of responsibility to be a small part of a much larger network involved in the development and training of church leaders. And the church felt that it had numerous resources, gifts, and people to help shape and supervise a significant learning experience for a young student. It was a congregation open to being "tested on," a congregation eager to be enriched by these students.

The model for this program very consciously became a "supervised experience in ministry" model. This was not to be merely a summer job in a church. It was meant to be a rather intense experience in ministry, with the significant learning occurring within an "action-reflection" model. Supervision was the key to the reflective component. Each major experience in ministry was to be complemented by a supervision process. Thus, for example, after every time the student preached a sermon, I led a debriefing group made up of lay people giving almost immediate feedback. I also met weekly with the student for supervision. At the beginning of summer, the student would develop a "learning covenant" covering three areas of hoped-for growth: professional goals (skills in ministry), personal goals (personal issues needing attention), and theological goals (reflection on ministry issues). Our weekly sessions included helping the students process their experiences, learning, challenges, and further goals. We always included a time for worship and prayer.

CMBC gave enthusiastic support to this initiative, then encouraged other churches to develop similar opportunities for their students. Our first summer student minister came in 1976. When I moved to Toronto in 1987 to become pastor of Toronto United Mennonite Church, that congregation also quickly embraced this program. Altogether it has been my privilege to supervise a total of thirty-one students. This has given me immense satisfaction and joy. And it seems that both the students who participated and the churches that hosted them have been enthusiastic about the program. My own reflection on what makes for a good pastor-congregation relationship was certainly stimulated by the questions of students and the responses of the congregation.

Parochialism

Not all that is satisfying in life happens in church or even with people. I discovered in Alberta that fish are apparently parochial. While Ontario fish refused to bite on an Alberta lad's hook, Alberta fish had no such qualms. First Mennonite Church in Edmonton had some avid fishermen, and I received many invitations to spend time with them on a lake. Sometimes I even caught my limit of fish. And I introduced my children to the joys of fishing. I discovered that moose, too, are fussy about provincial jurisdictions. Unlike the moose in Ontario, one Alberta moose even allowed me to fill our freezer with its meat.

Reaching for Some Creativity

One of the growing edges for me, an edge very much encouraged by the First Mennonite congregation, was to develop an emerging creative side of my spirit. I enjoyed writing small worship pieces, including monologues, dialogues, and short plays to fit into a worship service setting. During my time in Edmonton, I submitted a number of creative worship pieces for publication in Mennonite publications.

And then the church's young people and young adults decided to tackle something much bigger. We put on the Andrew Lloyd Webber musical *Joseph and the Amazing Technicolour Dreamcoat*. A professional drama coach in our congregation gave us some acting lessons, and then left the directing to me. As amateur as we were, this experience helped us bond and unleashed much enthusiasm and joy. We even took the musical on tour to Calgary.

One memory stands out for me. The musical required a rather large cast, and we were finding it difficult to fill every role. One of our young people, though a fine actor, claimed to be a monotone. He couldn't distinguish notes, he said. He could only sing one sustained low pitch. Well, he would still make a fine Potiphar. At every rehearsal we had the whole cast sing his part, aware that he would not and could not sing the notes. During the performance he would recite his lines, not sing them. But at the dress rehearsal, to our total shock, as he entered into the spirit of his role, he started singing his lines, perfectly in pitch. And he did this in every performance. Outside of that role he continued to be "pitch-challenged." I marvelled at the intricacies of the human mind.

A Sabbatical

One advantage – and privilege – of being the pastor of an educated and professional group of people was that the request for a sabbatical leave was easily processed and approved. Several of the church's leaders had received sabbatical leaves in their professional work. I had been in Edmonton for seven years when the church graciously offered me a year's leave.

A late invitation had come from the Mennonite Seminary in Asunción, Paraguay, to teach there for a year. Lydia was invited to teach Christian education and English as a second language, and I would teach Bible and pastoral psychology. The seminary was small, with about thirty students equally divided between those whose first language was German and those who spoke only Spanish. Since both Lydia and I grew up speaking German, teaching in German (though a bit overwhelming) did not seem impossible, even though we hadn't used our German for years. We bundled up our three children, then seven, nine, and eleven years old, and spent from January till December of 1979 in Paraguay.

In so many ways this year was life-changing. For one thing, it changed our family patterns. Our children left for school (a private Mennonite German-Spanish school) by 7 a.m. and came home at 1 p.m. My teaching schedule coincided with their schedule, while Lydia taught in the afternoon. I spent the afternoon with our children and sometimes made supper. I realized what a gift this was both to me and to Lydia – a deeper immersion in parenting for me, and a bit of a respite and chance for adult conversation for Lydia.

The other life-changing aspect of this year was that Lydia realized how much she loved teaching adults and living in the world of education. That is really where she made the decision to begin her graduate work in theology. She started these studies shortly after we returned to Edmonton. Our family life, and our marriage, would never be the same again. Our children, for the most part, thrived on the adventure, newness, and challenges of living and going to school in a totally foreign culture and learning two new languages – Spanish and German. Lydia and I also tried to learn some elementary Spanish. I learned enough to be able to read the daily paper superficially and to get the general idea of a sermon preached in Spanish, but not enough to feel comfortable in a conversation in that language.

I thoroughly enjoyed teaching the German-speaking seminary students. I taught in the fields of Old Testament, pastoral psychology, and homiletics (preaching). The biggest challenge for me was to teach in German – I knew none of the German vocabulary in psychology.

German-speaking and Spanish-speaking students took most of their courses together, but homiletics was taught separately. I became good friends with the professor who taught the Spanish students how to preach. We soon agreed that some of the stereotypical assumptions about our students were probably true. My German students produced finely researched "papers" but struggled to communicate their convictions persuasively. The Spanish students majored in rather exuberant communication but seemed not to pay as much attention to thorough exposition of Scripture. We brought the two classes together a few times, challenging them to learn from each other.

I did not know any Spanish at all when I encountered my first real crisis that I could not talk my way out of. I am a jogger, and a few days after arriving in Asunción I knew I needed to jog. It seemed that no one else in all of Asunción jogged, so it no doubt looked odd to see this white stranger doing so. A block from our apartment was a small park, a perfect place for jogging, I thought. The signs indicated that running on the grass was forbidden but said nothing about jogging on the sidewalk around the park. So early that morning, I set out. I came to the end of the block to find two big machine guns levelled at me, held by two distinctly unsmiling uniformed men. What to do? Perhaps foolishly, I just smiled, waved, and kept on running. I knew no words to explain myself. Maybe that shocked the soldiers enough that they didn't shoot. I went around the block and right back toward those two soldiers, who again raised their guns. The third time around they only raised them halfway, unsure of what to do with this stupid foreigner. For many days, they watched me rather uneasily as I jogged around the park each morning, but they kept their machine guns pointed down instead of at me. I learned later that they were guarding the home of an army general and weren't taking any chances. But at least they didn't shoot!

In Paraguay, we received many invitations to visit the various Mennonite colonies to teach and to preach, or just to be tourists. Never to be forgotten was a tenting trip to the Chololo Falls with another family. We pitched our tent on the downslope of the creek – a scenic spot that was very inviting. In the middle of the night we woke up, soaked through and through. A rain storm and flash flood had raised the creek level dramatically, and we were in danger of floating away. We spent the rest of the night drying off in the car.

I was invited to be the guest speaker at the all-Paraguay Mennonite annual conference, held in the Chaco. Our host family was very hospitable. Mennonites in Paraguay had embraced the Paraguayan culture of drinking maté. You sit in a circle and the maté cup and pipe are passed around – and around and around. That was happening here, and so I, as an appreciative guest, partook each time the cup came to me. Whatever was in the maté effected my innocent body deeply. I sweated all night and never really fell asleep. This before I was scheduled to make four presentations in two days – in German yet – to a large audience. These presentations, on the theme of the Mennonite peace position, were later printed in booklet form under the title *Die Friedfertigen – Teilnehmer an des Lammes Krieg* (translated as "Those Who Pursue Peace – Participants in the War of the

Lamb").[3] The editor of the booklet smiled at me as he acknowl-edged that he had edited the German quite severely.

Despite misadventures, sleepless nights and cultural insensi-tivities, and smiling editors, our sabbatical year in Paraguay was everything I needed to regain my momentum for ministry. It was an amazing gift from my congregation. I had worked as hard – perhaps harder – than before but felt renewed, refreshed, and energized for the next stage of my work and development. During that year in Paraguay I made the decision to enter a Doctor of Ministries program when we returned to Edmonton. And Lydia would enter graduate studies in theology.

New Visions

Meanwhile, First Mennonite Church had also moved forward with its vision for the future. A part of the congregation's plan-ning for the year I was away was to hire another pastor mid-year who would assume pastoral duties but also help the church work toward a new church plant in another part of the city. After I came back, the two of us would work together for a while and continue planning for the church plant. Then the congregation would help decide which one of us would stay as pastor of the mother church and which one would become pastor of the new one. It was a delight to work together with Jake Froese. In the end, he helped found Faith Mennonite Church, and I stayed as pastor of First Mennonite.

Now, with the encouragement of church leaders, I was ready to enter a Doctor of Ministries program at St. Stephen's College, connected with the University of Alberta in Edmonton. I knew I needed to grow as a pastor, and I knew that the challenges of

---

3   The booklet was published in 1980 by the Asociación Evangélica Mennonita del Paraguay.

such a program would push and pull me beyond my comfort zone. I especially welcomed the ecumenical nature of that pushing and pulling.

The congregation was very generous with me when the demands of these studies sometimes took me away from church work for short periods of time. When the time came for me to write my dissertation, after I had collected my data, the congregation graciously gave me a partial four-month sabbatical so that I could devote more time to writing. My daily work routine was to write from 8 a.m. till noon, and then do pastoral care and/ or committee work in the afternoon and often in the evening.

The title of my project dissertation was "Touched by Transcendence: Shaping Worship That Bridges Life and Faith," with the sub-title "The Worship Committee – An Idea Whose Time Has Come." I was particularly interested in how the congregation, through a committee dedicated to worship planning, could help nurture its spiritual life. In recent Mennonite practice, worship planning was the responsibility of the professional pastor. But this seemed to break from our larger tradition of the priesthood of all believers, where lay people were deeply involved in all aspects of church life, including spiritual life. Some Mennonite churches were beginning to experiment with committees that would work with the pastor in planning worship. But it seemed to me that the foundational thinking for this kind of partnership had not yet been done. First Mennonite Church did have a worship committee that worked with me, but we weren't always sure what its primary function was. Was it just to carry out all the organizational details that the pastor didn't want to be bothered with, or was it genuinely to give voice to the congregation's needs in planning worship? It was exciting to discover how the worship committee was becoming a vital aspect of the life of the congregation, bringing the insights and experience of lay persons into the worship life of the congregation.

Among the many concerns that surfaced during our meetings were the issues of patriarchy and sexual abuse. This effected both my public ministry and the pastoral care that I offered people. One young couple from another province came to my office for some marriage help. As their story unfolded, it became clear that the underlying issue was that the woman's father had sexually abused her, and this had profoundly troubled her sexual intimacy with her husband. I knew I was over my head in this situation and referred the couple to a professional counsellor.

At another time, I was asked to speak in a neighbouring Mennonite church. There I named the issue of sexual abuse and how the church's silence about this was hurting many women. That week I received a long letter from a woman who had heard me. She wrote that finally, finally, the subject had been opened in church, and that now she had the courage to name her own abuse at the hands of her husband.

Leaving Edmonton

We were ready to leave Edmonton for Toronto. I had been the pastor of First Mennonite Church for fifteen and a half years. We loved our time there. We loved the church. We were deeply involved in that community. Our children had grown up there. But it was time to leave. Toronto United Mennonite Church had invited me to be its pastor. Lydia had been accepted into the doctoral program in theology at the Toronto School of Theology.

Despite these positive reasons for leaving Edmonton, the move was wrenching. Some months after starting ministry all over again in Toronto, I entered into a deep depression. I almost never get depressed – at least usually not for longer than a few hours, or at most a day. But now I was depressed for a week. And finally, lying on our couch, unmoving and unproductive, I understood what this was about. I hadn't finished mourning what I had lost by leaving Edmonton. I had unfinished grieving to do. I cried. And the depression lifted. I was ready to fully embrace my life and ministry in Toronto.

My depression was an indication of how much I loved First Mennonite Church and, I think, how much I was loved in return. That congregation gave me so much. Its members supported me, encouraged me, and challenged me to grow as a pastor and as a person. They offered friendship and sabbatical leaves. Even now, thirty years later, my heart warms when I reflect on my time in Edmonton. That church provided many melodies for my retirement songs of praise.

3
Toronto United Mennonite Church

We were gathered in the home of the chair of the congregation of Toronto United Mennonite Church. I had been invited to Toronto to meet with the church council and pastoral search committee as a candidate for the position of pastor. Snacks were served, as was wine. This was new to me – no, not being served wine, but being served wine at a church council meeting. Was this normal here in the big Eastern city of Toronto, for urban Mennonites who adopted a more relaxed attitude toward alcohol consumption? Or was this a test of the candidate's sophistication level and whether he would fit into this highly urbanized congregation? The gesture did probably identify where the congregation was at and gave at least some indication of whether I was up to the challenge of being a pastor in this context.

First Mennonite Church in Edmonton was also situated in an urban context, of course, but that congregation included far more transplanted rural people than did this church. Toronto United Mennonite Church (TUMC) carried a much deeper urban imprint. I had grown up on a farm near the very small village of Rosemary, Alberta, with no urban instincts or longings at all. Even as an adolescent, I found the nearby very small town of Bassano overwhelmingly large. Both the TUMC congregation and I needed to process my readiness to enter the milieu of the biggest city in Canada – an Eastern city for this Western man.

This church was even open to inviting Lydia and me to come as co-pastors. By this time (1987) there were several female pastors in Mennonite settings in Ontario – though not in Alberta – and my marriage journey had opened me to affirming women in ministry. But this invitation still seemed to be a bit on the radical edge. And though I wholeheartedly affirmed women as pastors, I was not quite ready to be a co-pastor with my wife. It was perhaps too easy for me to say no to this suggestion by declaring that Lydia had her heart set on doing doctoral studies at the Toronto School of Theology. Which was true, but not the complete story. Part of her heart longed to be a pastor, a longing not fulfilled because she was a woman. It would take a few more years for me to become emotionally ready and self-confident enough to become partners in ministry with Lydia, first in teaching together and then as interim pastors together after my retirement from full-time pastoral ministry.

I did drink some wine at that meeting. And the church did invite me to be its pastor. After fifteen and a half wonderful years in Edmonton, we uprooted ourselves emotionally and physically and entered a challenging new world. For the next twenty years, I would be pastor of TUMC.

There was so much to learn in this new setting.

Learning about Myself

Some of this learning was about myself. I worked too hard that first year. I tried too hard to please everybody in the congregation. I see myself as reasonably confident and quite disciplined, able to structure my work and my life. On the farm I had learned to enjoy working long and hard. As a pastor, I've always prepared fully for preaching and teaching and for meetings. But that first year in Toronto I went overboard in preparing. Somehow, I felt that I needed to prove myself all over again. I was no longer fully confident in myself. The new context and new people were nibbling at my sense of self-worth. And my temptation was to solve this inner anxiety with over-preparation. My rationale was that there was so much to learn about the congregation and the city, and this learning demanded extra effort. But why would an established, confident, veteran pastor and leader suddenly have an attack of the jitters? Why would he feel that he had to prove himself all over again?

It wasn't that the congregation was pushing me and putting unrealistic expectations on me. Yes, church members did expect me to be competent and professional and to prepare well. But they were affirming my ministry more than I was. They were not putting extra pressure on me; I was putting the pressure on myself. I needed a deeper sense of self-worth and acceptance than overwork alone could provide.

Maybe that is why the story of the baptism and temptations of Jesus spoke to me so deeply at that point in my ministry. The Gospel of Mark brings three stories of Jesus together in a sequence I find quite profound. First Jesus is baptized, then is immediately taken into the wilderness by the Spirit to be tested by the devil for forty days, and immediately following that begins his public ministry (Mark 1:9–15). Baptism, temptation, and the beginning of ministry are grouped together in a careful sequence by Mark – grouped together for a purpose, I think.

The first of this trio of stories intrigues me. Jesus has just been baptized by John the Baptist. Then, Mark writes, "Just as he was coming up out of the water, he saw the heavens torn apart and the Spirit descending like a dove on him. And a voice came from heaven, 'You are my Son, the Beloved; with you I am well pleased.'"

I think that Jesus, like all humans, needed to hear this blessing, this affirmation from God. Even Jesus in his humanness needed to know that he was truly, deeply, profoundly loved by God. He needed to hear this voice and this word so that he would be strong enough within himself to deal with all the temptations of ministry, and certainly to deal with the temptations in the wilderness. And he needed to hear this blessing before he began his public ministry. And that is a key point: Jesus didn't need to earn the blessing and love of his Father God through successful ministry. He was assured of this before he began his ministry. The blessing came as gift, not reward.

The temptations in the wilderness, which follow immediately, are all temptations for Jesus to use his power in un-godlike ways to achieve personal recognition and fame and power. They are temptations to use ministry for his own glory, not God's glory. They are temptations to live out his vocation in self-serving ways, in culturally acceptable and self-aggrandizing ways. It is Luke who fills in the details of these wilderness temptations (Luke 4:1–13). Turn stones into bread and feed the masses, a sure-fire way to become hugely popular. Throw yourself from the pinnacle of the Temple, be rescued by angels, and surely you will be proclaimed a spectacular wonder worker. Worship Satan and be given the world's Kingdoms and splendour – and wealth. Had Jesus given in to these temptations he would probably have been spectacularly successful, and would no doubt have avoided the cross.

But the voice from God – "You are my Son, the Beloved; with you I am well pleased" – gave Jesus the inner grounding and strength and self-worth to resist the evil one. And having resisted, he was ready to engage in God's ministry, in God's ways.

Our deepest need as humans is to be loved and to be valued. We need to know, need to hear, that we have infinite value, that we are loved, that we are named in blessing. "You are my beloved son, my beloved daughter, my beloved child, with you I am well pleased." This is the essential beginning to any call to ministry or any call to service in the name of Jesus.

This was the voice I needed to pay more attention to that first year as pastor of TUMC, when I was tempted to earn my self-worth by overworking. I suppose our sense of self-worth and esteem is always precarious at best. And the temptation to protect or defend our self-worth in unhealthy ways is always before us. We easily become defensive, or strive for perfectionism, or overwork, or attack those near us. The Mark story reminds me that healthy self-esteem comes as a gift, given by a God who loves us. Part of this gift from God to me was to be placed in a congregation where a healthy, responsible, covenant-like relationship could develop between pastor and congregation. But at the beginning I still needed to learn to welcome robust feedback, including criticism, and not feel threatened by it.

I was recently struck by an article written by César García, general secretary of the Mennonite World Conference. García describes unhealthy leadership patterns that contribute to conflict. He talks specifically about pastors whose personal needs have not been resolved, who are driven to "extreme perfectionism," and who insist on enforcing uniformity.[4]

Unhealthy conflicts and abuse of power by leaders (pastors) comes when the personal needs of the leader have not been resolved. That is, they haven't heard that voice from God naming them "Beloved." Then they get thirsty for recognition and power in order to fill their inner needs. They strive for extreme perfectionism, because they can't risk being vulnerable. And then they try to enforce uniformity so that everyone agrees with them. Only then do they not feel threatened inside.

Jesus began his public ministry immediately after he had resisted the temptations in the wilderness. It took me longer, here in Toronto, to resist the temptation of earning my self-worth by trying to please everybody.

Learning about My New Congregation

There certainly was much to learn about my new congregation. Most of what I learned pleased me. Some of it threatened me just a little. Members of this congregation were more likely than

---

4   César Garcia, "A New Pattern of Leadership" *Courier* (Oct. 2014) 16.

folks at First Mennonite had been to give me direct feedback and challenge me. I knew I wanted this and needed this, and invited it, even when I felt somewhat defensive. In the long run, this was a huge gift to me. (And wasn't this also what I had learned to value so deeply in my marriage: a spirited give and take, challenge and affirmation, talking and arguing out issues?)

The congregation had in place two committees that delighted me. In writing my project dissertation while in Edmonton, I had advocated that churches have a strong worship committee. TUMC already had this and had put into place two additional committees that we did not have in Edmonton: a preaching team and a caring team. These were established when the previous pastor, Darrel Fast, began his Doctor of Ministry studies. The committees were probably seen as a temporary way to help the church meet its preaching and pastoral needs while the pastor was devoting significant time to his studies. But the committees worked so well and were so much affirmed that the congregation wanted to keep them going even after Darrel finished his studies and came back to full-time ministry. When I came to Toronto, I recognized how great a gift these were, both to the congregation and to me.

The Preaching Team

Four people from the congregation were chosen, by a special discernment process, to work with the pastor to meet the preaching needs of the congregation. These four lay people functioned as much more than occasional preachers scheduled to spell off the pastor. They were to oversee the preaching ministry of the church. They were to assess the spiritual needs of the congregation that could be addressed by preaching. It was understood that this team approach would also help us "grow" new preachers for the congregation.

At every monthly meeting, we shared our responses to the last month's sermons. We encouraged feedback and suggestions. We talked about helping each other find our true God-given preaching voice. I as pastor was only one of five teammates helping each other grow as preachers. Sometimes one or the other of us would share with the team what we were working on for our next sermon, inviting response and suggestions.

We then spent time looking further ahead, planning for the longer term, especially when we as a team wanted to work on a series of sermons. I have very warm memories of times when we preached a series on a particular book of the Bible, and did in-depth Bible study as part of our meetings. In this way, we prepared a series on the letter to the Ephesians, one on the Sermon on the Mount, and one on the book of Revelation. The last part of our meetings involved scheduling preachers for the next time period. We five members of the preaching team did not do all the preaching; other lay people were also invited to preach, as were outside guests. I continued the pattern I had established in Edmonton of preaching twice a month.

The Caring Team

The congregation also chose four people, again by a special discernment process, to work with the pastor to meet some of the caregiving and pastoral needs of the congregation. One pastor working alone cannot be all things to all people in the congregation. One pastor doesn't have big enough ears to hear what the needs and pains and joys of everyone in the congregation are.

The caring team's role was to help in this aspect of ministry, sometimes by alerting the pastor to someone who needed a visit, sometimes by helping structure support networks around a person or family, and sometimes by making visits themselves. The members of the team might be assigned to give special attention to a particular segment of the congregation. We were always careful about confidentiality issues.

One of the things I especially appreciated about the monthly meetings of the caring team was how we began by connecting with each other. We shared what was happening in our own lives. We cared for and prayed for each other. I felt cared for and nurtured as a pastor. This sustained me as I offered pastoral care to the congregation.

I have deep appreciation for both the preaching team and the caring team at TUMC. Both supported me in that long ministry.

The Seniors

When Lydia and I came to TUMC in 1987, there was a large group of seniors playing a significant role in the life of the church. In the Edmonton church, there had been very few seniors. A number of these Toronto seniors were living at the St. Clair O'Connor Community, an intergenerational housing complex recently built in partnership by two Mennonite churches, TUMC and Danforth Mennonite Church. These seniors (mostly seventy years and up) totally reshaped my understanding of growing older.

They were active, feisty, and anything but conservative. I had known seniors with a more-or-less rural mentality who happened to live in the city, not always out of choice. In contrast, most of these seniors had chosen to live in the big city because at heart they were urban people. They loved the city. They thrived there. They participated fully in the life of the city and of the church – and often challenged the conservatism of us younger folk.

At that time, Lydia was working on her doctorate in theology, and writing about and speaking about Christian feminism. The seniors invited her to speak to them about her research and her convictions, and then engage her in dialogue. They wanted to learn and explore new ideas. They were amazingly open. They were a delight to work with and to visit.

Changing Ethos – Extending the Parameters of Our Hospitality

The ethos of any community keeps changing, sometimes very slowly over time and sometimes more rapidly, spurred by events or opportunities or crises. The question for me was what role a pastoral leader plays in navigating or initiating a change in ethos. The issue TUMC faced was how to enlarge its scope of hospitality to people not like us and to create space for everyone to enter fully into the community. How could the pastor be a catalyst in this reshaping of the congregation's attitudes and culture? What strengths and what gifts did I have to offer to the congregation to help it process this change? What would be my pastoral approach?

I was beginning to understand more fully that a congregation is a system, more than just the sum of its parts. A systems theory understanding of the congregation was a helpful tool for ministry. A pastor's role is greater than providing pastoral care to individuals and families, preaching and praying and leading worship. Pastors also need to "look from the balcony" to get an overall picture of the congregation as a system. They need to assess what is healthy and what is not healthy in the congregation, and offer perspectives and visions and tools for addressing health issues.

I was also learning to be less afraid of conflict. Conflict, if openly expressed and handled well, can lead to growth. I felt that I was reasonably good at opening a conversation, at listening to all voices, at inviting people to express their convictions and their feelings directly so that conflict could be out in the open, rather than hidden and festering underneath.

These, I thought, were pastoral gifts I could bring into play as TUMC entered a time of fairly significant changes in ethos and identity.

Children

I have named my appreciation for the very positive role our many seniors played in the church. But there weren't many children at TUMC when I began my ministry there. The worship atmosphere was much quieter than it had been in Edmonton, where the church included far more young families and young children. The Toronto congregation liked this quieter worship time uninterrupted by the commotion of children – until the 1990s, when some young families moved in, bringing with them rather noisy children. The atmosphere changed. The noise level during worship increased dramatically, as did complaints about the noise. "How can we really worship God in quiet contemplation when we're always surrounded by so much noise?" "Can't parents keep their kids quiet these days?" "Maybe we should have Sunday school during worship time so that the kids are otherwise occupied. We need peace and quiet to really worship."

"But," said others, "isn't having young families and lots of children what we have needed here, what we have in fact prayed for? This is an answer to our prayers and to our needs as a congregation. Let's embrace this new reality and thank God for it. Let's learn to live with the noise level and see children as gifts with huge blessing for us now and for our future."

Gradually the complaints stopped and the affirmations grew, and we became a much more intergenerational church. We were in the midst of an ethos change. Today the noise levels during TUMC's worship services are quite high. We smile and feel very blessed. But at first it was a challenge for us to extend a fully welcoming hospitality to young families and young children.

Those More Evangelical

Some of these young families with their many noisy children also brought about another challenge to TUMC's ethos. They were a bit more "evangelical" than was the main core of the congregation, more ready to speak enthusiastically about their faith. Many in TUMC had reacted against the strictures and rules, conservatism and piety, and even the hymnody of their home congregations. They were now in an urban congregation. They had embraced a modernity mindset that valued reason and logic and organization and order, a rational approach to worship. No gospel songs here. No appealing only to emotions. No tugging at heartstrings. None of that fundamentalist language, please. None of that moralizing on a simplistic reading of Bible stories.

TUMC also had a very strong tradition of peace and justice witness, but this was not fully integrated with a sense of spirituality and worship. For example, members of the congregation had participated enthusiastically in refugee support and sponsorship of refugees fleeing from Vietnam, but then were not sure how to express their Christianity to their new neighbours.

So now there was a bit of a clash of cultures, of mindsets, of religious orientation, of language, of worship needs, of an understanding of the mission of the church. Would this clash lead us to a healthier, enriched congregation, or would it drive us apart? Would it stimulate the kind of engagement and discussion that would challenge both sides of the clash to grow and change, or would it alienate portions of the congregation? It seemed to me that this was a fertile, God-given moment, fraught with both great potential and some danger. It was an exciting time to be a pastor.

As pastor, I wanted to see every new person and every new family brought into the church as another gift of God for us. I saw what was unfolding as a part of embracing a fuller trajectory of hospitality and inclusion. This was expressed in a number of ways during those years.

TUMC initiated the development of a project called Lazarus Rising, a ministry to street people. The church gave full encouragement and support to Circles of Support, a ministry to sex offenders released from prison. For many years TUMC was deeply involved in an annual Advent festival highlighting Ten Thousand Villages (fair trade stores) sales and peace witness at Toronto's Harbourfront Centre. When folks from the church envisioned and created an inter-Mennonite choir, which soon became an ecumenical choir, they named it the Pax Christi Chorale – the "peace of Christ choir." When TUMC built its new building, it invited the New Life Centre, a Mennonite refugee services ministry, to be one of its partners. When the opportunity came to host a small Korean worshipping group, the church was again enthusiastic. The ministry of Christian Peacemaker Teams, standing with oppressed and threatened groups of people, was embraced by the congregation.

Peace and justice and service ran very deeply through all aspects of TUMC's church life and ethos. With the coming of new families in the 1990s, some of them from more evangelical traditions, it seemed to me that there was an opportunity for this life and ethos to be both broadened and deepened. It would be deepened if we could overcome some of our reactions to an evangelicalism that had wounded us, and if the newcomers could share with us the best of their more evangelical tradition, creating a more holistic approach to the church's mission in the world.

To the credit of the congregation, and to the credit of both sides in the clash of ethos, there was an eventual blending of cultures and religious language and approach to the Bible, of hymnody and worship styles. And TUMC continues to have the strength of very diverse perspectives and experiences, needs and gifts, brought together under one people of God.

A New Church Building

Our new church building, dedicated in 1996, would also test our hospitality and our readiness to change. The congregation was growing — a building, of course, cannot grow. It became apparent that our facilities would soon limit our potential. Our facilities were inadequate for our needs, and yet the church building was much loved. It had served the congregation very well. It had been designed by church members and constructed with the help of many church volunteers. They were emotionally attached to it and found it difficult to let go of it.

After much processing and visioning, we were finally ready to explore new facility options — and soon discovered that this would be a daunting task. We explored option after option, each of which fizzled out. Altogether it took almost eight years to come up with a plan and a proposal. This proposal would come with an emotional cost.

There were two main parts to this proposal that needed significant time to work through. One was that we not embark on a building project by ourselves, but invite two partners to join us. To some extent this idea reflected the financial challenges faced by a relatively small congregation in fulfilling a huge project. But more importantly, some of us in leadership valued the partnership concept for its own sake. We would invite the smaller Toronto Mennonite New Life Church, a Spanish-speaking congregation, and the Mennonite New Life Centre of Toronto, a refugee services ministry, to partner with us. They would become full partners with TUMC in that we would co-own the facilities, each partner owning a percentage of the building according to its size.

Emotionally, this was difficult for TUMC. It meant giving up sole ownership and full control of the property. It meant working together with people from other cultures, languages, and religious understandings. Personally, I was excited by this possibility and felt that as the pastor I should encourage us to explore this avenue very seriously. It would, I thought, continue our trajectory of radical hospitality.

The second part of the proposal was the building plan itself. The same architect from within the congregation who designed the first building would now design the new building. We would basically tear down the old building to the basement, extend the footprint to the edges of our property, and build a new three-story facility with dedicated space for all three partner organizations.

As expected, there was both enthusiasm for and resistance to this new plan. The cost would be quite high, and there were questions about the viability of the partnerships. We delayed final approval of this plan a further year so that we could work through these reservations more fully. And then we started building.

Our plan included a major contribution of volunteer labour. What is so striking to me is what this volunteering meant for our church and for our partnerships. Young and old worked side by side. Latin Americans and long-time Canadians worked side by side. And many of our older folk, who perhaps had more at stake in wanting to keep the old building, now gave an enormous amount of time helping to build the new one.

One particular workday stands out for me and for everyone who volunteered that day. Our contracted drywall installer resigned, leaving the main sanctuary bare to its framing. Some seventy of us, of all ages and from each of the partner organizations, spent an entire Saturday replacing that company. We had already put up the scaffolding. Now we installed the electrical work (we had electricians in the congregation), put in the insulation, and drywalled the entire sanctuary, including the high ceiling – all in one day. We did hire someone for mudding and sanding the drywall to prepare it for painting, which was also done by volunteers. Through volunteer labour, we completed an estimated half a million dollars' worth of work. This was an amazing community-building and hospitality-extending venture.

There also seemed to be some divine humour at work in this project. When the church had first bought its small lot at the corner of Lark and Queen in the 1940s, the concern had been the Greenwood racetrack across the street (sports enthusiasts, especially Canadian ones, may remember the famous Canadian racehorse Northern Dancer, who raced here. Northern Dancer won the Kentucky Derby and the Preakness Stakes in 1964, and – according to Wikipedia – became the most successful sire of the twentieth century. The street next to TUMC is now called Northern Dancer Boulevard). Patrons of horse racing would take up all the available street parking, and since the proposed church lot would be too small to include parking, this was a major concern. Another troubling issue for the church was the huge grandstand directly across the street from its new building. Not only did this further complicate parking issues, but the grandstand also reflected the noise of passing streetcars directly back to the church.

The congregation had lived with these inconvenient hindrances. And it had looked for options to relocate. None were viable. The racetrack and grandstand next door were among the huge stumbling blocks to our plan to rebuild on our present site. Finally, we made the decision to go ahead on this site anyway. Several weeks later, out of the blue, came the media announcement that the racetrack had been sold to a developer. The grandstand would be coming down. A housing development would take its place.

The real humour was in the huge billboards. The demolition company that took down the grandstand advertised its name in massive letters: PRIESTLY DEMOLITION. Not to be outdone, the company that put up the steel superstructure for our new building erected its own billboard directly across the street: PARADISE STEEL.

Can We Welcome People Who Are LGBTQ?

The trajectory of inclusion, welcome, and radical hospitality was alive and growing in TUMC. But it would be very severely tested in the years 2002–2003 as we wrestled with the issue of homosexuality. Not everyone felt included in our hospitality.

During that time we fought over how to respond to my associate pastor, a woman who had publicly said that she had fallen in love with another woman. How would the church respond? In the end, we released her from her pastoral duties, wounded her and each other in the congregation, and wondered where God was in all of this. I felt that I had failed as a pastor, unable to lead the congregation in a healthier process and discourse. I felt personally wounded and broken. I will say more about this in chapter 12.[5]

The Congregation Moves into the Future

Toronto United Mennonite Church was changing, and embracing the future. It was learning to process both visions and conflict in healthier ways. Having learned how important this could be, the congregation implemented "rules of public discourse" that have since guided and facilitated far more collegial decision making. These rules are read at the beginning of every meeting, and adherence to them is monitored. The way we express ourselves – our ideas, our disagreements, our concerns – is so important for healthy dialogue.

Healing did take place at TUMC, including in the life of this pastor. Relationships mended. Reconciliations happened. In the end, what saw us through our crisis and what helped us to

---

5   I have also written about this story in my previous book, *Dancing through Thistles in Bare Feet.*

essentially stay intact as a congregation was our conviction that our worship of God and our commitment to Jesus was more basic and more essential than our agreements and disagreements and conflicts. We confessed that our decisions were not yet our final ones, that we had much to learn from each other, and that we had hurt each other deeply. We agreed to keep the question of what it meant to practise radical hospitality as a central agenda for our congregation and to move together into the future with God's leading. In the long run, the congregation did move toward a much fuller welcome of people in the LGBTQ community.

The trajectory toward radical hospitality continues. It is never complete. Some folks have not experienced this fully enough and have withdrawn from the congregation. We hesitate along the way and fail along the way. But TUMC is now a more diverse congregation than it used to be. We have more people of colour, more people from other cultures and other faith traditions, more people who identify as LGBTQ, a greater variety of faith expression, a fuller intergenerational mix of people, and a wider spectrum of musical expression. I like to think that my earlier pastoral leadership contributed at least a bit toward this growing, radical hospitality.

An Amazingly Generous Congregation

Sabbaticals

During the twenty years that I was pastor of TUMC, the church offered me three sabbatical leaves. The first one was a four-month leave in 1994. Lydia had just finished her doctorate at Toronto School of Theology when Canadian Mennonite Bible College (CMBC) invited us to spend a year there teaching as a sabbatical replacement for a professor. Lydia was obviously excited about this opportunity to teach right after graduate school. But reality intruded. I was not free to move to Winnipeg for the year to be with her. Could she go on her own?

We assembled a discernment group of trusted friends and church leaders with whom to share this opportunity and this dilemma, and to seek advice. After a rich, intense evening of talking, listening, and processing, the group essentially said, "Your marriage is strong enough to withstand being apart for the first semester of four months, and we will ask the congregation to give Gary a four-month sabbatical so that he can join Lydia for the second semester in Winnipeg." And that is what happened: Lydia started teaching at CMBC in fall; I joined her after Christmas, also taught a course, interacted with students, did some preaching, and generally had a very refreshing break from my ministry in Toronto.

And yes, our marriage did survive, though we had a bit of a crisis when we rejoined each other after Christmas in our small on-campus apartment. Lydia is a terrific organizer, but her desk does not always reflect this organization. I am a bit of a neatness freak. From an earlier trip, Lydia had received a free flight voucher after being bumped to a later flight. I set about cleaning up the desk, putting some order into the papers strewn about. Vaguely I thought I heard her say she would review my litter pile. Before she had time to do this I threw the pile, including that voucher, away. (We still argue about whose fault that was.)

A second sabbatical took us to Cairo, Egypt, for six months from January through June 2000. Our son Kendall was in Egypt serving a three-year assignment with Mennonite Central Committee (MCC). It happened that the Evangelical (Presbyterian) Seminary in Cairo needed a professor for a semester to teach in a new master of theology program. Kendall brashly suggested that his mother was qualified to teach it, and so it happened that Lydia was invited to come to Egypt to be a professor at the seminary. And of course, I tagged along. I had already been discussing sabbatical possibilities with the church, and this all seemed to line up.

Cairo, and Egypt, proved to be a fascinating place to be for six months. We enjoyed many of the usual tourist activities. We climbed Mount Sinai with a group of Kendall's Coptic Orthodox students. We rode camels and crawled inside the pyramids. One of Lydia's students invited us to spend a weekend at his home village, a four-hour train ride south of Cairo. We explored the tombs of the pharaohs in Luxor. We scuba dived in Dahab, a resort on the Red Sea.

And while Lydia taught the MA students, I – well, I was a kind of "presence" at the seminary and at the Mennonite Central Committee (MCC) unit, without an official role. I interacted with students. I preached a few times. I met with other evangelical pastors. I met with MCC personnel as an unofficial pastor. I journaled. I walked and explored the streets of Cairo almost every afternoon. Together Lydia and I were resource people for the annual Middle Eastern MCC retreat in Cyprus. And at the end of our time, we spent two weeks in Iran representing MCC there. It was, in every way, an ideal sabbatical. I came back to Toronto re-energized.

One of the first things I realized when I came back to TUMC after six months was that the church had made some important and wise decisions while I was away. One of these decisions was to initiate a congregational prayer time of "sharing joys and concerns" as a central part of worship. In some preliminary explorations of this possibility before I left for sabbatical, I had resisted this move. Over the years, as I visited other churches that had instituted this practice, I had not been impressed with it. So often it felt trivial to me. I did not experience it as a deep sharing or as a meaningful prayer response (probably because I was not a part of those communities and didn't know the people). I was convinced that some people would "over-share" while most others wouldn't share at all. I did not encourage TUMC to move ahead with this.

To my surprise – and later delight – the church had moved ahead with this. And to my relief, this sharing time had become, and continues to be, a very important and often powerful moment in our corporate worship. It is anything but trivial. The sharing goes deep, often into vulnerable places. Often there are tears. People know that they are being cared for and prayed for. Community bonds are deepened. This foolish pastor is grateful that his church made a wise decision while he was away enjoying a wonderful sabbatical leave in Egypt.

My third sabbatical at TUMC came near the end of my time of ministry there, not a logical time to be granted a leave because, after all, I was getting ready to retire. Why would a pastor need time off to rejuvenate himself if he was just going to retire anyway?

But this sabbatical really did come at the initiative of the church. I had announced my retirement plans a year and a half in advance. Some in the church said that they wanted to encourage me to write a book that I could offer the church as a kind of retirement gift – a parting gift of words. I think they probably had in mind that I should go over my twenty years' worth of sermons, pick what I thought were the best ones, and publish them for posterity.

And frankly, I had thought of this too. But to do so I would need some time. It's hard to write a book in one's spare time. The church graciously offered me a three-month partial sabbatical to get this writing underway. I would have no preaching or teaching responsibilities but would continue providing pastoral care and participating in committees. I spent full mornings writing and became a pastor again for the rest of the day. I gathered a support and feedback group from the church and re-read all twenty years of my old sermons. And realized that I wasn't quite as enthusiastic about them now as I thought I had been when I first preached them. It just wasn't in me to publish a book of old sermons. My support group advised me to "just write what is on your heart." And so I did. Herald Press even agreed to publish it under the title *Dancing through Thistles in Bare Feet: A Pastoral Journey*.

I don't know if the congregation saw this as the gift it wanted from me upon my retirement, but that sabbatical, as were the others it they gave me, was another in a long list of gifts that TUMC gave me over those twenty years.

Teaching at Conrad Grebel College

In the mid-1990s, Conrad Grebel College (now Conrad Grebel University College), invited Lydia and I to co-teach the course "Church and Ministry" to their master's degree students in the ministry stream. Lydia would provide some of the more academic components, and I the more practical and ministry-based components. This of course would take some of my time away from ministry at TUMC. Again, the church graciously offered me the extra time to do this. TUMC liked the idea that it could, in this way, be a partner in helping to prepare future church leaders.

And by this time, I was ready to partner with Lydia in this kind of ministry. We were each confident enough in our own realms that we enjoyed the give and take of designing, planning, preparing for, and then teaching this course. The students seemed to enjoy, and hopefully benefited from, the times when we disagreed with each other in class and challenged each other.

For me this was the opportunity I needed to read more broadly in the areas of systems theory, models of doing church, changing expectations of what people want in a pastor, and conflict issues in the church. We later realized that this teaching experience, which we loved for its own sake, also helped prepare us for our joint ministry as intentional interim pastors following my retirement from full-time ministry.

Singing

I have always loved singing, though my voice teacher in college probably despaired at my slow progress in bringing my squeaky voice under control. I have sung in many choirs and conducted choirs, but I certainly don't have a solo-quality voice. Nonetheless I was invited to sing bass in TUMC's male quartet. Two of the others sang professionally. For pure joy and pleasure, and sometimes moments of profound spiritual encounter, those many years of singing with Dennis and Ed and Bob stand out. Thanks to them, and thanks to the church, for inviting us to sing so often in church. Singing energizes me. It plays a large part in my spiritual nurture.

Retirement

As I approached sixty-five years of age, I knew it was time to retire from full-time pastoral ministry. There was no obvious sign in the sky telling me to do this. It wasn't that I was burnt out. It wasn't that I no longer enjoyed my work or found it less than rewarding. It wasn't that the church was hinting at my reduced effectiveness (or if anyone was, I wasn't hearing it). It was more like a quiet inner voice suggesting that I needed a change of pace – and perhaps location for ministry – and that perhaps TUMC needed the renewed vision and energy and impetus a new pastor could provide. I had been there for two decades now. It was time for both church and pastor to move on, to embrace a new future.

And still my retirement was a wrenching time for both Lydia and me. June 2007 was filled with emotional intensity, grieving a huge sense of loss and celebrating twenty years of a deep, mutually supportive relationship between congregation and pastor.

4

Intentional Interim Ministry

After retiring from full-time ministry at Toronto United Mennonite Church in June 2007, I rested for some months. I needed a break. I needed a time of no responsibilities apart from a few guest preacher appearances in other churches. I read, jogged, gardened, golfed, cleaned up files, and travelled a bit. And I grieved. I grieved the loss of a vocation I had loved and a worshipping community I had loved. There is something deeply unsettling about such a transition, even though I had chosen it, even though I felt nudged to do so by God's Spirit, even though I knew in my heart that this was the right thing to do and the right time to do it.

But there was also something very freeing and enjoyable about that transition. It was a huge release to be freed from the heavy demands of full schedules and from the weight of heavy responsibility. There was now time for reflection, some writing, and a renewed appreciation for how much I have cherished my calling. And no doubt new opportunities would come.

The first of these was to spend four months at Associated Mennonite Biblical Seminaries (AMBS) in Elkhart, Indiana. Lydia and I went to AMBS in January 2008, intending to stay through April. There we attended chapel services and student forums, interacted informally with students and professors, taught one course, attended local Mennonite churches, and played Scrabble with SOOP volunteers (Service Opportunities with Our Partners) consisting of seniors who came to AMBS to help in a variety of jobs that needed some extra attention. We were also exploring the idea of writing a book together about weddings and marriage. We even presented a book proposal and outline to a student-faculty forum and were encouraged to start writing. We did start writing. But life intervened. We were invited to be intentional interim pastors at Wideman Mennonite Church in Markham, Ontario, a thirty-five-minute drive from our home in Toronto. We began our work there in March 2008. Our book idea died.

By this time, Lydia and I were ready to be co-pastors. I was refreshed after an eight-month resting period. We both wanted further involvement in ministry, but only if it was part-time. Our experience in teaching the "Church and Ministry" course at Conrad Grebel College so many times had, we thought, given us some of the analytical tools we needed for intentional interim ministry work. We happily began this ministry at Wideman Mennonite Church, followed by a term at Hagerman Mennonite Church, and finally at the Montreal Mennonite Fellowship.

Intentional interim ministry is a very different thing than regular pastoral ministry. The assignment is short term (no more than two years). The church is usually in transition and between pastors. Sometimes there is a great deal of conflict, either openly expressed or coursing just beneath the surface. The "intentional" part of the interim assignment means that it carries a focused agenda, more than just a "fill-in" role between pastors. Adding "intentional" to the name implies that the church has some specific needs that must be addressed. These may be to help process the ending of the previous ministry, whether it was a positive or unhappy ending, deal with unresolved conflict, or focus on a healthier future. Often the members are looking for a new direction, a new vision, a new reason for being where they are. Mostly the church needs to know again that it is deeply loved by God and be given the tools and encouragement to do the hard work of moving from its present to its future story.

We were aware that there has been much debate about the personal style of the interim minister. Some would argue that for the sake of objectivity and professionalism, it is better that the interim minister resist developing friendships and personal engagement with the congregation. After all, there is a hard job to be done, the timeline is short, and then the interim pastor leaves. Especially if there is conflict to be worked through, it is better to be professional and not allow personal investment and feelings to cloud one's thinking and get in the way of the confrontational work that needs to be done.

This approach doesn't work for Lydia and me. Partly this is because of who we are. We see ourselves as very relational people who need to be true to ourselves in order to be effective. And in our experience, so much of the pain in congregations going through a transition is personal and relational pain. We are not convinced that an objective approach will necessarily get to the heart of that pain. Perhaps a more relationship-based ministry can more easily lead to healed relationships. The temptation in using a more relational style, though, may be to avoid naming and saying the difficult things that need to be aired for the sake of the relationship. Our view is that ministry can be both relational and confrontational. One can be very direct in naming what needs to be named within a relationship that is both caring and honest.

Lydia and I did not come to this kind of partnership in ministry easily. Both of us needed to gain some confidence in our own abilities and sense of self-worth. Only in these later years of our marriage did we dare to work together professionally, though we had team-taught a course at Conrad Grebel College. And now we were embarking on interim ministry as a team. Mind you, we still got in each other's way sometimes, and continued to challenge and critique each other, and tried to fob off on the other things we didn't want to do.

We each brought our own experience and style in ministry and teaching to this challenging work. That is helpful as interim ministry is a unique role that needs different approaches than those used in longer-term ministry. The weekend workshops on interim ministry offered by Mennonite Church Eastern Canada (MCEC) were very helpful, but we still had much to learn.

Wideman Mennonite Church, Hagerman Mennonite Church, and Mennonite Fellowship of Montreal

It would not be fair to identify the specifics of our work in these congregations, but I want to name the gifts that this experience gave me in the last formal part of my career as pastor.

One can hardly imagine how radically different these three congregations that invited us to journey with them into their future were from each other in ethos, background, and faith language, though all three are part of the regional MCEC conference, are of a similar size, and located within a largely urban setting. And yet we enjoyed our work in each of these congregations, coming to love them just as we were loved in return. Each had invited us because of particular issues that needed attention – conflict, unhappiness from the ending of previous ministries, uncertainty about the future, or all of these. When there is a heavy agenda and big issues to work through intentionally, it seems surprising that the word "love" can describe the relationship between congregation and intentional interim pastors.

These small congregations (forty to sixty members) impressed us with their resilience, their tenacity, their networks of relationships with the broader community. They had issues to deal with and crises to overcome, but overcome they did. They stayed together despite conflicts. They were ready to personally invest in sorting things out and moving into the future. They weren't as dependent on a pastor as many larger congregations are. Each congregation was a gift to us in very particular ways.

Two things stand out about Wideman Mennonite Church (Markham, Ontario). The congregation has an amazing mission to and relationship with the Alcoholics Anonymous groups that meet in their church basement. That ministry continues to grow and deepen. And we were particularly impressed with the inter-generational relationships within the congregation. There were not enough children to form all the age-group classes that larger churches can, but children and seniors especially connected beautifully with each other. These gifts inspired us.

Hagerman Mennonite Church (Markham, Ontario) also has two unique ministries that could be a model for the wider Mennonite church. They have had a wonderful, mutual relationship with the Markham Chinese Mennonite Church, which has shared their facilities for over twenty years now. And more recently, a similar arrangement has been established with a Tamil Mennonite church. These congregations meet separately for worship but the Sunday school is shared, as is coffee hour after the services. The Chinese young people move easily between the two communities, often leading the music in one or the other. At baptism, they may decide to join one or the other of these churches, and are always at home in both. The Chinese Mennonite Church wisely encourages these dual relationships, knowing that their children will grow up speaking both Chinese and English, and in the long run will need to connect with an English-speaking church.

Hagerman Church has also been able to incorporate into its congregation several persons with mental disabilities who come from a group home, a ministry even now expanding. These adults feel fully at home in the congregation and feel valued.

The Mennonite Fellowship of Montreal (Quebec) is known throughout its neighbourhood, and the city, for its peace and justice work. Its members are deeply connected with several very significant social ministries, some of which were initiated by the Maison de l'amitié (House of Friendship), with whom they share a building. This social agency offers community services, classes, peace activities, and housing for young adults. The Fellowship itself has been able to draw in people from other than Mennonite backgrounds, and from Africa and Latin America. It is a vibrant community. In this church the sacred-secular divide is not as sharp as it sometimes is in other Mennonite churches, and God's presence in the city can be acknowledged and celebrated.

Each of these three churches offered something special to us beyond the personal relationships that were formed. Lydia and I treasure both the relationships and the unique ministries that are at the heart of these churches' lives in their respective settings.

Ending on a High Note

It keeps on surprising us that given the very intense, intentional, direct, and sometimes confrontational naming of issues and conflicts in these three congregations, Lydia and I can say that we ended our professional ministry on a high note. We like to think that we helped each of these congregations move into a healthier future. And we felt a sense of fulfillment in our own ministry. Being able to spend seven years in part-time intentional interim ministry together with Lydia has been an immense gift to me, and has been what I needed so that I could move more gently into full retirement.

INTERLUDE
God's Gifts Have Overflowed

I preached my final sermon at Toronto United Mennonite Church (TUMC) on June 10, 2007. In it I named some of the gifts I had received from that church over the years. I am including most of that sermon here because it expresses the theme of this book: how the churches I have pastored nurtured me and helped sustain my love for my calling.

This is a very rich, full, and wonderful Sunday morning. I celebrate the fact that God continues to call people into pastoral leadership. Witness the licensing toward ordination service this morning for Maureen and Jonathan, our youth pastors. I celebrate the fact that God continues to invite people into the fellowship of God's church. Witness also the membership service this morning for Ernie and John. I celebrate the incredible giftedness of this congregation – all of you. Witness the amazing things this congregation has done over so many years. I celebrate the invitation – the open, loving invitation of Jesus – to eat and drink at his table. Witness our communion table ready for us. And I celebrate the awesome privilege I have had of being your pastor for almost twenty years, a time now in its ending phase.

I have been overly nostalgic this week, and that has coloured this sermon unduly. My apologies. I do want to reflect on my experience of being your pastor, but only as a kind of lens through which to celebrate the much larger picture of what God is doing and what God's people are doing.

There is a deep irony, and maybe even a deep mystery, that almost overwhelms me as I am about to preach my last sermon here at TUMC before retirement. The irony and mystery has to do with the fact that when I began my vocation as pastor forty-two years ago, I was terrified of preaching. I feared that I would have nothing to say after my first sermon or two at Waters Mennonite Church.

It was in the town of Wawa, northern Ontario, on our way to Sudbury that July of 1965 that my panic boiled over. I was going to be a new pastor. I was twenty-three years old. I felt very insecure. I had been quiet for several hours already while driving, brooding away – quiet on the outside, in turmoil on the inside. Suddenly I burst out, right in the middle of Wawa: "Lydia, I think I know what the theme of my first sermon is going to be. But what am I going to preach on after that?"

"What am I going to preach on after that?" And here I am, forty-two years later, still preaching. And the amazing thing is that I have never run out of topics or themes or texts to preach about. Always there have been more than enough, more in fact than I can preach about. There is still panic, often, on an individual Sunday when nothing seems clear. Tuesdays are still my miserable day, when I try to begin preparing and realize again that I have no idea whatsoever how to begin preparing this particular sermon. But always, mysteriously, the pool of possibilities and themes and texts and ideas is bigger than I have time to use, with leftover crumbs filling many baskets (as in waste baskets). I don't know where many of these ideas come from.

It was my oldest son, Mark, who put me in my place about some of the preaching ideas that do come. He was at Canadian Mennonite Bible College, taking a homiletics or preaching course. I was there for meetings and sat down for lunch with him and a table full of other students who had just come from that class. And of course, they were talking about the class offerings that day. They had been studying the classic Princeton three-point sermon. I foolishly entered the conversation and confessed that I very seldom preached a three-point sermon. To which my son replied, "Yeah, Dad seldom makes any points at all."

And here I am at the end of almost twenty years of ministry here in this place, maybe still pointless, wondering which of the many unexplored themes and texts to preach about in this my last sermon here. I have had almost twenty years here to try to find the words. Surely, I must have run out of them. And I think I have. What more can be said in terms of challenge or comfort or inspiration or understanding of a text or our context? If I haven't managed to say what is important over the past twenty years, it is too late now.

But the other part of my heart cries out that the mystery of how God works in our lives and in my life is so big that we will never run out of themes and texts, and we do keep on reaching for language to try to understand it. Words are never going to be enough for this awesome task, but words are all that a preacher can offer. The irony, and the mystery, is that when I started my career as pastor I was terrified of preaching. I panicked about not finding themes and words for the next week, let alone for the next forty-two years. And now, at this ending, there are far more themes and texts than time to preach them. There is a mystery of God's grace at work here, I think. But don't blame God for my lack of points.

Today I celebrate the church – this awesomely gifted group of God's people who do the primary work of the church. I am eternally grateful to God for calling me to be a pastor and for inviting me to exercise my gifts by providing pastoral and spiritual leadership. I am eternally grateful to God for all of you – for each of you – for each of you has been a gift to the church – and to me.

Naming Your Gifts to Me

I want to name some of the ways in which you have been a particular gift to me – a particular blessing to me – and will, I'm sure, continue to be a gift and blessing to any new pastor who will come.

You Have Let Me Be Authentically Me

You have let me be me. You have not squeezed me into a "pastoral" mould. You have let me be Gary first, not Reverend Harder first. And that has been a huge gift to me. One of the things I have been reflecting on as I prepare emotionally for retirement is to ask, "What is my core identity? How central is 'pastor' to who I see myself being?"

We all wear many hats that are each a part of our identity. The pastor hat is certainly a very big one for me. It is a hat I have loved wearing, and which I will find difficult to lay aside. I'm sure I will be tempted in many places and situations to reach for it. I hope I will have the grace to stop myself from planting it on my head in any context related to TUMC. I think I can lay it aside, despite that temptation, because it is not yet central to who I am. Other hats are bigger. Being a husband, a father, a grandfather. Being a friend. Being a follower of Jesus. These all continue after I take off my pastor's hat. These, and others, are more at the core of who I am.

One of your gifts to me has been to let me be Gary first and pastor second, and not to presume how I should wear that pastor's hat. And you are, I think, ready to offer that same gift to your next pastor.

Gary Harder

You Have Opened Your Lives to Me

Another enormous gift is that you have opened your lives to me in remarkable ways. You have welcomed me when I called to invite myself over. Or you have taken the initiative to come to me as your pastor. And so often it has been a sacred moment when you have opened your lives to me – whether in sharing struggle or pain, or in celebrating special moments and special joy and special grace. Often you have made yourselves vulnerable to me, and often there have been very intimate and very sacred moments where God's Spirit is at work in a way that transforms both parishioner and pastor.

I am already grieving giving up pastoral care. I think that of everything I do, I will miss this the most. I am fully aware that pastoral care was what I dreaded most when I first became a pastor, and what I will now grieve the loss of most. Continue to open your lives to each other.

You Have Honoured My Integrity as a Preacher

I will miss preaching too, of course. I will miss it a great deal. Partly this is because you have honoured my integrity as a preacher. You have given me the freedom to speak what is on my mind and on my heart. And that is not to be taken for granted. I have always felt that I could be honest with you: honest about how I interpret the Scriptures even when my interpretation is not conventional or traditional – as, for example, on the issue of homosexuality; honest about how I analyze our context, the world in which we live; honest about my theological views when they are orthodox and when they aren't; honest about what is going on in our lives and in my life.

You have not tried to make me conform to what you think or to what you think is orthodox. You have rightfully challenged what I have said, differed with me, disagreed with me, critiqued me, and sometimes been angry with me, but you have never challenged my freedom to say what is on my heart. You have honoured my integrity as a preacher.

The other gift is that you listen so carefully. You are a listening congregation. Every preacher who preaches here realizes how carefully you listen to a sermon. And I can see your response in your faces. It is an enormous gift to be listened to like that. And that can't be taken for granted, either. In many other settings, it has sometimes felt like I am preaching into a void, not knowing whether anyone is listening, whether anyone is responding at all.

Here you honour us preachers with a keen and attentive listening. You honour us by allowing us to find and express our own voice. You respect our integrity as preachers. That is a wonderful gift that you will, I'm sure, extend to any pastor, and in fact to every person who preaches here.

You Have Nurtured Me and My Family

I have felt well-nurtured here — emotionally, relationally, spiritually, and intellectually. One of the huge temptations for us pastors is to think that we are the primary nurturers, the ones who are always giving, never receiving. We look to help meet others' needs, and forget our own. The huge temptation for the members of a congregation is to see themselves primarily as receivers of nurture — especially from the pastor — and thus become passive recipients, drawing in everything the pastor may have to offer, not realizing that no one can keep on giving without also receiving.

If we pastors only give and don't receive, we will dry up and wither away — wither away spiritually. You have not been passive recipients. In so many ways and in so many settings, you nurture each other and you nurture me. In many committee meetings, we have shared our immediate stories around the table, listened to and cared for each other, and prayed for each other. You have given me three sabbatical leaves in which to renew my energy and vision. Lydia and I have been a part of wonderful small groups. We have known deep friendships here.

This is a very alive place. I keep on being amazed at the gifts that are offered and shared here by so many people – public gifts like worship leading, preaching, music ministry, storytelling, teaching, and ushering. Administrative gifts in leading meetings, organizing projects, and planning events. People-related gifts in forming friendships, caring for each other, touching people's lives, expressing love and acceptance. Behind-the-scenes practical gifts in fixing things, building things, and preparing food.

So often I have felt nurtured here by worship, by wonderful congregational singing, by organizational efficiency, by the open, caring heart of this congregation.

I feel that I can retire, not because I feel dried up and depleted and exhausted but because it is the right time, and I look forward to other ministry opportunities God may have in mind for me. Take to heart the gift of nurturing your leaders and keep on nurturing each other.

You Offer a Rich Diversity to Each Other and to Me

I thrill to the diversity in this congregation – a theological and denominational diversity, a cultural and ethnic diversity, a racial diversity, and an economic diversity. It is hard, sometimes, to see such diversity as a gift. Certainly such diversity is always a challenge. But you are learning well how to name your own story, your own thought, your own convictions, your own interpretations, without demanding that the other agree fully with you. I think we are seeing more and more that our unity is in following Jesus Christ. It is not in agreeing with each other. Our worship can be Christ-centred even while we give each other the freedom to share diverse interpretations and convictions and opinions.

I continue to be fascinated with Jesus and his absolute radicalness for his time and for ours. We Christians differ enormously in how we understand Jesus, of course. How could it be otherwise if he is the fullest expression of a God who will never be fully disclosed or understood? The Christian church over the centuries has done its best to tame down this Jesus, to domesticate him, to make him an ally in our human causes and often for our human wars.

It was the Anabaptists of the sixteenth century who dared a major reconsideration of the Jesus of the Gospels, unleashing a radical movement that sought to follow this Jesus in life, not only to believe in him. And this following included a commitment to peace and non-violence, a commitment to justice and service, to befriending the marginalized and poor and abused, to building a caring community of support. The symbol of this movement was adult believers' baptism. But at its heart this movement brought a new understanding of who Jesus was and what it meant to try to follow him in life. This movement was so radical, so countercultural, so threatening to existing structures that a horrendous persecution was launched to try to stamp it out.

We are the heirs of that movement, and I think the identity of being Anabaptist-Mennonite is still central to us. Many of you come from other than Mennonite heritages, but I think you too resonate with this core identity.

Our diversity, such a blessing, still has some rather solid foundations that hold us joyfully together: a centring on Jesus the Christ, and an understanding of this largely through the lens of Anabaptist identity – holding as very basic a radical following of Jesus into peace and justice and community and inclusion.

Our diversity – played out from solid core convictions – is an immense gift to a congregation. It has been an immense gift to me. And I think it is an immense gift to our world.

Above All, You Have Offered Me and My Family Your Love

Being here as your pastor has always been more than only a job, more than only tasks that needed doing, duties that needed to be fulfilled, responsibilities that needed to be carried out. This has been a place to live life in its fullness – to grow, to fail, to feel safe, to make mistakes, to be challenged, to be supported and encouraged, to struggle, to follow God's mysterious invitation to be God's people.

In the end, I have experienced this as a very loving place. Not always, of course – no humans and no community of humans ever has this love thing completely figured out. But in the end, I have felt loved and have felt empowered to return that love. I have felt immensely blessed being here.

A Prayer of Celebration and Blessing

I will retire from being your pastor feeling that this is a good time to retire – good for me and, I think, good for you as a congregation. You have an amazing potential to be God's hands and God's voice and God's love, here and in many parts of the world. You are an immensely gifted congregation. You are a growing congregation.

I celebrate the privilege it has been to be your pastor. I celebrate what God has done among us and through us. I celebrate what God will still do in and through Toronto United Mennonite Church.

I close with the prayer of Paul for the church at Ephesus. This is my prayer for you:

> For this reason, I bow my knees before the Father, from whom every family in heaven and on earth takes its name. I pray that, according to the riches of God's

glory, God may grant that you may be strengthened in your inner being with power through God's Spirit, and that Christ may dwell in your hearts through faith, as you are being rooted and grounded in love. I pray that you may have the power to comprehend, with all the saints, what is the breadth and length and height and depth, and to know the love of Christ that surpasses knowledge, so that you may be filled with all the fullness of God.

Now to him who by the power at work within us is able to accomplish abundantly far more than all we can ask or imagine, to him be glory in the church and in Christ Jesus to all generations, forever and ever. Amen. (Ephesians 3:14–21)

PART TWO
DEVELOPING MY OWN VOICE

It sometimes seemed to me that the pastoral role wanted to consume my entire identity. I knew this was dangerous. I knew that I needed a strong inner core that was separate from my vocation. If my sense of self and of self-worth were tied too closely to my success or failure as a pastor, both my professional and personal life would suffer. Professionally, I would be tempted to cater to what people wanted rather than needed. Personally, I would become hollow inside. But how does one retain a strong sense of self and self-worth apart from one's professional calling? How can we pastors let our core self shape our ministry rather than allow our ministry to totally shape who we are? (Although it will, of course, shape us in some ways.)

I knew I needed to pay attention to my personal life. I needed to develop my own voice. I needed to pay attention to my physical needs, my inner spirituality, my love for music, and my personal relationships, especially my marriage. Only then could I partner with a congregation in a duet that would bring joy, love, and healing to everyone who heard the congregational song.

If one part of paying attention to my personal voice, sense of self, and self-worth was learning to respond to feedback and critique in non-threatening and dialogical ways, another part was to acknowledge and develop those things that gave me joy and fulfillment. These included music and sports.

I have always enjoyed singing. All my life I have sung in the congregation, in choirs, in small groups, in quartets, and even in duets. But I have been shy about singing solo. Part of this shyness is knowing that I don't have a professional quality voice. My voice lessons persuaded both me and my voice teachers of this. Singing with others seems to free me from my self-consciousness and lets me fully enjoy music making. Singing solo seems to expose my inner discomfort in having a voice that is not professional quality – and thus not quite worthy of exposing, even in very informal, non-professional settings like church.

And so I have sometimes missed out on opportunities when singing solo would have been appropriate and would have been appreciated. In fact, the few times I actually risked singing pieces of songs as a part of my sermon, the response was very positive. Perhaps I felt freer to sing when the focus was on the sermon, not on my voice.

My singing story, metaphor as it is, serves as a warning to me in my personal story. As a pastor, my personal voice could easily be consumed by the people I worked for and with. I was sometimes tempted to quiet my own inner voice. But doing so would hollow me out, both professionally and personally.

In this section I reflect on what nurtured my spirit, what gave me joy, what helped me develop a personal "solo voice," what shaped my identity apart from the professional hat I wore. I needed to value my uniqueness as a person. I needed to be responsible for my personal wholeness and growth.

I have profound respect for colleagues who don't share my good physical health and yet continue to offer a wonderful ministry. Likewise, I have a deep appreciation for colleagues who are single and can't rely on a partner for support or for helping them maintain a healthy self-image. Their stories of attending to their inner spirit and self-care would be very different than mine.

Yet here I want to share my story. This part of the book includes reflections on caring for my physical health and well-being (which includes my love of sports), nurturing my spirit through music, and recognizing how my marriage, family, and friendships profoundly shape who I am.

INTERLUDE
Dialogue with a Mirror – While Shaving

An important part of caring for one's well-being means attending to self-worth and self-image. Here I offer a short dialogue, previously written for a youth audience.

Face: Oh, what an ache in my gut! Perfect for such a God-awful morning. Oh, right, wasn't supposed to say that. Grin and bear it, they say. Hello, Mirror, what do you have to say for yourself?

Mirror: Nothing!

Face: Huh, could've expected as much from a mirror. Well, what have you got to say for me then? Come on, straight from the shoulder, ever seen a more handsome face?

Mirror: Face – not bad. But what's behind it?

Face: Look, just answer my questions, OK? How do you like my smile?

Mirror: Not much.

Face: You've got to be kidding. What's wrong with it?

Mirror: It's only a face smile.

Face: And what's that supposed to mean?

Mirror: It's a smile that hides more than it reveals.

Face: You're rather bold today, Mirror. I'll thank you to mind your own business.

Mirror: You look. I reflect.

Face: I didn't want to look that closely.

Mirror: But I've noticed you have looked at your face image a little differently the last while, Face, as if you were seeing beyond those pimples and that droopy eyelid. What are you seeing?

Face: I'd prefer if you reflected back what I want to see, Mirror.

Mirror: Sure, Face, you'd really like me to be a magnifying glass, building you up twice as big as you are; make you come across as a hero-type good guy, if not so much to others, at least to yourself. Well, let me tell you something. I add nothing to an image. I work with what I've got standing in front of me. Right now, that's you, the way you are. I don't reflect the pretend you.

Face: And I've hated you for it, Mirror, like I sometimes almost hate myself. Funny how I try so hard to be somebody I'm not and end up not liking the image I try so hard to create.

Mirror: And yet you keep on trying to fake yourself and everybody else.

Face: I'd get away with it too if it weren't for you. If only you would play my game.

Mirror: I've been watching you pretty closely the last while as you shave. You get all lathered white, faceless blob, expressionless eyes, waiting the razor's edge. And then you start to shave. One stroke after another, your white mask is ripped off and your face emerges. And then you sort of look at yourself as if saying, "I wish I could shave off the big mask – that big smiling blob that covers me, that I hide behind everywhere I go." A few times I really thought you were beginning to pull a razor through that mask.

Face: I did make a few strokes. But I lathered up again. I was scared.

Mirror: Of what?

Face: Of myself. And of what others would think.

Mirror: What do others think now?

Face: That I'm confident, sure of myself; that I'm in command of myself and of my world; that I'm a pretty decent guy; that I have a lot of friends.

Mirror: And you don't have a lot of friends?

Face: Sure, I have friends. Quite a few in fact. But a lot of them have masks on too.

Mirror: So, your masks are friends with each other! Should be quite a budding little friendship.

Face: They can carry on a lively conversation. And sometimes it's quite a lot of fun.

Mirror: And yet you're lonely?

Face: I'm lonely. Sometimes real lonely.

Mirror: Anything else you saw when you lifted that mask?

Face: Look, I've had enough for one day. I'm getting tired of you poking around.

Mirror: You're still looking at me. You can leave any time. And it's called reflecting, not poking.

Face: I don't want to look, but I can't leave.

Mirror: You really didn't like what you saw, eh?

Face: I've never been able to measure up to what I've wanted to be or what my parents wanted me to be. I try to prove myself over and over again that I'm worth something, and it just doesn't seem to work. I feel like a failure, like everything I do turns sour. I guess I'm programmed for failure.

Mirror: Do I detect a note of self-pity?

Face: That's what l am. I'm not good. I'm not worth anything at all. I'm all bad.

Gary Harder

Mirror: You do go to extremes, don't you, Face – from confident wonder boy to abject nothingness. I really don't think I'm reflecting either of those.

Face: Well, that's what I see.

Mirror: Then you still don't see what is really there, what is really you.

Face: What is really there, then? Isn't my loneliness, frustration, shyness, insecurity, worry, all there? Isn't that all a part of me?

Mirror: Sure, it is. But what has that to do with badness and failure and nothingness?

Face: Never thought of that before.

Mirror: You know, Face, being a mirror, I've studied up on reflections and images. A big mirror told me once that humans are a kind of reflection of God. Made me envious, that did.

Face: You mean like I was made in the image of God? I wish I could believe that, or at least recognize what it is of God's image that I have.

Mirror: One thing I can tell you. It's not the mask that is the image of God.

Face: Not the wonder boy, or the nothingness. Seems like there's only me left.

80

Mirror: Say, that's more like it. It feels good to be able to reflect something of substance for a change. What I want to know now is whether this has been only a private showing or whether you'll let others see inside of you, too.

Face: Will people still like me if they know who I really am?

Mirror: Let them know and find out, then

5

Nurturing Physical and Emotional Well-Being

My life as an adult has mostly been lived indoors. But I have had a deep need to also be outdoors. Growing up on a farm kept me outside most days. Throughout my working life, I knew I needed to spend time in God's creation. My emotional well-being suffers when I am confined too long inside walls. In being outdoors and physically active, I find a balance in life, an outlet, a place where I gain energy. There I find a key to maintaining my physical and emotional and relational well-being.

In this chapter I tell a number of sports stories. Although I am an introvert by nature, these stories have a "relationship" theme woven through them, often relationship with strangers. Somehow, on a golf course or in an arena, almost despite myself, very interesting engagements happen. This relationship world extends beyond my church world, another gift to me. Here I can be a bit more relaxed, not really caring about my competence, at how well I am playing the game. The point is engagement and interaction.

Enjoying Sports

I feel particularly blessed by my good physical health, surely a gift from God. I have always felt energized by my calling and my work, even when there were stressful, energy-draining demands placed on me. I think that my overall excellent health has been an important factor in sustaining my energy for my calling. I have never had a serious illness. When I was a teen, surgeons made two unsuccessful attempts to remove a baker's cyst from my left knee. But the cyst never really bothered me, apart from looking rather ugly. In my twenty years of ministry at Toronto United Mennonite Church I missed less than a week of work for health reasons – and that was mostly to deal with an ankle broken playing slow pitch baseball on our church team (I stepped awkwardly on second base trying to stretch a double).

My good health has been a gift, but I like to think that my enjoyment of sports and many outdoor activities has contributed to that health. One of the sports (among many) that I really enjoy playing is hockey. By good fortune, a Baptist pastor friend of mine invited me to join him and a casual group of players who played hockey every Thursday afternoon (yes, I still play with them). They are a wonderful group of hockey enthusiasts, mostly middle aged and older, though there are a few players in their thirties and forties whom I certainly cannot keep up with. Hockey can be a bit rough. Not in this group. There is no "hitting," no body checks allowed, though slap shots are. And amazingly, there are almost never any flashes of anger – or if there are, they are gone in a few seconds.

But one Thursday afternoon an opposing player had a short outbreak of temper. He is a much better player than I, but I managed to take the puck away from him. On impulse he checked me, his shoulder hitting my left knee (I still don't know how), and I limped off the ice. The doctor told me that my ACL was damaged, and I would need to be off skates for at least a month. I was upset with this development – until I realized that the baker's cyst on my knee had disappeared. Two surgeries couldn't expunge it. The thing just grew back. And now an angry, out-of-character check did the thing in for good. It never grew back. I do love to play hockey.

And Al and I have become very good friends. For a number of years, we would arrive early before almost every game so that we could go to the nearby Tim Horton's for a coffee, donut, and chat. We often talked about our respective challenges and joys in ministry. We sought each other's advice. We encouraged each other. We preached in each other's churches. And we always played against each other on the ice, much to the delight of our teammates, who enjoyed joking about the Baptist and the Mennonite pastors fighting each other in the corners.

A year ago, Al moved to another ministry in London, Ontario, and I have missed our weekly coffee time – and our tilts on the ice. We met recently in London, and our conversation again went deep. When I retired from full-time ministry in 2007, Al became one of my confidants as I processed that journey. Along the way, I had walked with him as he went through surgery and radiation for tongue cancer. And now I listened to Al and his wife talk about the challenges of transitioning from one ministry and city to another. It was the ministerial that brought us together, and the hockey that kept us together as we forged this close bond.

Another contributor to my good health is the gift God gave me for sleeping. Essentially nothing disturbs my sleep – apart from a few middle-of-the-night crisis calls. There were some of these over the years, including a few from con artists who thought that a half-awake, compassionate, gullible pastor might be an easy mark. To me this ability to sleep is a huge gift. No matter how intense an evening engagement is, when I lie down for night it is gone and I fall asleep immediately. I wake up refreshed. I wake up ready to tackle the new day, with whatever challenges or routine it may bring (with aging there are now one or two understandable interruptions at night, but even so I easily fall back to sleep again).

I feel that my love for sports has also contributed to my good health – even if I sometimes spend too much time watching them on TV. From childhood on I have participated in a wide variety of sports, though I am not particularly good at them. I am on the clumsy side. I am not particularly well coordinated. I look awkward.

It may be that one of the reasons I still love sports is precisely because I wasn't particularly good at them. I was never good enough to play at an organized high level, where coaches were demanding and pressure built up. I just played for fun on lower-level teams. I sometimes regret that I never got the coaching that might have helped me develop better skills. But I also know people who were much more skilled than I and who received this kind of coaching, then quit sports because they couldn't deal with the pressure and burned out. Meanwhile, I still play hockey and still look forward to games every Thursday afternoon all winter. Next winter I hope to add curling to my sport activities. I've never curled, so I will be very poor at it.

Lydia does not share my love of sports. She decided years ago that she really didn't need to be an obedient wife by watching sports with me. In the last years we have agreed to have two television sets so that we could each watch what we wanted. We tried golfing together but that wasn't very successful. Maybe golf is too close to being a sport.

But we do share a love for the outdoors. We have always enjoyed camping. Our most relaxed vacations were those spent tenting beside a lake. We share a love for canoeing, hiking, swimming in a lake, barbequing freshly caught fish. We have always enjoyed gardening together, though more recently, since Lydia has had both hips replaced, I do most of the physical work. We did have a rather good gardening partnership. She managed the flowers and I the vegetables. She has much more of an eye for the beautiful in nature, and I am inclined to be a bit more practical.

It may be that jogging has been a primary factor in maintaining my good physical health. I started jogging with several classmates at seminary and since then it has been a part of my life. I run far too slowly for racing. But I am tenacious enough and disciplined enough to sustain jogging. I have needed jogging, not only for my physical health but also for my emotional health.

Most people would say that I have an even temperament, not really given to explosions or excesses. While that is true, I do get tense and out of sorts and a bit edgy with those closest to me. Jogging helps me sort things out. It is hard to stay tense when you are physically close to exhaustion.

Sometimes I have figured out a whole sermon outline while jogging, and I hurry to find paper or computer after I get back. Sometimes my mind simply stays blank and I have no idea what I was thinking about while running. And sometimes I marvel at the sights and smells of my environment, especially in spring and fall. Lydia wonders why I like to jog by myself. She needs company to exercise, which she gets at her early morning swim. I welcome the time alone that jogging affords.

I know that I cannot take my good physical health for granted, especially now as I age. I am also aware, from many sources, that pastors generally have a rather poor health record. Apparently, most of us are in poorer health than our parishioners.

Gary L. Harbaugh, in the foreword to Gwen Halaas's book *Clergy, Retirement, and Wholeness*, makes this claim: "Twenty years ago, in 'Pastor as Person and The Faith-hardy Christian,' I reported the research results after thousands of administrations of my holistic Faith-hardiness Inventory. When asked to put in rank order the physical (body), mental (thinking), emotional (feeling), social (relating), and spiritual (believing), clergy consistently ranked the physical lowest."[6]

Gwen Halaas reports her own recent study of pastors in the Evangelical Lutheran Church in America (average age fifty). She says that "two out of three were overweight, one in three was obese, one in four had high blood pressure and high cholesterol, and nearly one in five had suffered from serious depression in

---

6   See Gwen Wagstrom Halaas, *Clergy, Retirement, and Wholeness: Looking Forward to the Third Age* (Herndon, VA: Alban Institute, 2005), foreword.

the past year ... These health issues appear to have a higher incidence in pastors than in the general population."[7]

I am overwhelmingly grateful to God for my good physical health. I like to think that had I had serious health issues to deal with, my congregations would have supported me and walked with me through them. I like to think that a good, covenantal kind of relationship between congregation and pastor would always mean a caring support for each other that nurtures health in both, and is especially sensitive when that health is threatened in the other.

Not Always on the Straight and Narrow – Golfing Stories

I like to think that the sport of golfing has contributed to my good health, even if I am a very erratic golfer. I sincerely hope that I was a better pastor than I am a golfer. If not, I would be in some despair. But I have thoroughly enjoyed being both, partly because of the company I get to keep along the way. As neither pastor nor golfer have I been able to stay consistently on the "straight and narrow."

During the fifteen and a half years I spent in Edmonton being a pastor and pretending to be a golfer, I had pastor colleagues and friends as golfing companions almost every Monday through the golfing season. One Mennonite Brethren reverend hit the ball farther than I could, but had an awesome hook. The other Mennonite Brethren minister was much more laid-back and modest in his swing, and didn't have nearly as far to go when looking for his lost ball. And the Swiss Mennonite padre, true to his background (we called them "Old" Mennonites, and they were generally known to be stricter and more straight-laced, though that didn't really apply to this particular individual)

---

7   Halaas, *Clergy, Retirement, and Wholeness*, p. 15.

usually stayed away from the dangerous rough. Since he was content with a shorter drive, he sometimes had to hit the ball more often to get to the green. I was known for having a magnificent slice.

We played and conversed and argued and laughed through almost every golf course in the greater Edmonton area, and sometimes travelled a hundred miles to try a new one, especially one that offered a good special. Perhaps our camaraderie on the golf course contributed to the close working relationships among the churches we led.

Alas, in my twenty-five years of living in Toronto I have not been privileged with that same depth of golf companionship. My ministerial colleagues here are too wise to be looking for lost golf balls when they could be searching for straying sheep, so they resist my invitations to go golfing. Most of my other friends don't have Monday as their day off, so we golf together only very occasionally. Usually I sign up as a single, ready to be teamed up with strangers.

But There Are Compensations

One compensation has been access to "clergy privileges" on Mondays, on a very fine private/public course forty minutes away. The Pheasant Run Golf Club near Newmarket, Ontario, lets clergy play a full round of golf for the princely sum of $11.30, a "donation" the club apparently gives to charity. Pheasant Run tends to be full of clergy of every stripe and tradition on Mondays, and since I usually come as a single (apart from the rare time my clergy son from Kitchener can join me), I get paired up with an impressive diversity of fellow reverends.

The "clergy privileges" story has an air of mystery around it. Over the years, I have heard various explanations for that largess. An article in a local newspaper, *The Era* (August 12,

2012), offers what seems to be a legitimate story. Journalist Simon Martin writes that when the founding owner, Gordon Evans, was developing the golf course in the late 1970s, he had trouble finding a sufficient source of water and was looking for divine intervention.

Said his son and present president, Mr. Evans: "Dad was getting a little panicky. He said if he found water, he would look after the clergy." He soon found a very abundant water source, and, true to his promise, has "looked after" us clergy ever since. And that does explain, somewhat, the clergy privileges at Pheasant Run. But it doesn't account for the persistent legend that a certain Catholic priest "witched" for the water, and, finding an abundant aquifer, reaped for all clergy this privilege.

Whatever the story, Mondays often see me heading north by myself and getting teamed up with an assortment of fellow clergy – or sometimes just perplexed club members – in pursuit of the elusive straight drive. All I am required to do when signing in is show my Ontario government–issued certificate of registration that authorizes me to officiate at weddings, plus my driver's licence to prove that the certificate and licence belong to the same person. (It feels a little ironic that I as a Mennonite come from a tradition that has championed the separation of church and state, and yet now reap the benefits of an official connection to the state. Even more ironic is that the Pheasant Run Golf Club has, completely coincidentally, chosen to display a photocopy of my certificate of registration on their counter as a way of informing all clergy of what they are required to produce to benefit from this clergy privilege. There it is: my name and registration number, prominently displayed in the clubhouse. If only they knew how inadequately I represented the golfing abilities of the clergy!)

Occasionally, I go to a local city golf course much closer by. There too I get paired with strangers, for better or for worse. On both courses, I am amazed at the stories that emerge in our pursuit of a little white ball with a mind of its own. I share a few of them here.

The Cantors

On this day, on the public course, I was paired with two Jewish cantors, one of whom was very extroverted and talkative, the other much more introverted and quiet. I, by personality, am much more like the second one and can be quite content minding my own business and rationing my words, especially when walking side by side with strangers. I do engage in the expected pleasantries, of course, which always include exchanging first names and claiming to be glad to be partnering with the other, whether we are glad to do so or not (is casual golf known for its honesty?).

The problem is that these opening pleasantries usually include the question, "So what do you do?" My fellow golfers that day found out that I was a Christian clergyman, and after further questioning, that I was a Mennonite one. They were quite intrigued. And I learned that they were Jewish cantors and was likewise intrigued. I have a Mennonite friend who is a very fine voice teacher, who happens to coach some Jewish cantors and has brought some of that Jewish musical influence into our church occasionally. So, I was quite easily hooked into conversation.

They gladly talked about their unique role, which included not only "canting," or singing the Scriptures, but also a fair bit of teaching the Scriptures. As we chased balls and chased threads of thought, they (especially the extroverted one) talked so easily about different schools of biblical interpretation. I had heard this before, but it probably hadn't registered in the same way it did now. Their tradition in the Talmud and Midrash, for example, they said, recognizes that there are often diverse, even opposite interpretations from different schools of thought. These are placed side by side, the tension between them not needing to be resolved. It could be hundreds of years before one interpretation or the other gains prominence. In the meantime, they could teach both.

There is so often more than one way to interpret a text. I admired the ease with which they could acknowledge that, and their humility in not needing to have a final authoritative conclusion. It seemed to me that so often we Christians insist there is only one way to read a text, especially a controversial one, and that "my reading is the only right one." We are so often reluctant to chase an interpretation down a different fairway, even when the argument we are pursuing is getting narrower and narrower and running out of space. These cantors were teaching me a more relaxed, modest, and much more patient approach to biblical interpretation.

I have no memory of how well or how poorly any of us hit the golf ball. In the end that seemed to have no importance. I do remember a very animated, enjoyable discourse as we traversed that course that day.

The Healer

Rarely do I resent the partners arbitrarily assigned me. There are certainly times when the conversation doesn't go much beyond the pleasantries of the introduction. For whatever reason, there are games when we mostly stay at the "great shot" level of engagement. It may be my mood, or the other's mood, or just the realization after learning our respective prejudices that there isn't much point in pursuing our differences if we want to enjoy our game. Most of the time, though, I keep on being surprised at how enjoyable, and even deep, the conversations are with colleagues from other traditions.

One Monday I did struggle with the playing companion I had been paired with. Our foursome was made up of two fortyish-looking club members and two clergy. The club members knew about the "clergy privileges" and were possibly intrigued to be playing with a self-defined charismatic, and a Mennonite who wasn't wearing a beard after all. They joked about needing to tame their normal, more colourful language when they hit an errant ball, and about needing divine intervention when faced with an impossible lie.

And then one of them sprained his ankle. Coming out of the woods on a decline, he lost his balance and twisted his ankle. He was in considerable pain and thought he would have to abandon his round. I offered sympathy. My charismatic clergy companion offered much more. In fact, he quite insisted on holding a "healing prayer service" right there. The injured man was deeply uncomfortable with the idea and said he wasn't ready to be thus prayed over.

I too felt very uncomfortable, which is surely perplexing since I do believe in prayer and in God's healing. And yet here I was, distancing myself from my colleague. My colleague wouldn't take no for an answer. In fact, he grabbed that offending ankle, held it in his hands, and offered a loud prayer for God's healing.

The healing didn't happen. The two club members got into their cart, visibly embarrassed, and left to find a doctor. We two clergy finished our round, mostly in silence. I was upset with my colleague, and then with myself. Why hadn't I been ready to confront his disregard for our wounded companion's discomfort? And he? I don't know. I can only imagine that he may have blamed the injured man's lack of faith, or his clergy companion's lack of faith, for God's reluctance to restore that ankle.

But why did I not have it out with him? Was there that big of a gap between our respective understandings of prayer and healing and engagement with non-believers that we couldn't converse about them? A day's-off enjoyment of a game of golf is probably not the time or place for a confrontation. But surely, I could have at least invited some conversation. Why didn't I say something like, "I felt a bit uncomfortable with what you just did. Can we talk about it?" But I didn't. And because I didn't, we probably both felt uneasy as we finished our game of golf.

The Unordained

It was at the public course where I got into a stimulating conversation with a former Catholic priest. We again were four strangers, four "singles" brought together as a foursome. But somehow this former priest and I became a kind of twosome, almost ignoring the other two. And since the other two didn't seem interested at all in our conversation, this felt all right. We were drawn to each other's stories and to each other's "theology of the church."

Following ordination to the priesthood, my golfing companion spent years in Brazil as a missionary. Gradually he began to question his own calling to the priesthood. Upon returning to Canada, he entered a very deliberate two-year retreat to sort out his sense of calling and his commitment to the church. Following that period of soul-searching and discernment he withdrew from the priesthood, but not from the church. He kept his faith and still loved the church, though he offered many critiques of it.

Leaving the priesthood was a wrenchingly difficult decision for him. If I heard him right, there were two basic reasons – the power a priest had and the loneliness a priest experienced.

I thought his argument against the rule of priestly celibacy was quite insightful. "It's all about intimacy," he said. The issue for him and, he insisted, for many priests, was not the lack of a sexual partner. The issue is not abstinence from sex. The issue is a lack of deep personal intimacy with another person, a void that intimacy with God still cannot replace. A priest has an extremely busy and full life, carrying out the demands of that vocation. "And then you come home, emptied, to an empty room. I experienced extreme loneliness. I couldn't survive that way. And this is true for many of the priests I know." Several years later he did marry, though he insisted he didn't leave the priesthood in order to get married.

The other issue that troubled him was priestly power – his own as a priest, but even more basically the power of the hierarchy. "Basic church decisions are always made at the top, and then forced down. Our lay people are disengaged. And they are getting angry. There is a huge gap between the pronouncements from on high and the lives and beliefs of ordinary Catholics. The hierarchy is totally out of touch."

And then we rambled over other topics such as birth control, abortion, homosexuality, closed communion, church schools, and how to be church in a post-modern world. We wandered across different fairways of thought and sometimes got lost in the woods as we acknowledged the complexities of these issues.

What surprised me again in the end was that this former Catholic priest, in some ways very critical of the church, still functioned as a priest in an unofficial way in a local church. He loved teaching the Scriptures and engaging with young adults around their faith issues. His priest welcomed these ministries.

I was also surprised by how much we had in common as we talked about the various issues all churches, regardless of denomination, face. We did not hear each other primarily as disenchanted and critical churchgoers but as fellow followers of Jesus who loved the church and were looking for its renewal. I did not come away from that conversation with an anti-Catholic bias but with a deep appreciation for the way local churches live their calling faithfully, sometimes despite orders "from on high".

I pondered again the tension between leadership and followership, and the temptation of leaders – pastors or conference personnel – to make decisions that do not resonate with the grassroots. How do people who have been given the power to lead use that to empower and engage the whole church? And I pondered the mystery of profound intimacy. How is that for an innocent game of golf?

The Insider

One of the few recurring golfing companions I had was a member of my congregation. I was his pastor. Other people in the congregation smiled when they heard of our golfing partnership. It was public knowledge that he and I saw most things differently when it came to theology and how we read the Bible. He represented very well the most traditional voice of the congregation and the most direct and literal interpretation of the Bible. And I? I like to think that I hold our best traditions dear, but confess that I am more ready to explore new understandings of how Scripture and context meet.

The reality was that we disagreed with each other on a whole lot of subjects. We each held our positions with deep conviction. And yet we respected each other, talked easily with each other, and enjoyed golfing together. And we enjoyed each other's humour.

Our theological disagreements came into sharp focus over a particularly controversial issue the church was wrestling with. He became the focal point for a position very different from mine, very publicly delineated.

Unfortunately, shortly after this he was diagnosed with terminal cancer. He welcomed my pastoral care during this time, and he wanted me to officiate at his funeral when he died. The challenge was for me to find a way to honour and celebrate his life at his funeral while being honest about our many differences of opinion. The whole congregation was aware of these differences and wondered what I would do with them on this solemn occasion.

His daughter gave me a key. As I was meeting with the family to prepare for the funeral, she said, "Dad always enjoyed your humour, Gary. I think he would have wanted you to show some of that humour at his funeral." And so, along with reflecting on some of his favourite passages of Scripture, I ventured into the rough with some reflections on our golfing companionship. I included the following in my funeral sermon:

> This I would say about golfing with "Jim." I could hit the ball a few yards further than he could on a drive. But never as straight. This became a metaphor for me. [By this time the congregation is smiling – they see where this is going.] His golfing, like his theology, was more straight and narrow than was mine. He thought me too wild in both golf and in my theology. I kept on exploring adjacent fairways in both, while he stayed in the centre.
>
> Sometimes he totally disagreed with my interpretations of Scripture. He had very decided opinions on many things, and often took a straighter and narrower path through the Scriptures than I did. He read in a very direct, straightforward, simple way, and was a bit impatient with nuanced interpretations. He certainly knew his Scriptures, based his convictions and life on them, and tried to live out his faith without compromise. And that I respected very deeply in him, even while we disagreed with each other.

The whole congregation chuckled, and knew this to be true. I still miss him.

My Blue Mood Companion

This would be my last golfing round of the year on a beautiful Tuesday afternoon in early November. But I was in a rather blue mood. I call it my "loner" mood. I wanted to be alone. I had had enough of people. Life had been busy and full of people. I felt the need to get away and be by myself. I also felt the need for a game of golf – by myself.

I reasoned, reasonably enough, I thought that if I went to the course later in the afternoon, after all hope of playing all eighteen holes was past, I would be alone. Surely no one else would be foolish enough to start their round knowing it would get dark before they could finish.

Alas, one other person was just as foolish as was I. He was already at the first tee, ready to drive his ball. Who knows, maybe he was in a "loner" mood as well, just as upset as I was when he saw me coming. I was told by the starter to join him. I tried to hide my disappointment. My about-to-be golfing companion looked older than I. And he was Chinese. "Probably can't even speak English," I muttered to myself.

But etiquette says you must engage with the other. It's both the human thing to do and the expected thing to do on the golf course. I tried to smile nicely as we met and exchanged names and drove the first tee. But I did feel resentful.

It turned out his English was very good, after all. We exchanged names. And then he asked me the question I didn't really want him to ask: "So, what do you do?"

"I am a clergyman," I replied, "and I also do some teaching at our college."

"Oh, and from which denomination, and where do you teach?" (Another set of questions I did not want him to ask.)

It came out a bit reluctantly, but I managed to say, "I am the pastor of a Mennonite church, and my wife and I teach a course at Conrad Grebel University College." And then his face broke into a huge smile.

"Our family is Catholic," he said. "My son went to Conrad Grebel and loved it there. He graduated with a music degree and is now a Catholic priest. He had a wonderful experience at Grebel."

And the conversation just took off from there. He told me his story. He had been a high school math teacher. He experienced a tragedy in his life – I think it was because his wife had died – and he, in despair, entered a deep depression. Because of that his own physical health failed, and he felt his life was at risk. He moved to Toronto because his elderly father said he would take care of him.

Sometimes, during despairing and sleepless nights, through the thin wall, he heard his father praying for him. And that started his healing journey. He wanted to refocus his life, find something that could give him meaning again and a reason to live. He remembered how much he had enjoyed the piano lessons he took in Hong Kong when he was a child, a love for music he had long neglected as a math teacher. He would go back to music studies and music making. And he would go back to church.

At the time of our conversation, he had recorded five CDs of spiritual songs for the Catholic church, music he had composed and performed. His face, his heart, his life breathed joy.

By now it was getting dark, increasingly hard to follow the flight of a golf ball. We cut off three holes and crossed back into the first nine so that we could finish our game on hole number nine at the clubhouse. There I turned to him to shake his hand in farewell. He would have none of that.

"Gary," he said, "this has been such a special round of golf. We have had an amazing fellowship here on the course. Would you join me in praying the Lord's Prayer together? I think that is something that Catholics and Mennonites can do together."

We put our hands on each other's shoulders, there in front of the clubhouse of this very public course, and prayed the Lord's Prayer together.

What an incredible gift that round of golf was to me. My wife marvelled that I came home smiling when I had left frowning.

Gratitude

Paying attention to my physical well-being has played an important role in nurturing my inner voice and personal sense of self-worth. I feel very grateful for my excellent health – and for a metabolism that seems to deal with any of my caloric excesses. As I write this I am recovering from a minor head cold, the first I have contracted in years. It serves to remind me again of my good fortune. Good health has been a major factor, I think, in sustaining my emotional health and my energy for and love of ministry.

6

'Tis Music That Nurtures My Spirit

I made one of the worst decisions of my life while only in grade three: I quit taking piano lessons. My parents were very upset. They pled, remonstrated, argued, tried to bribe me – all to no avail. I insisted on quitting. Practising piano, after all, was interfering with playing hockey. No matter that music making and music education and piano playing were seen in our family system as having far higher value than chasing a puck on the ice. Mom was a pianist. Dad was a choir conductor. An older brother was excelling at piano and would later excel in voice. Our newly bought record player breathed out a steady stream of classical music.

And still, I quit piano lessons. Much later, as I approached grade twelve, I deeply regretted that rash choice. My regret may have been tied to an enormous growth spurt, which had made me so physically awkward that I felt useless playing hockey anyway. (My brothers teased me mercilessly during that time: "Gary, you are stumbling around so slowly that we have to measure you against a fence post to see if you are actually moving forward.") But more likely, I was beginning to understand in myself that music was something that I loved, and now didn't have the skill to express via the piano. My changing voice hadn't settled down yet, so I certainly couldn't produce any pleasant music by singing.

I started taking piano lessons again in grade twelve. I knew this was too late to make a pianist out of me. My fingers, muscled but stiff from irrigating and pitching hay, couldn't respond adequately anymore. But I wanted to study music anyway. I continued with piano lessons at Canadian Mennonite Bible College (CMBC), fully aware that I would never make a good pianist but wanting to gain enough skill to at least play hymns and read a choral score so that I could conduct it. By then I had realized that my musical passion was actually conducting music. Somehow, I passed my Royal Conservatory grade eight piano examination, though not with a mark I could boast about.

At CMBC I was in two degree programs, graduating with a Bachelor of Christian Education and a Diploma of Sacred Music. I was following two loves that have stayed with me throughout my life: thinking biblically and theologically, and making music. These two passions have at times competed with each other. It took me a long time to make that final decision, acknowledging that God was inviting me to be a pastor and not a professional musician. My voice lessons quickly showed me that I would never be a soloist. But I knew I would always love to sing and would always love to make music. At CMBC I sang in the touring choirs, mass choirs, and quartets, and conducted music where I could. Later, when I went to Goshen College to finish my BA, I graduated with a major in music.

I knew that music would constantly sustain me and nurture me and inspire me throughout my ministry.

My "Pow-Wow" Music

It was one of my grandsons who thus named my musical passion. As a young lad, this Indigenous grandchild was quite deeply involved in traditional dancing, an expression of First Nations spirituality. He was an amazing sight in his gorgeous regalia, dancing his heart out to the haunting singing and drumming of traditional pow-wow music. Mitchel and his siblings were at our house one Sunday morning, and as I was engrossed in my usual Sunday morning routine of listening to Bach, I heard him explain to the younger ones what this strange music was all about. "Oh, that's Opa's pow-wow music."

"Right on, Mitchel, that's a great insight." Traditional Indigenous pow-wow music, with its drumming and singing and dancing, expresses the heart of Aboriginal spirituality, a profound connection with the Creator. For me, the music of Bach expresses a deep part of my spirituality, a profound connection with God. For the last fifty years, almost without exception, I have listened to the music of Bach every Sunday morning. (Lydia first put up with this idiosyncrasy and eventually fully tuned in to my Sunday morning habit). Mostly I listen to Bach's choral music – cantatas, masses, chorales, motets – but also to instrumental works. Sometimes, but not nearly always, I follow the texts thus explored. But really, it is the music itself that touches my spirit. During all my years of ministry, listening to the music of Bach on a Sunday morning seemed to ground me, put me in touch with my spiritual centre, as I prepared to lead worship or to preach. It seemed to give me the spiritual energy required to lead others in worship. And now that I am retired, we still listen to Bach on a Sunday morning.

As a choral singer, I enjoy a wide range of repertoire (not quite all of it with the same enthusiasm). The Pax Christi Chorale, in which I have sung for thirty years, has performed major works by a variety of composers, including works by more contemporary composers. I am grateful for this wide embrace of wonderful music. But I feel particularly inspired when the choir sings a Bach cantata, motet, or the B-minor Mass – or when the congregation sings a Bach chorale in church.

The Conductor as Preacher

It was Robert Shaw who was preaching the sermon. Singers from across Canada had gathered in Winnipeg to sing Brahms's *German Requiem* under the baton of this famous choral conductor. His preaching surprised me, because I had only known him as a conductor. In my home when I was growing up, the records of the Robert Shaw Chorale were prized and almost worn out by their many playings. Robert Shaw was our musical hero. And here he was, preaching at our CMBC chapel time, and these words, as I remember them, are etched into my consciousness:

> What is the nature of great music? What is the nature of good worship? What are the attributes and states of being that allow it to happen? For me its absolute minimum conditions are a sense of mystery and an admission of pain.

Worship is a place to bring our pain and to open ourselves to the mystery of God's presence and love and healing. Music, at its best, opens our hearts to both.

It happened that Robert Shaw was conducting both the *German Requiem* by Brahms and *Christ lag in Todesbanden* (a Good Friday cantata) by Bach that weekend. And through it all I was reliving my grief over my father's death. The *German Requiem* was Dad's favourite piece of music. We read the text at his funeral. We listened to the music in our grieving. And here I had the opportunity to sing it, a powerful experience of re-entering pain and experiencing a healing mystery. After the concert, George Wiebe, our music professor and friend to Dad, knowing Dad's love for this music and for this requiem, sought me out and said, "Wasn't it as if heaven itself opened up this evening?"

And Yet

Yet at the most basic level, it is still congregational singing that most inspires me and most nurtures my inner spirit. In the long run this is more basic and more important to me than singing in choirs and quartets, which I love to do, or listening to great music, which I also love to do. Congregational singing moves away from performance to total participation. It expresses the heart of a congregation's spirit, and the many moods and dynamics of the Spirit's work among us. I feel very fortunate and blessed that the primary churches in which I have been pastor have had exceptionally good, strong, spirited, mostly full-harmony congregational singing with a wide range of hymnody.

The Pax Christi Chorale, in which I still sing, was started as an inter-Mennonite choir thirty years ago by music leaders from our church, together with leaders from several other Toronto-area Mennonite churches. It began as a modest, amateur choir; over the years it has grown into a splendid interdenominational choir of close to one hundred singers that can perform the great choral works with relative ease. I knew, at its beginning, that if this choir succeeded, it would probably mean that we would never be able to have a standing choir at Toronto United Mennonite Church. The good singers would not have the time to sing in both the church choir and an outside choir. And since I had conducted our church choir in Edmonton for many years and felt that it made a good contribution to our worship there, I struggled with how enthusiastically I could support this new venture.

I liked having a church choir. I knew that there were enough fine singers in the church that it was relatively easy to put together a very fine occasional choir for special services. But that was not like having a choir sing regularly. In the end, I did support the formation of the "Peace of Christ" choir, and in fact joined it. The congregational singing in the church was so strong and the potential of the new choir so huge that these factors outweighed my wish for a standing choir in the church. Good congregational singing is even more important to me than having a good choir performing regularly.

I don't have much knowledge of music in the early church. Did they have cantors singing the Scriptures? What we do have is the admonition the Apostle Paul gives to the churches in Ephesus and Philippi to sing:

> But be filled with the Spirit, as you sing psalms and hymns and spiritual songs among yourselves, singing and making melody to the Lord in your hearts, giving thanks to God the Father at all times and for everything in the name of our Lord Jesus Christ. (Ephesians 5:18–20)

> Let the word of Christ dwell in you richly; teach and admonish one another in all wisdom; and with gratitude in your hearts sing psalms, hymns, and spiritual songs to God. (Colossians 3:16)

To me this sounds like congregational singing.

A text that intrigues me is the story of Paul and Silas singing away while in prison:

> About midnight Paul and Silas were praying and singing hymns to God, *and the prisoners were listening to them.* Suddenly there was an earthquake, so violent that the foundations of the prison were shaken; and immediately all the doors were opened and everyone's chains were unfastened. When the jailor woke up and saw the prison doors wide open, he drew his sword and was about to kill himself, since he supposed that the prisoners had escaped. But Paul shouted in a loud voice, "Do not harm yourself, *for we are all here.*" (Acts 16:25–28; italics added)

It's surprising that Paul and Silas, stripped of their clothing, beaten and flogged, and put in the innermost cell of the prison with their feet in the stocks, are singing at midnight. It is surprising that the other prisoners, supposedly criminals of some sort, are listening attentively to their singing. And it is almost shocking that, given the opportunity to escape, those prisoners choose to stay put with the singers. Something powerful was happening in that "congregational" singing.

I have no idea what kind of voices Paul and Silas had. I doubt that they were trained singers. But there was a power in their singing. There is a power in good congregational singing. Maybe two people singing in prison – or in my case, a small family singing together – do not yet a congregation make. But both scenarios can be settings where singing together can have a powerful impact.

A Family Singing Together

When our three children were growing up in Edmonton, Alberta, we made long car trips to Niagara, Ontario – home to Lydia's parents – and to Clearbrook, British Columbia – home to my mother – almost every year. These were immense distances to travel in a relatively short time. Often, to pass the time, we sang together. We sang many of the songs in our hymnbook and in the *Sing and Rejoice* collection. Our two sons, both pastors now, loved singing. They have a deep appreciation for our hymnody. They are fully at ease in choosing, and often leading, music for congregational singing. Perhaps some of this came from our cross-Canada car trips.

'Tis music indeed that enlivens this pastor's retirement life, still giving me joy until that time when I will hear the angels themselves singing.

INTERLUDE
Congregational Singing as a Pastor Sees It

I originally wrote this piece on congregational singing as a chapter for Music in Worship: A Mennonite Perspective, *edited by Bernie Neufeld.*[8] *The chapter is reproduced here with minor modifications.*

I write this chapter as our congregation is on the verge of moving into our new facilities. For ten years, we have discussed, debated, explored, argued, researched, fought, reasoned, voted, and re-voted our way toward this moment.

"It has to be multifunctional," some said. "We've got to be able to use our building every day of the week to justify the million dollars. And that means getting rid of the pews and having movable chairs."

"But we insist it has to be a worship space first of all," others said, "with the look and the symbols that draw us to God. We don't want just any old gymnasium look. Better keep the pews."

"We've got to be practical though," others argued, "and design a serviceable building that will accommodate all our needs. With land costs as they are in Toronto, we have to use every inch of space available."

"We shouldn't go it alone," was heard loudly and clearly. "We have an exciting opportunity to partner with another ethnic group, perhaps with our Spanish brothers and sisters."

---

8   Scottdale, PA, and Waterloo, ON: Herald Press, 1998.

"We think it should be 'simple' in truly Mennonite tradition," others theologized, "so that we remove our class consciousness and make both our rich and poor neighbors feel welcome."

"And what about acoustics?" cried many loud voices. "Good congregational singing is so central to our worship life that acoustics must be a primary concern." Some folks told horror stories of how badly many new Mennonite facilities they had visited worked acoustically. "All the music has to be amplified. Absolutely dreadful." One voice was even heard to mutter, "When you push a microphone in the face of everyone who sings, you not only change the music style of the church, you change its theology."

And so it came to pass that "acoustics" became a significant theme in our new design. Our worship space even underwent a modest redesign after acoustical engineers had had their say (though we don't fully trust them. "Do they have any idea about 'Mennonite' singing?"). Our old building "sang very well." We take pride in our strong and vibrant congregational singing. We are aware that singing is close to the heart of our spirituality, our soul. Our interim worship space at St. Clair O'Connor (a Mennonite intergenerational housing community), while offering a wonderful connection with many of our seniors, was absolutely dead acoustically. We struggled to retain any joy in our singing.

On Christmas Eve we will move into our new "meeting room." Our ears are on full alert. We have planned a "lessons and carols" style of Christmas Eve service. We will know immediately "whether it will work for singing."

Societal Context

We hear much these days about pre-modernism, modernism, and post-modernism. "We are living in post-modern times," say the analysts of social culture. Like it or not, worship life is being dramatically affected and altered by the winds of post-modernism.

"There is an increase in the search for a deeper spirituality," say the analysts, "but a decrease in expressing this spirituality in the organized church. Unless our worship styles change dramatically, the organized church will become totally irrelevant to the spiritual search of our younger generation."

"Our Western world is dominated by a consumerism mentality," observe some, "and so we are tempted to buy into religious consumerism too. People, especially seekers, are viewed as a market, consuming objects that must be entertaining. Music especially is used as a commercial tool, part of an entertainment package catering to people's (younger people's) likes and acculturated tastes." The buzzwords are "seeker sensitive" and "visitor friendly."

"I'm not a Mennonite. I can't sing like that," said a visitor to our church. "I love the sound of the harmony. I'm in awe. But I feel totally left out. Can't you sing at least one song each Sunday that has only the melody so that I can follow along and hear what I should be singing?"

"But do we have to totally sell out to our culture in order to be relevant?" argue others. "We shouldn't have to enlist the popular music of a consumer culture in order to attract a younger audience today. Aren't Christians (especially Mennonite Christians) supposed to be counter-culture rather than slaves to culture? Besides, the 'throw up' music today is musically boring and theologically simplistic."

"Many young people today are growing up musically sophisticated," observe some. "They are highly trained and enormously talented. And they are fully at home with diversity. Let's finally move beyond the fruitless 'chorus versus hymn' dichotomy and embrace a variety of music styles."

"Nah, I don't buy into that 'return to an acoustical sound' you young adults are talking about," said a high schooler. "Give me a highly amplified beat any day. But do I want that in church? Nah, I think church should be different and special."

Our social context is a post-modern one. What do we embrace? What do we challenge?

Personal Context

I bring a huge personal bias into the discussion of music in worship. My musical tastes were shaped by a family that loved classical music. I grew up with Bach, Handel, Mozart, and Brahms. Even as a teenager, I thumbed my nose at pop music. As a teen, I wanted to emulate my father, who was a farmer and the church choir conductor. I went to Canadian Mennonite Bible College to study music so that I could go back home to Rosemary, Alberta, to farm and conduct the church choir.

Musically I got stuck some two centuries ago, feel most at home in the classical tradition, and prefer a natural to an amplified sound. But the pastor's musical tastes (or lack thereof) and preferences are not an adequate basis for choosing the musical repertoire of the church. Professionally, I think that music needs to be fully integrated into the worship service as a whole. Theologically, I believe that worship is not a performance but a participatory act of encountering God.

Is here any hope, then, of saying anything significant or even interesting about music and worship in a consumer-oriented post-modern world?

The Participatory Nature of Public Worship

Anabaptists have stressed that worship involves the whole community. The gathered people are not an audience of individuals gathered to be fed or entertained by leaders set apart. Worship gains its Spirit-led power when the people as community enter the presence of God, led there to be sure, but coming as a participatory community (Colossians 3:12–17; 1 Corinthians 14:26). This would suggest to me that when it comes to music in worship, the most important music in the church is congregational singing. As much as I enjoy and am often led to encountering God by a good choir, an instrumental ensemble or solo, or a well-played piano or organ, these, in my mind, are not the center of a church's music ministry; congregational singing is. This means to me that participation and vitality are key factors.

Our congregations are, for the most part, intergenerational. All ages, from children to the aged, need to find their voice and their identity reflected in what they sing. All ages need to be encouraged to fully express and/or develop their musical gifts. Most congregations, especially urban ones, are increasingly cosmopolitan and cross-cultural. This fact would already make a case for enlarging our musical expression and style to include hymns from other cultures (*International Songbook* and *Hymnal: A Worship Book* do a great service here[9]) and to include some unison singing for those who are not used to reading parts. We can only be enriched by including the global church in our hymnody. And hopefully we can be fully "gender inclusive" in our singing. Inclusive language has been and still is divisive in some of our congregations. I would plead for sensitivity here, but for a sensitivity that moves clearly in the direction of inclusivity.

Vitality and energy and creativity are key here. Sameness and tameness kill the spirit. The problem that many young people have with traditional hymns is not the music itself, nor, for the most part, the text, but the lethargic way these are often sung. Congregational singing needs a power, an "aliveness," regardless

---

9 See Doreen Helen Klassen, ed., *International Songbook* (Carol Stream, IL: Mennonite World Conference, 1990); and *Hymnal: A Worship Book* (Elgin, IL: Brethren Press; Newton, KS; Faith and Life Press; Scottdale, PA: Mennonite Publishing House, 1992).

of which musical style is chosen. (Worship leaders and preachers, regardless of their musicianship or singing ability, are so visible that the congregation often takes its emotional cue from them and reflects their enthusiasm, or lack thereof, in its own singing.) Congregational singing is, I think, a barometer of the spiritual vitality of the church. It is an indicator of how deeply faith is experienced. Energy and animation and full participation are more important than choral purity. If congregational singing is central, then we must put our best musical efforts here, whether it is in selecting appropriate hymns, leading them well, or training the whole congregation to sing as well as possible. For me this means encouraging even the "musically challenged" to sing out and to love singing. Let even the monotones praise the Lord in full voice. But training the whole congregation should also include teaching children and young people how to sing in harmony and teaching them the joy of singing.

At some level, we in the Mennonite church are probably still somewhat suspicious of professional musicians in the church. We are afraid they will be elitist or too esoteric for us, or they will intimidate us amateurs. But we urgently need both their leadership in our worship and their gifts in leading and training the whole congregation musically. My experience is that many of them share their gifts gladly. They teach, help, model, mentor, and encourage.

Hospitality and Inviting Outsiders into Our Home

As a family or as a congregation, we have an identity, an atmosphere (culture), a set of house rules, and certain comfortable ways of doing things. Musically, each congregation has an identity, including a hymnody, which reaches to the core of its being. But if it is hospitable, it will take into consideration the hymnody of the outsider it is inviting in. This doesn't mean that the congregation changes its own identity to cater to the stranger. It does mean, however, that it is sensitive to the experience of the stranger. Over time, the newcomers will join with the old-timers to gradually forge a new identity and a more inclusive hymnody.

When we invite persons from other cultures into our homes, we gladly serve them special Mennonite foods (though not exclusively, especially if there are repeat visits), just as we enjoy being served their specialties in their homes. We enrich each other's culinary experience. With hymnody, the problem comes not from having an identity but from being too narrow and exclusive in our musical diet. For example, it seems to me that the "choral versus chorus" battle is a loser all around. We have visited many unhappy choices and dichotomies on our people, whether that be choral versus chorus; music that is "seeker sensitive" or for regulars; music for youth over against music for the gray hairs; amplified versus acoustical sound; traditional versus new; harmony versus unison; and music for the mind and heart or music for the whole body (especially the feet).

In the words of one of my sons (another closet musician who is professionally involved in church ministries other than music – yes, the sins of the fathers are visited on the next generation):

> The dichotomy between "hymns" and "choruses" is limiting and unhelpful. It reduces the vast musical and textual richness and variety of both centuries of musical development and hymn writing and of the many different contemporary musical expressions to only two categories. There is quality and legitimacy within each of these many styles, just as there are poorer examples of each. Healthy vibrant worship integrates a diversity and variety of musical styles and

expressions, even though congregations may lean in certain directions.[10]

I find it significant that young people and young adults are often far more eclectic in their musical tastes than my generation is and can enjoy a much greater diversity in styles than I can. They move easily from Bach to jazz to pop to chorus. So, let's not get them stuck on either only hymns or only choruses. There are rich resources from various styles and traditions. Many of our children are growing up with far greater musical sophistication and skill than my generation had. Many of them are enormously talented and trained. Let's challenge them to use all their musical powers in the service of our Lord. If we do, the boundaries around "hymns" or "choruses" will never be able to contain them.

In choosing music we do need to take into account the history and present context of our churches. There are important traditions and memories and faith expressions that give meaning to a group. We can't abandon these, but we can push out the edges. We can become more inclusive. We can broaden our congregational repertoire. We do need to be hospitable to the stranger. For me personally, and for our congregation, I think, the core hymnody remains the more traditional hymn style, enriched and broadened by an amazing variety of wonderful new music resources. I am so pleased with many of the new hymn texts in *Hymnal: A Worship Book*.[11] I am glad to be able to turn to the new texts to find themes and poetry to connect with my preaching.

Much more can still be done to develop and incorporate good, solid contemporary hymns into our worship. We can encourage the poets and composers among us to unleash their creativity here. We can try to incorporate the best of the new hymns in our worship; hymns that speak relevantly to our context; are

---

10 Mark Harder, notes from a workshop, March 1, 1997, St. Jacobs, ON.
11 See note 9, on page 111.

integrated, holistic, thoughtful; and offer wonderful visions of what God is doing in our world.

Longing for Wholeness and for Integration

We want to love God with all our heart and mind and soul and strength. We want to combine belief and experience and action in our faith. We resist compartmentalisations that separate and segment our faith or our worship into small boxes. When it comes to worship, my orientation is to insist that music must be at the service of worship. It needs to be integrated into the larger theme or liturgical structure or spiritual/emotional tone of the whole.

I chose my Doctor of Ministries dissertation ("Touched by Transcendence: Shaping Worship That Bridges Life and Faith") based on a rather disturbing experience. It occurred at a Mennonite music seminar. Two hundred and seventy musicians from across Canada, Mennonite Brethren and General Conference Mennonites, gathered in Winnipeg in February 1985 to sing Brahms and Bach under the baton of Robert Shaw. The week was a musical, emotional, and spiritual mountaintop for me. But I was dismayed with the answers to a very innocent and unpremeditated question I asked some twenty to twenty-five of these Mennonite music leaders during several lunchtime conversations in groups of six or seven around a table.

"How do you coordinate your music ministry with the overall worship ministry of your church? How do you work at integrating music with the worship theme of the morning?" To my dismay, they all said they didn't. Without exception, the people I asked said they did their own thing (chose music they happened to like), and the minister did his own thing (none of them had women ministers at that time). They never got together to plan or coordinate their ministries. The music leaders, of course, all laid the blame for the lack of consultation on the minister. "He doesn't know anything about music anyway." Or, "He chooses his theme the last part of the week and that doesn't give us enough lead time." Or, "He's not interested in our suggestions." The point was that in the churches represented by these music leaders, there was no planning that included the major worship participants. The music was a separate island disconnected from any meaningful integration with whatever else happened in worship. The result then is that the order of worship is not dignified by a coordinating theme, and the various components of the service become a collection of more or less interesting and/ or worshipful pieces. The bulletin has become a program and the worship leader a master of ceremonies.

In Toronto United Mennonite Church, we are trying to find new ways to plan worship that is more integrated. Most recently, we are both excited and frustrated by a worship-planning format we are trying. Our preaching team (four lay members of the congregation plus me as pastor) explores themes and texts and, of course, schedules preachers. One member of the worship committee then acts as a coordinator and gathers all the major worship participants for a given service one week in advance during our coffee hour (preacher, worship leader, song leader, accompanist, and children's storyteller). The preacher gives the text and a short explanation of the theme. Then everybody brainstorms around these. It's amazing how creative this process sometimes is and how integrated the worship services sometimes are. But the process often breaks down, sometimes because we preachers don't have our act together early enough, but more often because one or more than one of us is away on any given Sunday and just not available. Yet when we meet, the results are very satisfying.

It is immensely satisfying when music contributes a key element to worship. Perhaps what is needed at a given moment is a Taizé short piece, or a Bach chorale, or a guitar-led chorus or folk hymn, or a song from Guatemala or Africa, or a chant, or an

African-American spiritual, or a gospel song, or a Brian Wren or Bradley Lehman contemporary hymn. A team can cast the net widely and help make the music serve the rest of the worship. I long for such wholeness.

Transforming Our World, Not Being Conformed To It

Chapter 12 in Romans, with its challenge to "not be conformed to this world" (Romans 12:2), has always had a significant place in the Mennonite canon. My interpretation today is that we need to be responsive to our culture but not controlled by it. Some of the old dualisms of the clear separation between church and world or of "Christ against culture" are surely unhelpful.

When it comes to music, we can't help but notice that our children and young people are being profoundly shaped by the pop (rock) culture of our day. But does it mean that we bring this music into the church wholesale so that we will keep our young people? Do we really need to cater to the popular music of our commercial and consumerist culture just to survive? Is there a way of being "in the world" but not fully "of the world" that has integrity and that has worship appeal? Can we engage the culture without becoming the culture?

My reading of young people is that they are often bored with traditional hymnody. But neither do they want, as an alternative, the church to fully embrace pop culture. They may choose that as their music to listen to at home. But they know it is commercial, meant to entertain, and often espouses values incompatible with their faith. They do not want to take it wholesale into church. They do want some recognition that some of the sounds and rhythms of contemporary culture are now a part of who they are. But they also want the church to be different, to reflect Christ more than the culture. They want energy and life and a beat, but they also want depth.

Perhaps we always need to be in the process of creating a new culture in the church. We always need to be in the process of naming our experience and transforming our culture in the light of Christ. We bring with us a tradition, in the best sense of that word, but continually create a new vision, a new reality. That is why we urgently need new hymns that express the reality of our experience and our faith in some of the musical idioms which can bridge the older world and the newer world.

Depth in Worship That Fully Embraces Mystery, Joy, and Pain

"What is the nature of great music? What is the nature of good worship? What are the attributes and states of being that allow it to happen? For me its absolute minimum conditions are a sense of mystery and an admission of pain."[12] In these words, Robert Shaw, musician, is striving for depth. Life is the most whole when we acknowledge a deep sense of mystery – in great music, in good worship, in life itself.

There must be a deep sense of mystery in worship. We come before a God whom we cannot control or manipulate or even fully understand. Of course, God is revealed in Scripture, in Jesus Christ, and in our experience. Even so, we see only "in a mirror, dimly" (1 Corinthians 13:12). We await a time when we still see God face to face. In the meantime, we acknowledge mystery. In the meantime, we struggle with perplexing life situations, with unanswerable questions, with the unfathomable reality that God does indeed work in mysterious ways. Our worship will have depth if we open ourselves to the mysterious God.

---

12 Robert Shaw, "Worship and the Arts," sermon preached February 1, 1985, in Winnipeg, Manitoba.

Worship is also a place to bring our pain. Each of us comes to a worship service with a whole backlog of feelings and experiences, joy and pain mixed, hopes and fears struggling with each other. We all carry some hurt, some strained relationships; some physical, emotional, or spiritual unwellness; some anxieties or fears or worries; some unfulfilled hopes or plans or expectations; some sin or guilt; or grief over one kind of loss or another; or questions about life or about death or about faith. To live is to experience pain. In worship, we bring our pain to a healing God in the context of a healing community.

If we are in touch with mystery and with pain, then joy and celebration will come naturally and even spontaneously. But if we attempt to develop an isolated praise and celebration culture disconnected from pain and mystery, it will in the end be shallow and hollow. Surely, we need more joy and praise and more celebration of God's love and power in our worship. But we don't want just froth. Mystery and pain and joy are all experiences of depth. Music in worship must reflect that depth. I do not think that depth equals complexity. Sometimes a very simple melody or a very simple text can be very profound. But there is much very shallow music out there (both musically and theologically). Little ditties and little pieties won't reach through to the core of our being.

The Psalms are a model to me of bringing together mystery and pain and joy at a very deep level. They embrace all human experience, the lovely and the unlovely, and dare bring it before God. They even dare bring God before God in accusation. In worship, we long for depth. We long for a place where mystery and pain and joy are all recognized, all experienced fully. I think we want our worship music to help take us there.

Conclusion

Our congregation had its first service in our new facility on Christmas Eve. We chose a "lessons and carols" kind of service so that we had every opportunity to sing together. A flute broke the candle-lit silence with the melody of "O Come, O Come, Immanuel." The congregation ventured the unison opening lines, held its collective breath, and then plunged into harmony at "Rejoice." The sanctuary filled with an awesome sound. Smiles broke out all over the place. The acoustics were wonderful. We sang with smiles, with joy, with some tears, with power, with love for our Savior. The place works acoustically. Now it's up to us to continue to create a music ministry that fully utilizes this worship space for the full glory of God.

7

The Many Rhythms of the Marriage Duet

A good musical duet involves two voices with very distinct timbres and ranges, but with equal power. The two voices complement each other. They take turns leading, sometimes in solo freedom. They come together in harmonic union. The two voices interact with each other in an intimate way.

At Goshen College, the music department in which I was enrolled performed Mozart's opera *The Magic Flute* (I had a very small part in it). Two of the main characters, Pamina and Papageno, sing a wonderful duet. Pamina leads out by singing, "The man who feels sweet love's emotion will always have a kindly heart." And Papageno responds, "The joys of love shall be our own; we live by love, by love alone." At the climax of the duet the two of them sing in beautiful harmony: "Wife and man, man and wife, reach the height of godly life."

I think of my marriage as a duet of mutual and equal voices. Lydia and I take turns leading out. We are okay with some dissonant sounds when we come together again, but usually find a way to make harmonic music that satisfies both of us.

Marriage has played a huge role in sustaining my energy for and love of pastoral ministry. This is much more than a polite nod to a supportive wife. In so many ways we have been soulmates, and this has been a primary factor in energizing my ministry. It has also played a huge role in nurturing my inner voice and my sense of self.

In many ways intimacy is a gift we are given when we are open to relationship. Marriage is but one of many spheres of intimacy. A number of my colleagues and friends in ministry are single, and exemplify a life rich with deep and intimate relationships. All of us pastors, whether married or not, need to cultivate meaningful relationships with family members, with colleagues, with people inside and outside of their congregation, and with people in the community.

I neither want to idealize my marriage (like most marriage partners, we know that intimacy can never be taken for granted) nor hold up married clergy as the ideal. The ideal is rather that pastors, like all people, need to be nurtured by healthy relationships. We need to love and be loved. All pastors need to develop and nurture relationships that are deep and fulfilling. The sphere of these relationships and friendships is wide – certainly including family, colleagues, people they work with, community contacts, and people within the congregation. Some traditions suggest that pastors should not develop friendships within the congregation they are serving. They might then play favourites. I'm not sure a pastor can maintain emotional wholeness without having friendships inside the church. The challenge is to know which hat – pastor or friend – to put on in a given situation.

My story is unique in the way my partner has helped me grow in my ministry. The story I tell of my marriage relationship is a kind of symbol of the larger role that intimate relationships play in living out God's call to be an agent of God's love. I focus on that story, but am also very aware of how deeply this story is complemented by the stories of my larger family circle and my many friends and co-workers.

Intellectual Companion

It feels a little presumptuous on my part to say that my wife and I are "intellectual companions." Lydia is a much more competent scholar than am I. And yet I think we are intellectual soulmates – at least some of the time. We have thrived on discussing and arguing over theological and biblical and contemporary points of view. We challenge each other, support each other, and edit each other's writing. And sometimes we just enjoy being intellectual sparring partners. And since retirement, we regularly play Scrabble together. We do play quite competitively, and seem to be a good match for each other. When we add up our wins, we are almost exactly fifty-fifty.

We have always argued with and challenged each other. Lydia will hold me accountable when she sees superficiality in my biblical, theological, or contemporary analysis. And mostly I appreciate this. Sometimes it does upset me. And yet I also know that when I am stuck, when something isn't working in a sermon, a paper, or a ministry proposal, she can quickly spot the problem and point to a potential solution. She has always pushed me to find my fuller potential as a pastor, as a biblical student, as a writer, as an administrator.

I sometimes feel threatened by her sharp critiques. As an introvert, I am inclined to keep things inside. In my family of origin the pattern was to be respectfully nice to each other and never argue or even register disagreement. Lydia is an extrovert, as is her whole family. Her family pattern was to engage in loud, heated conversations and arguments and challenges. I have this mental picture of Lydia and her dad, plus a sibling or two, all on ladders picking peaches from one tree, engaged in a loud and spirited "discussion-argument" as they filled basket after basket of fruit. And they loved doing this. It only deepened their family bonds. To me, entering her family, this was a shock. It seemed counterintuitive to forge good relationships by engaging each other so forcefully. And it was totally opposite to my growing up family pattern. I sensed that this was healthy, but I found it very difficult to enter that kind of give and take. I was tempted to withdraw into my shell for protection.

Of course, Lydia brought her style of engagement into our marriage. Even though I knew deep inside of me that this was healthy and was what I – and we – needed, I still felt threatened and defensive when she challenged my thinking and my way of working. I would close up, withdraw emotionally, and become quiet, sometimes even resentful. Yet I knew our relationship (and my ministry) needed these challenges. Gradually I learned to "fight" back, to become a sparring partner, to join the dance of debating and arguing ideas and interpretations and insights.

This has been immensely important to me in sustaining my love for ministry. There is something very energizing about the constant challenge to read a Scripture text with new eyes, and to try to engage new theological awareness, and then ask how these apply to our contemporary place in life. When I was tempted to coast on old sermons and old frameworks of thought and an unexamined interpretation of a biblical text, Lydia pushed me to go deeper and read more broadly. Doing so helped me thrive on the many challenges of sermon and teaching preparation. And then she encouraged me to enter a Doctor of Ministries program at St. Stephen's College, affiliated with the University of Alberta in Edmonton. This helped me continue my professional and academic development.

I like to think that I also entered her intellectual and academic world and challenged her to excel. I knew she was hungry to return to academic life after our children were less dependent on her as a stay-at-home mom, and I encouraged her to enter master's and doctoral studies in theology. This brought a whole new dimension to our intellectual table talk – including that of "feminism."

The world, including the theological world and the church world, was changing. Could I keep up? Our intellectual sparring had, I think, sort of prepared me for this. I didn't feel threatened when Lydia butted her head against old stereotypes, prejudices and exclusions, and old ways of reading patriarchal biblical texts, which she cross-examined ruthlessly. Instead, I could support and encourage her. Somewhat later, after she finished her doctoral work and after I had enough maturity and self-confidence as a pastor not to feel as easily threatened, we even became partners in teaching together (the "Church and Ministry" course at Conrad Grebel College, as well as a similar course at Associated Mennonite Biblical Seminaries in Elkhart, Indiana) and then in pastoring together (as intentional interim co-pastors following my retirement from full-time ministry). In both teaching and pastoring together we delighted in the rigorous intellectual partnership involved in organizing and thinking through classes and models for conflict resolution and church renewal.

I acknowledge that it took me some years to become comfortable with doing ministry together. When I was invited to become pastor of Toronto United Mennonite Church (TUMC) in 1987, the search committee suggested that they were open to hiring Lydia and me as a ministry team. But I wasn't ready for that. My excuse was that Lydia wanted to come to Toronto to do doctoral work in theology, not to be sidetracked by a job. Yes, she had been accepted as a doctoral student. But I did not really encourage exploring the joint ministry opportunity.

But once at TUMC, as my ministerial confidence grew, I gradually became more open to more forms of partnership in ministry. This shift took place as we learned to be equal partners within our family context. Yet we realized that we needed to be careful of power issues in the church, lest we overwhelm people with our ideas and proposals for change. We were aware that because of our respective positions as pastor and professor, and because of our personalities, we carried quite a bit of power and might intimidate others and perhaps stifle discussion and debate. We started teaching together outside of the church, leading workshops together, occasionally preaching sermons in dialogue fashion, and writing articles together.

And then Lydia was invited by TUMC, where I was the pastor, to join the preaching team and became a part of the dynamic of that ministry. Her participation in this way was welcomed and affirmed by both the team and the congregation – and by me. And it felt like a gift to me. By the time retirement came from full-time work, and with it the opportunity for us to do intentional interim ministry together, I was fully ready to embrace this new partnership. It helped that Lydia was ready to take on some of the administrative planning that I had become weary of.

I am fully aware that many of my pastoral colleagues would not want, and might even resent, a spouse looking over their vocational shoulders. They are quite happy having a partner who is not interested in meddling in their work world. Keeping professional and family worlds separate is just fine with them. I certainly respect that choice. But for me this intersection has been a gift.

Partners in Redefining Role Expectations

The new wave of feminist sensitivity that Lydia – and I – got caught up in also brought some changes to our living together. Our marriage had started out with role definitions that were becoming outdated: the kitchen was a woman's domain; I might very reluctantly do some vacuuming; parenting duties fell mostly to the mother. Neither of us were really satisfied with this arrangement, but we didn't have either the models or the intellectual frameworks to change it.

But there was already a small change happening in our parenting patterns. A pastor's work has a certain amount of time flexibility built in. One of the time challenges for me was the need for evening work, whether for meetings or pastoral visits. I am much more of a morning person than an evening person at the best of times. But often I could come home by mid-to-late afternoon. Partly through this happenstance, and partly through Lydia's complaint that she needed both a parental break and time to make supper, we developed a pattern of me spending time with our children when they came home from school, often even putting them to bed after supper, and then leaving again for evening work. I was gradually becoming more of a participant dad.

Gradually, I also started to do some of the cooking and some of the other housework, especially after Lydia started graduate studies. I discovered that I quite enjoyed cooking, and even baking. At this point in our marriage we share meal preparation and housework quite evenly. We kind of made the intellectual and practical journey into feminism together.

But still we spar and argue and live out of our personal realities. Introvert meets extrovert. Sloppy scholar meets thorough scholar. Conflict avoider meets conflict engager. Feeling level controller meets feeling level venter. Aren't these sure signs of a dysfunctional marriage and of professional catastrophe?

I suppose there is something to the notion that opposites attract. Why would I be so attracted to a girl who was so extroverted and who would challenge me so deeply? To be truthful, she wasn't attracted to her opposite nearly as quickly as I was. Our joint story started with very little promise.

Unlikely Beginnings

Lydia and I met, very briefly and uneventfully, around a Ping Pong table at Canadian Mennonite Bible College (CMBC) in Winnipeg during our first week there in 1961. A week later another newly made friend and I thought it would be fun to find some girls to go with us to a football game – the Calgary Stampeders, my favourite team, was playing the Winnipeg Blue Bombers. But whom to ask? We perused the student list, hardly an auspicious beginning to our dating journey. As the various names of girls showed up in the list we thought we remembered a few names from that round robin Ping Pong game. We called them. And they both said yes. So, John and Marie and Gary and Lydia watched football together. Or, as Lydia complained, Gary watched football intently and John and Marie enjoyed conversing with each other. (By the way, John and Marie also got married).

We had a few more dates, and then Lydia had had enough of this introverted non-talker who loved football and opera more than conversation. She dated others. I sulked. Maybe I wore her down with my persistence. Eventually we studied Greek together. For me this felt a bit risky because Lydia was clearly the better scholar, got better grades than did I, and would soon, no doubt, see herself as more of a coach or teacher than a fellow learner of Greek. I saw myself as her intellectual inferior. I carried the emotional baggage of having been a very poor – make that failing – high school student. But at least we were doing something together.

Something changed on choir tour at the end of our second year. After not dating for many months, we sat together on the long bus ride from Saskatchewan to Winnipeg that ended our tour. We decided to resume dating.

Maybe it was easier for her to say yes to dating because she knew that we would very soon part ways again to go to our respective provinces to farm. During that summer, we communicated via letters, and then resumed dating back at CMBC in fall. She even invited me to come to Ontario for Christmas to meet her family – surely a good sign. But I was not able to put my best foot forward. Partly it was because I had caught a severe cold on the car trip there. We drove to Ontario in a small Austin car with essentially no heater. I did most of the driving, most of the way through a blizzard. The combination of cold and exhaustion did me in. But I was also a bit intimidated by her overly extroverted family. I was certainly not the life of the party. By the time we took the train back to Winnipeg I think she had pretty much decided that this farm boy from Rosemary, Alberta, really didn't show marriage potential after all.

But neither could she quite break off our relationship. In fact, by the end of February we were unofficially engaged. How our relationship turned and then developed so quickly still mystifies me. Together we planned our official engagement announcement. We were both in the CMBC touring choir that spring, which that year was touring Montana and Alberta. The itinerary listed the Rosemary Mennonite Church for Easter Sunday morning. Rosemary is my home church. Perfect, I thought. We can announce our engagement in my home church on Easter Sunday morning.

But. A huge but. The first problem was that our touring choir had been divided into two choirs in order to accommodate all the churches in our itinerary. And initially Lydia had been placed in the larger choir, which was scheduled to be in Calgary on Easter Sunday morning, while I was put into the smaller group singing in Rosemary. We brought our dilemma and divulged our secret to George Wiebe, choir conductor and tour organizer. His eyes twinkled as he exchanged altos, no doubt to some consternation on the part of the one who suddenly found herself in the large choir singing in Calgary. What an Easter Sunday morning – singing together and then making a public engagement announcement in my home church.

The much deeper problem was that my father was dying. He was in hospital following a second heart attack, his weakened body not able to fight off the pneumonia that followed. Lydia had not yet met him. I took her to introduce her to Dad and to announce our engagement to him on that Saturday. My dad gave Lydia such a warm welcome and blessing – in Low German, no less, which Lydia could understand but not really speak. Lydia has immensely warm feelings about that emotional and holy moment. And then on Easter Sunday afternoon our small choir came to the hospital to sing for Dad. He was deeply moved by our singing and loved the fact that Lydia and I were part of that very small choir.

I'm not sure if I was fully in touch with all the roller-coaster emotions of that moment in time. What I am clear about is that Lydia and I experienced an emotional and spiritual intimacy in that weekend of joy and fear.

Spiritual and Emotional Soulmates

We did announce our engagement that Sunday morning in my home church. But there was a second significant moment for us that Easter Sunday. This was a note my dad had put into the bulletin, a greeting to the congregation from a man who probably was aware that his end was coming. "Jesus has risen, and lives. That is my testimony." Life and death are so intertwined. In our case, grieving loss and celebrating love were intertwined. Both took us to emotional depths.

Our small choir rejoined the larger choir in Edmonton, finished its tour, and returned to Winnipeg. A day later came the phone call from Mom. "Gary, Dad has only a short time to live. Please hurry home." I rushed to find Lydia, both to share the news and to find some comfort. We both knew we wanted to go the "prayer room" together. We knew we wanted to and needed to pray together. And that has had profound implications for us. Yes, Dad still died. But we knew a spiritual and emotional intimacy there, a putting our story into a bigger story. We knew we could, and wanted to, pray together. And that part of our relationship has endured throughout our marriage. It still is a powerful part of our intimacy, along with many other intimacies in our relationship.

Praying together as husband and wife is not always easy, and surely it sometimes feels like only a superficial routine, a too-easy voicing of generalities and platitudes. And yet there is always the opportunity and the challenge, if we are open to them, for us to go deeper inside of ourselves to where our real pain and joy and fear and hope and anxiety and love and compassion can be expressed. And then we know again that praying together, over the long haul, does express and nurture a spiritual intimacy that feels foundational to our relationship.

I did get home to spend two days with Dad before he died. And then Lydia came to the funeral, encouraged to come after some hesitation by our mutual good friend Rodney Sawatzky. It was also Rodney who inadvertently put his finger on an issue I was not yet quite ready to deal with. As I was getting ready to fly home, I overheard Rodney say to another friend, "I hope Gary will find a way to express his grief and sorrow. He will be tempted to keep too tight a control over his emotions." That memory has stayed with me. I knew it was a truth. And I knew that Lydia could help me deal with it.

Ours was a small house. Lydia slept with Mom. And Mom needed to talk. She talked and talked, about Dad and about their life together. Lydia got to know my Dad in a rather intimate way from Mom's stories about him. And Lydia formed a bond with Mom that was deep and lasting and life-giving for both. And this deepened our marriage intimacy.

One of the lasting memories I have of Dad's dying was that at one point he was quite agitated and not quite ready to let go. Then Reverend Nickel, a long-time friend of Dad's, and the bishop (*Ältester*) of the church, came and prayed with Dad. Dad very noticeably calmed down, relaxed, and died within a few minutes. This has encouraged me in my own ministry with people who are dying. I have personal experience of how powerful prayer can be at a death-side.

Dad's dying, death, and funeral had a huge impact on Lydia's and my relationship and marriage, and, I think, on my ministry. Through this very painful time we forged a deeper emotional and spiritual intimacy.

Prayer, for a pastor, is both a personal thing and a professional duty. And that is a huge challenge. Even just to ponder the image of being a professional "pray-er" seems a bit off-putting, a bit contrived, and a bit "cold." A pastor spends a lot of time praying at public gatherings, as well as in innumerable private pastoral situations. A pastor, as a professional, is expected to be in touch with God and with the deep needs of the people and to have a way with words to express these. And to be able to pray for people day after day and week after week and year after year, without succumbing to clichés and routine and the predictable and boring. Is that even possible?

As a pastor, I realized that if I didn't have a personal prayer life I would dry up as a professional prayer. I'm not sure if I could have sustained a deep personal prayer life on my own. I think God knew I needed a spiritual and emotional soulmate to do this.

Some of my colleagues these days have turned to "spiritual direction" to help them integrate personal and professional praying. They invite a spiritual director to guide them in their spiritual and professional life. I fully affirm them in this. Some of them testify to being shaped and nourished and constantly renewed by it. Some have used it to shape their ministry in very important ways. Yet I have never invited a spiritual director to guide my prayer life.

Others have valued going on silent prayer retreats, sometimes a week or two at a time. They come back spiritually refreshed, they say. They value a quiet alone time to focus on their relationship with God and on prayer and meditation exercises.

I have not been able to fully enter this journey into prayer either. I have attended some spiritual direction retreats – as long as a day at a time. But that is not where I most deeply meet God. Maybe these retreats were too short to let that happen. Maybe there is something amiss in my soul.

What does renew and energize me (and I think Lydia also) is to retreat to nature settings. We have thrived on camping and tenting and hiking and swimming in a lake. Even puttering around in our garden feels renewing. This is not so much focused prayer or meditation time as it is letting the beauty of God's world penetrate my being – and having the time to relax into that world without time pressures and without agenda.

And then, of course, there is music. All my adult life I have sung – in choirs, in quartets, in the congregation. I have conducted church choirs. And I have listened to music. Every Sunday morning, I listen to the music of Bach. That settles my soul, prepares me emotionally and spiritually to preach and pray professionally that morning.

I do want my public praying to grow out of a meaningful private prayer life – which I experience more through marriage than through silent retreats or disciplined personal prayer. I want my public praying to be ruthlessly honest and vulnerable, something more than safe, nice, repetitious, politically correct generalities. I want to balance carefully crafted, sometimes poetic prayer with more spontaneous, in-the-moment praying.

But public praying is always a challenging thing, because it demands that you listen both to God and to the people – and to your own inner self. For me this challenge felt less intimidating because of what Lydia and I lived out at home.

Sharing a Journey of Crisis and Disillusionment

What if the Bible isn't true? What if the church is too human to allow God to work in and through it? What if everything we believe about God is an illusion?

I am deeply grateful that these questions came to me mostly in my second year at CMBC, and not in my third year when we were planning a wedding and attending a funeral. In my second year, I felt I was in some kind of suspended crisis – a faith crisis. And so was Lydia.

I was gradually becoming aware that the pre-modern lens through which I had been reading the Bible was leaving me empty and disillusioned. My inquiring mind raised far too many questions when reading the Bible so literally. I had, and still have, a great deal of respect for our uneducated lay preachers who journeyed from one end of the Bible to the other in most sermons, reading the Bible literally and faithfully retelling its stories. They were faithful to what they had been given. I did gain a lot of biblical knowledge that way – when I actually listened to the sermon. But I was finding it more and more difficult to believe and to pray.

In the 1960s two world views were clashing at college, and I as a student felt squeezed in the middle. Some of our professors had drunk from the well of a historical-critical way of reading the Bible, a methodology taught in their graduate studies. They were entering a modernity framework of thought, based on very different understandings of how the Bible came to us and how it must be read "in context." But others of our professors still taught the Bible from a pre-modern world view that was much more literal and un-nuanced by context. I felt both excited and confused.

I took a course in homiletics (preaching) taught by two professors – one from each of these perspectives. It was my turn to prepare and preach a sermon to our worship assembly. I don't think I was fully conscious of what I was doing, but I must have listed on the side of a historical-critical reading of my text. The one professor really liked it and wanted to give an A grade. The other really didn't like it, and had a D in mind for me. They eventually compromised and gave me a B.

I knew I couldn't go back to a purely literal way of reading the Bible. But neither was I even close to understanding the implications of a more scholarly reading. I was in some turmoil.

And then Billy Graham came to Winnipeg for a huge crusade. We Bible college students were expected to be very enthusiastic and supportive, and it was hoped many of us would sign up to be trained as counsellors to help lead people to Christ. I didn't sign up. I did want people to turn to Jesus. But I was uneasy with the politics of mass evangelism. We learned about how the campaign was strategized and planned and implemented. We learned about how numbers were crunched and the souls won to Christ were predicted. It was all professional and smooth and slick – and successful.

And I felt disillusioned with the whole thing. I attended several crusade evenings and listened rather intently to Graham's preaching. It seemed to me that it all came out of a pre-modern framework. I looked up the Scripture texts he used and quoted, and read the context around them. And realized that quoted text and context were often miles apart. To me this was very sloppy biblical work. I very foolishly put my critiques of Graham's use of Scripture in his preaching to paper and posted it on the "Wittenberg Door" (a place in the school hallway where students could post their opinions and concerns) for the whole school to read – and reaped a storm of protest and bewilderment. We were in the middle of a clash of world views.

I knew I couldn't go back. But I didn't know the way forward. I was in a faith crisis. And I worried that if I embraced that historical-critical way of reading the Bible I might lose my faith entirely, and would lose all my confidence in praying.

And yet, fearfully entertaining a new world view and hesitantly embracing historical- critical studies helped me to hold on to faith and hold on to prayer. Only much later did I become more fully aware of the limitations of that new world view and of that approach to Scripture, a limitation of any and all our human constructs.

In the end, what lifted this crisis for me were four things:

1. *Observing a lived faith.* I observed how several of our professors integrated their faith with their scholarship. Waldemar Janzen and David Schroeder especially, as well as others, impressed me with their scholarship – a world that was new and exciting to me. But they also seemed to be people of a deep and profound

faith. They were people of prayer. They could be both scholars and believers. They could analyze Scripture with all the scholarly tools available, and then still pray so simply and so personally.

Lydia, too, was struggling with faith. Her crisis grew out of a huge power struggle in her home church, one that was very hurtful to her parents and then to her. What do you do with a church you have grown up in and love when it shows itself to be very human and very hurtful? At the same time, she was studying the letters of Paul to the church at Corinth. Corinth too was full of huge conflicts. It too was so very human and very messy. With these stories comes disillusionment with church itself. But also, eventually, comes the recognition that God always works only in and through very human agencies, including an always fallible church. Lydia and I shared our faith struggles and our sense of crisis with each other. It seemed we were soulmates in faith crisis too.

2. *Discovering Anabaptism.* I heard the word "Anabaptist" for the first time at CMBC. I was Mennonite through and through. But I had never heard of our origins in the Anabaptist movement of the sixteenth century. I had never heard our core Anabaptist convictions articulated. I knew we Mennonites were pacifists. By then I had heard of conscientious objection to war. I knew that quite a few young Mennonite men refused to sign up to fight in World War II. But why?

A new identity world opened to me when I started to read the stories of Conrad Grebel refusing to have his infant daughter baptized, of Felix Manz choosing to be drowned in the river rather than giving up his faith, of Menno Simons articulating a new understanding of church and of discipleship, of a whole community committed to actually following Jesus, not only believing in him.

This both caught my attention and inspired me. This was a lived faith that I could identify with. I read the Gospels with new eyes. I read the stories of Jesus with new appreciation. I was beginning to make intellectual sense out of my heritage as a Mennonite Christian follower of Jesus. These were the beginnings of a new foundation of faith, and later, of ministry.

3. *Forging friendships through turmoil.* I had several very close friends in my home community in Rosemary, Alberta. But it took me quite a while to trust myself to develop deep friendships at CMBC. I had made a lot of friends, but not really intimate friends. During this year of faith crisis, I discovered other dorm mates whose faith foundations were also shaking. Gradually we shared this with each other and struggled together. Lydia and I were part of a rather small circle of students who became close to each other because we dared let each other into our faith questions and our disillusionment with oversimplified answers. There was a depth and an honesty in our searching and sharing and struggling together. The friendships forged during these times have endured and continue to nourish me. Several of these friends have already died. I grieved their passing, and gave thanks to God for how they enriched my life.

4. *Exploring worship in other denominations.* That second year at CMBC, my faith crisis urging me on, I decided to explore how other Christians worshipped. For most of that winter, I attended a different church each Sunday, exploring the way various traditions worshipped. I tried to cover the spectrum from ultra-conservative and fundamentalist to ultra-orthodox and liturgical. I observed that despite the radical differences between these two poles, people seemed to be genuinely worshipping. I reflected on my own responses, surprised that I could participate in quite a variety of worship styles, but aware also of worship that left me either uncomfortable or uninvolved. Most of all, I appreciated observing how Christians from various denominations could worship God so authentically.

In the end, I knew that the "congregationalism" of my tradition was my true worship home. In this worship home there is a great deal of lay participation – in planning and leading worship, in preaching and in public prayer. Professional clergy are not the entire show, as they seemed to be in most of churches I visited, whether "high" church or "low" church.

When Lydia started her graduate studies in theology she focused on the notion of "hermeneutic community." Every follower of Jesus is empowered to read the Scriptures and help interpret them. Every follower of Jesus is invited into community and invited into the discernment processes of that community. The many discussions and debates we had as she pursued and wrote about this notion with academic vigour helped me focus how I understood my ministry within an Anabaptist community. Again, our marriage impacted how I did ministry.

Our marriage duet, with its many layered intimacies, has profoundly shaped my ministry and has been a major factor in sustaining my love for my calling. It has been at the centre of many relationships that have endured over time. And it has given me the confidence to enter the congregation-pastor duet expecting growing, trustful relationships, depth encounters, and mutual conversions.

INTERLUDE
On the Wings of the Dawn: An
Invitation to Join the Metaphor

The following graduation speech is an example of a number of sermons, articles, and occasional speeches on which Lydia and I have collaborated. The invitation came from the 1995 graduating class of Canadian Mennonite Bible College, after Lydia had taught there for one year and I had taught a course for one semester.

> If I rise on the wings of the dawn, if I settle on
> the far side of the sea, even there your hand will
> guide me and your right hand will hold me fast.
> (Psalm 139:9–10)

Lydia: To those of you graduating, you who have invited
us to share this moment with you, our thanks!
You have given us a rare privilege. You endured
our teaching for a short while, and now you have
called us back for this, the moment of your sending
forth from this place called CMBC. It is an honour.
Your lives and ours touched each other, some only
routinely, others in deep places.

Gary: You also need to know that you have created no
small amount of marriage stress for us. You have
forced us to bring together two totally different
ways of working and preparing in making this

graduation speech. We have booked off a few days to help us sort this out!

Lydia: CMBC itself has always occupied a rather large place in our lives, from our own student days here, to many years of board involvement, to long-term friendships with faculty and staff, to the graduation of two of our children, to a short, exciting time of teaching here.

Gary: Yesterday I met with a dozen or so fellow classmates, graduates of exactly thirty years ago, reliving memories and stories and journeys since. What a motley bunch we were then, and still are now, as unlikely a collection of eager world shakers as ever stumbled out of this place, with high visions and low potential. But we all agreed it had been worth it. We all give thanks for our years here. And we all still have some vision left, despite whole years full of reality, including some pain and disillusionment.

Lydia: You, the class of '95, sitting in front of us in your black robes, hiding both blemish and great beauty, are a more imposing and gifted lot than we felt ourselves to be back then. But then the world we want to send you into and the church as well have become more complex and diverse.

You have chosen the image of wings as a graduation motif: "On the wings of the dawn." And you have chosen Psalm 139 as the text. It is poetry. It is filled with images. How important, after several years of mostly prose and papers and exams and academic rigour and analysis, and disciplined practice, and precision, to end with poetry. And to take wings. And to fly.

Gary: I can literally fly. In my dreams, that is, occasionally. I finally confessed that to a sub-group of introverts huddled off in a corner at a party, where a large number from our church had gathered. And, like in a therapy group or at an AA meeting, several others confided that they too could fly in their dreams. It feels a bit risky admitting that in public. I don't know what deep, hidden trauma or neurosis or unmet needs these dreams portend, and probably don't want to find out – at least not from any of you amateur psychoanalysts who will spend the rest of this speech-time diagnosing my psyche rather than listening to what comes beyond confession.

I can fly. There is a wonderful exhilaration in the flying. I soar lightly, effortlessly across the meadows, over trees, across rooms, above people bound to the earth. I feel free and spontaneous, and, I suspect, powerful. I can hover lightly. I can move forward or upward at great speed. And all without effort. I just will it, and it happens. I am not aware in these dreams of fleeing from anyone or anything as our psalm suggests. Neither am I aware of any great purpose to my winging about.

But the dream always changes before it's done. It goes heavy. It takes greater and greater effort to clear obstacles. I seem to lose power. I can't fly as high anymore. I can't get above the trees. It takes an immense effort to continue. Everything seems to slow down, and eventually I am earthbound again and left with some sense of disappointment and even exhaustion as my body just can't fly anymore. At least not until my next dream – which might be many months hence.

It may feel like bad news to eager graduates just getting their pilot's licence to tell them a story of wings clipped and flight aborted. But we think there is some good news hidden in this metaphor of life.

Lydia: Perhaps our psalmist also belonged to this club of dream flyers, the late-night club of nocturnal voyagers.

> Where can I go from your Spirit?
> Or where can I flee from your presence?
> If I ascend to heaven, you are there;
> if I make my bed in Sheol, you are there.
> If I take the wings of the morning
> and settle at the farthest limits of the sea,
> even there your hand shall lead me,
> and your right hand shall hold me fast.

On first reading, Psalm 139 is a wonderful poem of confidence in God, of faith and trust, and of the simple awareness that God is not absent even in the extremes of life. It lifts us on wings of faith. But in a deeper reading we do get hints of turbulence, of downdrafts, and maybe even of crash landings. Only as we enter the psalm more fully do we realize the challenge that this psalm gives to us, the challenge to take up flying in a more serious way, with new purpose and new power.

So today, on this your graduation, we invite you to join us in further exploring Psalm 139. We want to share with you three ways to read this psalm, three readings that reflect our own pilgrimage with this text. Your family, your friends, and the broader church are invited to listen in, to reflect on their own experience with this poem. But we warn you. Reading this psalm can be risky, for its poetic expressions and imaginative language invite us to an ever-deeper encounter with the One who can turn even our too-easy reading upside down.

1. A Theological Reading

Gary: A first reading of this psalm might be called a theological reading, which would be a very natural reading for most of us here, and especially for you students at CMBC. The first reading is a very "feel good" reading. It is very comforting. It is very inspiring.

> O Lord, you have searched me and known me.
> You know when I sit down and when I rise up;
> you discern my thoughts from far away.
> You search out my path and my lying down,
> and are acquainted with all my ways.
> Even before a word is on my tongue,
> O Lord, you know it completely.
> You hem me in, behind and before,
> and lay your hand upon me.
> Such knowledge is too wonderful for me;
> it is so high that I cannot attain it.

In this first reading we assume that this psalm is about God, and so what we notice first are the many things that the psalmist knows about God. The psalm affirms basic convictions, core beliefs that we also have been taught at home and at church and at CMBC. God is with us in all circumstances of life. No matter where I go or what I do or what tragedy or pain may befall me, God will be there with me. This is a beautiful and comforting reading for us because it affirms some of our most basic convictions and beliefs. It is an important reading for students who are facing major transitions and new challenges.

Lydia: The poet of this piece describes these convictions through various lenses. As I read these verses I was reminded of a movie that I saw at the Science

Centre in Toronto, a movie in which we are asked to look at life from two distinct perspectives.

First, there is a macroscopic view. Picture this scene. A person sits in a chair on a beach, filling the picture. But the camera moves further and further away. First you see only the person in the chair. Then you see the whole beach. Then you see the whole city nestled beside the huge lake. Then you see the province, and then the whole continent, and finally the entire universe and galaxy. The speck which is the person gets smaller and smaller. We are impressed with the immensity of the universe and the smallness of the person, whom we can now only imagine in the middle of the picture.

> If I ascend to heaven you are there;
> if I make my bed in Sheol, you are there.
> If I ... settle at the farthest limits of the sea,
> even there your hand shall lead me,
> and your right hand shall hold me fast.
> If I say, "Surely the darkness shall cover me,
> and the light around me become night,"
> even the darkness is not dark to you.

Then the psalmist uses a microscopic frame. Picture the same person sitting in the same chair, but now the camera zeroes in ever closer. The picture focuses on a hand. Then on the wrinkles on the hand. Then on a cell. And then – we run out of imagination.

> For it was you who formed my inward parts;
> you knit me together in my mother's womb.
> I praise you, for I am fearfully and wonder-
> fully made.
> Wonderful are your works;
> that I know very well.

My frame was not hidden from you,
when I was made in secret,
intricately woven in the depths of the earth.
Your eyes beheld my unformed substance.
In your book were written
all the days that were formed for me,
when none of them as yet existed.
How weighty to me are your thoughts, O God!
How vast is the sum of them!
I try to count them – they are more than the sand;
I come to the end – I am still with you.

Beautiful. Inspiring. Awesome. This theological or "church" reading of Psalm 139 soars with feelings of safety and protection and being known and being loved by God.

Gary: But we have left out some verses. They didn't seem to quite fit in. In fact, it seems to us that in most worship services where this popular psalm is read, verses 19 through 22 are left out. All that stuff about enemies and hate and revenge does not fit into church worship, and so we leave out those verses, just as we often leave our everyday lives outside as we enter the church door. We can stay with our first nice theological reading only if we suppress our questions and our doubts and the fear and the anger that are a part of all human experience.

But if we leave out these verses and stay with a more naive reading, we are in danger of building a distorted picture of a God who is always on our side and is always protecting us from any harm – and keeping us from any genuine introspection. With such a reading, we can even justify shutting out ideas and new people – ideas and people that might threaten our easy comfort. Our communities will then become safe only for us insiders.

Lydia: For those of you who have read philosophy, or taken a hermeneutics course, you may recall that Ricoeur calls this a reading in the "first naïveté." Walter Brueggemann speaks of a reading in which we are securely oriented, in a situation of equilibrium, in a state of being settled. It is a reading that can sustain us only if we ignore the critical issues raised by the world around us and if we suppress the pain, confusion, and despair that is sometimes within us. Though this first reading may seem like flying, it can be more like gliding, oblivious to the world beneath us ... until we crash.

2. An Anthropological Reading

Gary: It is the events at "the edge of our humanness," the events that threaten and disrupt our convenient equilibrium that ask us to reread the psalm, this time struggling with those times when God seems absent, when there is no comforting word, when we discover that the wings that we thought were upholding us are suddenly not there. The only reading that seems possible at this stage is an anthropological reading, a focus on our humanness.

In this second reading we focus on exactly those parts of the psalm that we usually feel very uncomfortable with, for it is these words that express the feelings that we have in our moments of despair and anger. It is these thoughts that express what we feel when we enter into solidarity with our world in its pain and hurt. For the psalm is not only about God, but also about us humans. And it is about us humans in a decidedly un-flying mode, when we have crash-landed, when life doesn't make theological sense anymore, when what we experience is the absence of God.

> O that you would kill the wicked, O God,
> and that the bloodthirsty would depart from me –
> those who speak of you maliciously,
> and lift themselves up against you for evil!
> Do I not hate those who hate you?
> I hate them with perfect hatred;
> I count them my enemies.

Lydia: Wow! Hold on a minute. If everything is so nice and our life so successful and wonderful and if God is always comfortably near, why this sudden, totally out-of-place outburst?

Here too there is both a macroscopic and microscopic view of harsh human reality and a harsh depiction of evil. Yes, there are wicked, bloodthirsty, abusive, evil people out there. There are political institutions and structures that continue to support violence and oppression. We will always have them with us.

These days we are reminded of World War II and the ceasefire of fifty years ago, the ceasefire that was not a peace treaty and did not really create peace. We are reminded of the Holocaust, the extermination of Jews by Christians. These days we mourn the car bombing in Oklahoma in which many people were killed and wounded, many of them children. We are becoming aware of the horrible abuse of the residential school system for Indigenous peoples across Canada.

The lens focusing on the evil out there seems to get bigger and bigger until it includes not only our city, but our country; not only Canada, but the whole world. We begin to speak about our attempts to solve the problems – we speak of bigger police forces, more security, more military weapons. But then we suddenly become quiet.

We suddenly realize that the psalmist is not content with looking only at the evil "out there." He is also willing to look inward. "Search me, O God, and know my heart ... and see if there is any wickedness there." And there is. We do discover and experience that there is evil, brokenness, and pain inside each of us. The microscopic lens focuses inward, clear, sharper, penetrating all our barriers and pretences. It takes courage to see the hatred and fear within ourselves and within our communities.

Gary: This second reading of the psalm, this anthropological reading, is also necessary. It tells us of the rawness of human life. It puts us in solidarity with all of humanity. It tells us that we can't fly around forever on our own power. It tells us that our lives, even lives surrounded by God's presence, will know enemies and evil and pain and crash-landings. It tells us that though we may seem powerful, we often feel powerless to change the world out there, or even the world within us.

Paul Ricoeur calls these times "limit-experiences" that create "limit-expressions" of hate and anger and despair. Walter Brueggemann speaks of times of dislocation, of disorientation, of dismantling of inadequate theologies. All of us, I think, recognize times when we come to the limits of our strength and ability to go on – we come to the end of our rope.

Many of you graduates have already begun to read this psalm with these counter-voices included. Perhaps a more thorough reading of the Bible here at CMBC has already shattered some of your certainties. You too have discovered that the knowledge you thought you had about God was suddenly not enough. Even in a safe community like CMBC, there may have been times when the world and its pain entered the community. A phone call from a friend or family member, an emergency in one of your service assignments or in the dorm, or just a routine reading of the newspaper – and you are faced with the seeming absence of God. But you kept on studying, struggling, searching, hoping that somehow the first and second reading could be brought together. And your intellectual struggle became a wrestling with God, much like Jacob's wrestling with the angel in the wilderness, or Hannah's wrestling in prayer in the temple courts.

3. The Psalm as Prayer

Lydia: And so, we come to a third reading – which is not really a reading at all. For we become aware that the psalm is really a prayer – a prayer addressed to the God whom we know only partially, but still intimately. And the prayer comes from all who are no longer naive about themselves and the world. We have looked outside of ourselves and inside of ourselves. And we have lost our innocence.

And now this psalm becomes a very different kind of psalm, now no longer primarily about theological or anthropological insights. It isn't really about nice theology or knowledge of God. It isn't about more aware self-knowledge. The psalm transcends each of these levels. We become aware that this psalm is really about God knowing us. Our lives are an open book to God. God knows us in the profound and intimate sense of the wonderful Hebrew word *Jadah* – to know. The psalm is about God being mysteriously present to us even in our "limit-experiences," even in our loss of naïveté, even in our disorientation, even in our awareness of evil and our own "woundedness." When we have crash-landed and lost even the answers we thought we had and are driven to prayer, almost desperate prayer, there comes the almost insane awareness that God does indeed know us – and still loves us – and we can go on again.

Gary: Search me, O God, and know my heart;
test me and know my thoughts.
See if there is any wicked way in me,
And lead me in the way everlasting.

At times, in personal and family life, and surely in pastoral ministry, I am driven to prayer – not the easy, comfortable, relaxed, confident prayer of the successful family man or successful minister, but the more desperate prayer arising out of overwhelming complexity and few solutions. "Search me, know my heart, test me, know my thoughts." And the future opens up again.

Begin to Fly

Lydia: On the wings of the dawn. Dawn has arrived. Morning is breaking. The dream is over. We are awake. Now the real flying begins.

Graduates, fellow wing seekers, believe that you can fly. Not because of the great knowledge of God you have gained here at CMBC, though we hope you have learned a great deal and that you will be very vigorous in your theological reflections and your biblical reading. Not because of the great anthropological insights you have gained, though we would push you to ever more rigorous learning here. Not because of remarkable self-insight, though above all you do need to be very self-aware.

But fly on the wings of prayer, on the wings of the awareness that God knows you and that God knows the world. This God will guide you in purposeful flight. This God will accompany you on your journey. This God will love you through your successes and through your failures.

Gary: Read the psalm again and again ... in a kind of first reading, a theological and perhaps naive reading, and find comfort and safety there. Read it in a second, more anthropological reading, and find there a profound understanding about our world and about ourselves. But read it also a third time, when reading turns into prayer, for it is on the wings of prayer that you can fly and soar to great heights.

Lydia and Gary: Bon voyage! God bless you all. Amen.

PART THREE
WHEN THE MUSIC IS FESTIVE

Special occasions in the life of the church drew out my more creative side. My first reaction when I learned of a funeral or wedding that I needed to preside over was to feel the heavy responsibility and time commitment this would demand. And in the case of a death, knowing that I would have to reach deep inside myself if I wanted to engage the grieving family in depth – deeper than I often wanted to go. My second response was to realize that I was often energized by this intense involvement with people dealing with life-and-death issues. There is something very holy about meeting people at the place of these major transitions in life. Then I would begin to ask myself how I could open myself to the conversations needed, and then to craft and create worship experiences that would be both important and personal for these people. I thrived on the opportunity to try to make public ceremonies such as baptisms, parent-child dedications, funerals, and weddings unique and personal.

Yet these events are also communal. They bring together personal pastoral care and community pastoral care. Or, more importantly, they bring the persons involved more fully into the community. The whole community becomes a partner in grieving together and celebrating together. Public observances open the door for the community to become caregiver, offering these individuals love and friendship.

Personal pastoral care must of course remain confidential. A pastor is often involved in meaningful and profound aspects of the lives of persons in the congregation. Of all vocations, I can't think of many that touch the real world in more places than does a pastor's. We tend to be there when life is pain-filled or even brutal; when someone who is dying or with the family of someone who has died; with those who are despairing and want to end their lives; when a marriage is in jeopardy; when relationships have disintegrated; when there is conflict in the home and children and parents don't get along; when people are desperately sick; when addiction issues are destroying a life and a family; when social injustice crushes someone; when the political process becomes inhuman; when people find it impossible to have faith, in anything – themselves, society, or God.

But this is only one half of people's experiences that pastors are involved in. The other half includes celebrating weddings and wedding anniversaries, the birth of babies, love and wholesome relationships, the joy of a life rich with meaning; marking a person's commitment to Christ in baptism, graduation from school, finding good employment; seeing individuals grow a deeper faith out of crisis, demonstrate a caring concern for others, or express a beautiful joy in living.

Very few vocations hold the possibility of entering both sides of the deep experiences of life as fully as pastors do. Public ceremonies give the opportunity for members of the church community to enter some of these experiences and become participants in offering care and love and support, to become partners in ministry.

The repeating events of the church year also create an opportunity for community building. Celebrating Christmas, Good Friday and Easter, Pentecost, and Thanksgiving year after year can become old hat for the pastor – especially after fifty years of it. Just go back to the same old sermons and repeat. And then something would draw me beyond the repetitious nature of these events. Something pulled out my more creative side and suggested that there might be a new way of telling the old stories again.

When faced with repeating events, I always experienced a tension between succumbing to routine and relying on old stuff, and challenging myself to seize another opportunity to explore new possibilities. Which impulse, which choice, always before me, would win out this time?

In Part Three I reflect on the celebratory events of church life – the festive seasons of the church year like Christmas, Good Friday, and Easter, as well as special occasions like baptisms and parent-child dedication services. Then I turn to weddings and funerals. I will devote a chapter to each of these. I want the public face of these liturgies to reflect the deep, mysterious heart of God's love enveloping both individual persons and the community as a whole.

8

Naming the Sacred in the Ordinary

My first Good Friday at Toronto United Mennonite Church (TUMC) exhausted me – and moved me deeply. I could hardly imagine the immense effort it would take to get our sanctuary prepared for that evening's service. There was a long and deeply valued tradition lived out here. Our Good Friday service included a meal held in the sanctuary. But our worship space was filled with pews. These pews had to be moved to accommodate the tables needed to have a supper together. What do you do with all the pews?

All the pews, I learned, had to be taken out and stacked somewhere – mostly in our office spaces. I was convinced there wasn't enough room. But it had been done before. And would be done many times again. It was exhausting – and exacting – work. Finally, the last pews had been manhandled and stacked into a space too small for them. But then we had to set up all the tables – with the growing awareness that after the service all the pews and tables would have to be returned to their rightful place.

The Good Friday supper, I learned, was the most important service of the year at TUMC, the highlight of the church year. It was a supper, with the story of the death of Jesus told, hopefully dramatically, as part of the meal. Scriptures and hymns and special music and communion would be interspersed throughout the meal until the story was complete. The story ends with the death of Jesus. We are left in the dark, all candles extinguished,

pondering, alone. Left with death. Left with no hint of the resurrection to come. That would come Easter Sunday morning.

For many years we wrestled with those pews and with that
drama. For me, with the help of the worship committee, the
challenge was to craft a fresh way of telling the Good Friday story
year after year. We wrote readers' theatre versions of the story
from the different Gospel accounts. We wrote monologues and
dialogues. We wrote dramas. The story itself never became old.

In 1997, TUMC dedicated a new worship space, the result of an
almost complete rebuilding of our old building. *We sold the pews.*
We filled the sanctuary with chairs. No more pews to squeeze
into impossible places. And there were also other changes to our
Good Friday traditions. One was that we were becoming aware
that there were more and more children in our congregation.
But our observance of Good Friday, especially because it was a
communion service, was understood to be an adult service that
wasn't all that child-friendly.

We began to hold a separate, children's version of the Good
Friday story in the morning in addition to our traditional
service in the evening. The children's service has now evolved
into a family service. But the evening service also keeps evolv-
ing and changing – as it must. Speeding this evolution was a
new partnership.

In the bigger picture, the way a particular worship tradition evolves is significant only if it happens because of how the
identity and spiritual maturity of the community is growing
and changing. Exchanging pews with chairs, which facilitated a
gradual change in our Good Friday worship tradition, was only
a very small part of the much bigger changes brought about by
a new facility.

TUMC had given up full ownership control of the new build-
ing. It was now a joint owner with the Mennonite New Life
Centre of Toronto (the refugee services arm of the Mennonite
Church) and the Toronto Mennonite New Life Church (a
Spanish-speaking congregation mostly consisting of refugees

from Central and South America). We had become full partners. We had worked together as volunteers in renovating the building. We worship together only very occasionally – but always on Good Friday. That evening service is led in English and Spanish, with leaders from both congregations. For me this adds depth to our reflections on the death of Jesus. In partnership, we enrich each other and change each other.

Baptism and Child Dedication Stories

The balance between stability and openness to the new is built into the routines of both the church year and the celebration of more personal transition moments. Every year we repeat the cycle of Advent, Christmas, Easter, Pentecost, Thanksgiving. Can these routines have meaning year after year? Along the way we bless babies and marriages, invite people to be baptized, and say a final farewell to those who have died.

In 1525, Conrad Grebel refused to have his infant daughter baptized – and precipitated a crisis that led to the birth of the Anabaptist movement. For over one thousand years the church had baptized infants. Grebel rejected the church theology that said an infant was born sinful and needed to be baptized in order for it to be "saved" and assured of going to heaven should it die. The church and the state were not happy with Grebel's presumptuous refusal and issued him an ultimatum. Still he refused to have his daughter baptized. On January 21, 1525, a small group of like-minded followers of Jesus met in the home of one Felix Manz and baptized each other as believing adults. The name "re-baptizers" or "Anabaptist" was born.[13]

---

13 C. Arnold Snyder, *Anabaptist History and Theology: An Introduction* (Kitchener, ON: Pandora Press, 1995), p. 54.

In keeping with their Anabaptist heritage, Mennonites practise adult believer's baptism upon confession of faith, emphasizing the personal choice of the one being baptized. In place of infant baptism, we offer a parent-child dedication ceremony, hoping that the child, when grown up, will make a personal claim of faith and request baptism. What then do we do with adult Christians who were baptized as infants and want to officially become members of the Mennonite church? Do we accept their infant baptism, or do we insist on a re-baptism, which would be in keeping with our heritage?

Answering this question became both more challenging and definitive when our son Kendall married Charleen. Charleen was Christian Reformed and had been baptized as an infant. She joined the Mennonite church in adulthood without being re-baptized as an adult. Her simple, and profound, disclaimer was that from as early as she could remember her church and her parents had named her baptism as the sign that she was deeply loved by God. That has enormous meaning for her. She saw no need to be re-baptized. It is striking that she is now a Mennonite pastor, happily baptizing people on their confession of faith – without at all denigrating infant baptism. What Charleen adds to our theology of baptism, I think, is a strong emphasis on the unmerited grace of God. "In baptism, we are named a beloved child of God," she says. She has also recreated the parent-child dedication to place more emphasis on the naming of the baby as "beloved," a sign of grace that comes even before an individual chooses to follow Jesus.

The Lutheran Couple Who Would Take No Chances

A young couple of Lutheran background started attending our church, drawn by their embrace of Anabaptism, specifically our peace position and our understanding of baptism. They had taken the faith exploration course I offered, and now wanted to both join our church officially and have their child dedicated. On the morning of the dedication service, the husband said with a big smile on his face, "You know, Gary, that if our child is ever in a life and death crisis, I will insist on her being baptized. I'm not taking any chances."

Baptism Pictures in a Museum?

I had heard the rumours. I needed to see it for myself. The Edmonton Museum featured a huge picture of three of our young people being baptized. The rumours were true.

The director of the museum had called me to ask if he could come to one of our services so that he could better understand who Anabaptist Mennonites were. He wanted to both interview me and attend a typical service. He had an interest in highlighting diverse religious heritages in some way. I suppose we Mennonites were about as diverse as he could find. We chatted together and he showed up, with his camera, on a Sunday morning – a Sunday when we happened to baptize three young adults. That baptism picture, along with a rather fine introduction to Anabaptism, graced a museum display wall for many years. (He did ask permission to post the display).

What Have Horses to Do with a Baptism?

A young woman who had grown up in our church but now didn't attend any more came to a wedding of friends of hers which I officiated. I had a chance to chat with her before the reception. In a teasing mode, she said that she had met a pastor who rode around on a motorcycle and even rode that bike to church occasionally. That really impressed her, she said. Then she challenged me, dared me, really, to also ride a motorcycle to church. If I did that, she said, she would come to church on that morning to witness the ride.

I confessed that I knew nothing about motorcycles and wouldn't know how to manage her dare. But, I added, I knew a lot about horses, and I would be glad to ride a horse to church. I was quite certain that I could borrow a horse from a church member who owned horses. I challenged her to come to church on a given Sunday morning, saying I would greet her on horse-back. Laughing, she said yes.

That Sunday morning, I borrowed a horse, rode it onto the churchyard, and greeted everyone who came, saying that this was the morning I would preach "the sermon from the mount" (Mathew 5–7). The young woman came, seemingly enjoying the dare and the fulfillment of our conversation at that wedding. A few years later she requested baptism.

How Much Water Does One Need for a Baptism?

After my retirement from full-time ministry, Lydia and I were intentional interim ministers in three different churches. In one of these, the mode of baptism tended to be by full immersion. One young man requested baptism by immersion and had a specific place in mind. A particular Mennonite-run camp and retreat centre had been very important to his faith maturation. It had a creek running through it. That is where he wanted to be baptized.

We invited the whole church to have the worship and baptism service there. The challenge was that we were in a dry spell, weather-wise. The creek was running very shallow. Was there enough water for full immersion? This young man would not be daunted. We tried to deepen a place just before the bridge. I baptized him there, by immersion, though it was really only his head that got fully dunked. He and everyone else were in great spirits. It felt like God was smiling and laughing with us.

A Rookie Pastor Messes Up His First Parent-Child Dedication Service

I was young, eager, but totally inexperienced, leading my first ever parent–child dedication service. Four parents brought their young infants to the front of the church for me to bless and pray over. Confidently, but foolishly, I hadn't written out my prayer of dedication.

One of the couples was relatively new to the congregation. They weren't of Mennonite background but had become friends with church members living in our community. The mother of the child was coming to church regularly. The father was a bit reluctant to get involved too closely with these strange Mennonites. But here he was on this morning, wanting his child also be blessed. I had met with all four couples to prepare for this dedication. I had almost over-prepared for the whole service – except for writing out that one prayer.

The ceremony itself went well – the questions of intent for the parents to answer, naming each child in that process. Finally, the prayer of blessing. And in my prayer, I forgot to name that one particular child. I just forgot one child. Theirs. I realized it the moment I sat down, ceremony finished. I felt torn apart inside. All my apologies and all their forgiveness didn't quell my inner turbulence. Was I really cut out to be a pastor?

But it seems that God's blessing on parents and children doesn't really depend upon the memory and expertise of the pastor. That baby, un-named in my blessing prayer, is now a Mennonite pastor, blessing other children and their parents, probably not forgetting a single name.

Two Dedication Services on One Sunday

A number of couples in the church had requested a dedication service for their children. But one of these children had spent his whole life — almost a year already — in the hospital, often in the intensive care unit. He had been born without an esophagus.

The dedication service at church that morning was filled with joy and smiles and a confident hope. Right after the service, a fairly large group of us headed to the hospital for another dedication, one that had a deep seriousness surrounding it. This child and these parents had spent the past months with a hospital as their primary context, nurses and doctors their immediate community. The child's biggest of many surgeries was imminent.

The dedication prayer for that child went deeper than the earlier prayer of blessing at the church. It was an urgent plea to God for that child to survive, to live. The child did live, thanks to a newly crafted esophagus, and hopefully has no memory of the angst and fears and prayers of the parents and the church. He is doing well.

The Gift of Hospitality

We are gathered in our living room. Five couples have brought their infants to our home in preparation for a parent-child dedication service on Sunday. We invite them to share their experience of parenting. What are their joys, their anxieties, their hopes and dreams, their fears?

Their responses begin a bit carefully, with some hesitation over how vulnerable they are ready to be with each other — and with us — and with God. But their experience of pregnancy and waiting and birthing and parenting is so precious, so consuming, so daunting that their stories and feelings cannot be held back. The experience of giving birth, of parents holding such a fragile new being in their arms, of being responsible for it, of loving it and being loved in turn is so powerful and so profound that stories and smiles and tears soon create a sacred space filled with holy conversation.

Two hours later, as we pause for prayer before a light snack, there is a spirit of intimacy, a sense that we have been encompassed by a sacred journey. On the surface, it was Lydia and I who opened our home in hospitality. On a much deeper level, our guests extended hospitality to us as they opened their lives to each other and to us.

Hospitality, it seems, is always a reciprocal opening of our lives to each other.

Advent and Christmas

This season is a month long. A whole month. And it comes every year without fail. In fact, commercially this season is much longer than a month, beginning already shortly after Halloween. How in the world can the church have any enthusiasm at all for dedicating so much time to one story – the birth of Jesus – amidst this long, gaudy season of flagrant excess? And how can pastors maintain their enthusiasm for retelling one story for a whole month, then repeating this year after year after year?

It helped me come to terms with the inevitability of the prolonged beginning of the new church year (Advent) by focusing on how the old church year ends. It ends with Eternity Sunday. In some Mennonite churches, the last Sunday of November has become a time to commemorate all members who have died during that year. It is a sobering end to the church year, and a sobering reminder that death is inevitable. This alone helps temper the excesses of the coming season.

Eternity Sunday turned into a very important moment in our church's life as a community of faith. On the one hand, it became an occasion to name death and grief and loss publicly and openly. Those who had experienced a death of a loved one during the past year (or longer) could bring a flower to the altar and name that person to the congregation (sometimes the liturgy was to light a candle). I was often surprised by how many people participated. Since TUMC is a very urban congregation, with many members who have come from other places, we are not always aware of the deaths and funerals outside of our immediate context that impact deeply on our members. This ceremony allows a sharing of that pain and loss, and invites support and prayer.

On the other hand, Eternity Sunday is a prime moment to reflect on eternity, on our belief that death is not the end of life but the gateway to eternal life. It is an expression of a profound hope. Eternity Sunday gives us a sense of grounding as we anticipate both the joys and the excesses of the coming new year, and our observance of Advent and Christmas.

And yet. There are four Sundays of Advent. There is Christmas Eve and Christmas Day (for those churches that still have a service on Christmas Day). How is a pastor supposed to retain any enthusiasm for this season or find anything new to say, year after year? Maybe there is no need for anything new or fresh. After all, the coming of God in the form of a human baby is a timeless message.

Perhaps it was only my own need that prompted me to explore more creative ways of telling a story that the Scriptures themselves do not spend a lot of space on. In comparison to the death of Jesus, the Bible doesn't dwell long on stories of his birth. But I did enjoy trying to find new ways to tell something of the old story.

INTERLUDE
The Morning After a Sign

Some of my attempts at telling old, familiar stories in a new way were published by The Mennonite. *This interlude originally appeared on December 18, 1984.*

"Look for a sign," they said. "God will give a sign." Long overdue, I would say. We've been praying, crying, begging, pleading for a sign from God. God has abandoned us. Maybe God is sitting on his throne up there somewhere in heaven, blissfully ignorant of the mess his "good" creation is in. He doesn't visit the earth often. A sign, that's all we want. A sign to let us know God hasn't forgotten us, that he sees and knows what our life is like. A sign that would tell us, "I, the Lord God, am still active in the world. I am a saving God. I am who I am. Do not be afraid. I am God."

They said there was such a sign last night. False hope, no doubt. Some stupid shepherds going on about angels and about a baby born in Bethlehem to a peasant couple, saying he was the Son of God. Every baby born – every male baby – is a son of God. Well, maybe all peasants need visions of grandeur now and then, some escape from reality – God knows their life is hard enough – but they don't need to get the whole town excited about it. Next thing you know we'll have the Romans nosing around again.

Speaking of which, that's why we need the sign so desperately. You know what they've done now, don't you? Filed, notified, taxed — forever on their lists. Once you're on, you never get off again. It's just the next step in their control over our lives. We are just another cipher forever to be taxed. But if you're not on their lists, you are worse off yet — you don't exist. With no identification, you can't live. "Everyone please be so kind as to return to their ancestral village in order to be enrolled." Or else!

My friend Ben Zadok refuses to do so. He will remain defiant to the end. He won't put his name down on any Roman list, not unless it's written with Roman blood.

We've often argued about "the sign." Zadok and I, and Shamiel and Ehron and Tobiah. We argue about what kind of Messiah God will send. We argue and argue.

Zadok can see nothing but Judas Maccabeus resurrected. He sees blood in every dream. Daydream, nightmare, it doesn't matter: he sees blood — Roman blood. The sign will be another Maccabean warrior smashing Roman might, just as Judas drove out Antiochus Epiphanes and the despicable Syrians 150 years ago. He gets positively wild about that. "The Romans are Satan's agents," he says, "the most vile and evil force in our world. There is only one way to deal with them." He says if God would only deal with that problem, life would be beautiful again.

The rest of us don't exactly disagree with Zadok, but we do see other things too. Shamiel says he is looking for a different sign. He insists God has promised a second Moses, a lawgiver who will tell everyone how to live. "If people would only know how they should live and would have someone to guide them in doing the right things — living by the laws of God — then the new age of God would be ushered in and the Romans wouldn't really matter. The root problem," says Shamiel, "is that people have too much freedom today" — a point of view totally incomprehensible to Zadok. But Shamiel has a point. The Roman thing is only an outward loss of freedom. Inwardly our people have too much. They do what is expedient to survive. There don't seem to be any absolutes anymore. Morality is not taken seriously. The laws of God are for private contemplation, but for public concourse you do what you need to do to survive. "A second Moses," says Shamiel, "is who we are waiting for – the Ten Commandments retold, reinterpreted, proclaimed. That is the Messiah we need."

Ehron says any amount of laws won't do any more good than more pigeons on the temple pinnacle unless we finally get a king to enforce them. "Anyone who is even slightly acquainted with Holy Scriptures," says Ehron, "knows that the Messiah God will send a king like one this world has never seen before. A king in the line of David, only more so," he insists. "The heart of the problem is that we have no sense of authority. Everyone does his own thing … OK, her own thing too. We Jews have no sense of final authority apart from our religious leaders. And all the authority they have is tradition and musty, pious platitudes. Another David would set things right. Iron authority. Make us a proud nation once more, a nation under God, a light to all the nations. The sign will wear purple robes and make us all proud again, and God fearing.

Tobiah is too polite to disagree with Ehron, but when he gets a chance, he talks enthusiastically about another prophet, like Elijah. I'm always surprised at that. A mild man like Tobiah gets stuck in one place in our Holy Scriptures, but he sure likes the story of Elijah killing the prophets of Baal on Mount Carmel. According to him, our problem is a religious problem and has nothing to do with the lack of kings or the presence of Romans.

"Kings can't bring about religious revival," he says. "Only a true prophet can do that. The issue is our loyalty to God, our inward heart, not laws or Romans or outward authority. Any time another enemy conquers us, we take on their gods too. Where are our martyrs who remain loyal at any cost? Whenever a new religious idea comes along, we swallow it. What we're getting is ecclesiastical diarrhea and nothing stays with us anymore."

Like I said, for a mild man Tobiah has some grit. And a way with words.

"We need an Elijah," he says, "to set our priorities right. Pledge total loyalty to Yahweh God and get rid of all the prophets of other ideas and false values."

It's all enough to confuse people. My friends all go to the Scriptures, and they all come out with different signs. They all picture different Messiahs, and these all trouble me, although I can't quite understand why. Each seems to catch only part of the promise of God. Each has its origins in our Scriptures. Why don't the pieces fit together? Why do each of those signs mean the destruction or defeat of someone? Can there be a Messiah who can come as a blessing to all people, to both Jews and Romans?

And there is still this thing of last night. Shepherds in unholy celebration (ever heard shepherds trying to sing?), visions of angels, and a baby born in some wretched stable. A Savior, they called him, Christ the Lord. Preposterous. And yet, why can't I dismiss the whole thing?

What have we got in the story? Bethlehem, a two-bit town; a young, poor peasant couple having their first baby; shepherds going on about seeing angels; a stable; a baby – it just doesn't add up.

A baby. Didn't Isaiah talk about a baby? Isaiah confronting King Ahaz? Ahaz so terrified he's desperate. Resin and Pekah nipping at his heels. And Assyria ready to devour them all. Ahaz in panic looks for a sign. "What is the Lord's sign, Isaiah? What is the sign of our deliverance?"

Isaiah says, "The Lord himself will give you a sign. Behold, a young woman shall conceive and bear a son, and shall call his name Immanuel, which means, God with us" (Isaiah 77:14). But that doesn't make sense, never did make sense. Ahaz is beset by Syrians and Assyrians and even cousin Jews, his own people are panic stricken, and Isaiah tells him the sign from God is a baby.

What kind of a sign is that? When things are dark and hopeless you've got to wait for a baby to grow up?

"Yes," says Isaiah, "a baby is a living sign from God." "For people walking in deep darkness, a light is beginning to shine … for to us a child is born, to us a son is given; and the government will be upon his shoulder, and his name will be called Wonderful Counselor, Mighty God, Everlasting Father, Prince of Peace" (9:2, 6). A baby. Immanuel, God with us.

They say that happened last night. Maybe I'm just letting those idiotic shepherds get to me. But today, the day after, our little world seems somehow to have a bit more light, a bit more love. A baby in a manger? Christ the Lord? I think I'll have another look at God's promise and …

9

Wedding Fanfares

We were gathering on the manicured lawn of a prestigious private golf club. The bride and groom, and their family members, were radiant with anticipation. A large congregation was finding seating in the open air. At the front, a lonely podium stood in the centre of a stage, supposedly for the pastor (me), under a protective canopy. There was just enough room on that stage for the wedding party, whom I would call forward for the actual ceremony. For now, they sat with the congregation under overcast skies.

There were some rather ominous clouds building on the horizon. The father of the bride looked nervously at the darkening sky. This was an outdoor wedding, after all, with no immediate shelter available. The service started. I preached a rather short homily – I thought. It wasn't short enough. I had just called the wedding party onto the stage under the shelter of the canopy to say their vows when thunder and a downpour of rain erupted almost simultaneously.

Nearly everyone stayed sitting where they were for the final "I do's." Almost everyone got soaking wet – except for pastor and wedding party. I marvelled that the whole gathering was quite willing to get wet in order to witness the vows the couple made. Later, at the reception, there were many jokes (and keen observations) about the drama of marriage and what to do when storms strike and rain and lightning replace the sunshine. The humour and the laughter reflected an important reality. Most marriages do endure some storms.

Why I Love Doing Weddings – and Why This Is an Important Ministry

Weddings offer both huge opportunities and huge challenges for pastors. Most of us struggle at times with requests to conduct weddings from couples outside of the church. And we almost always struggle with the trivialization of weddings by the "wedding industry." And yet it is a huge privilege to invite God's blessing on a couple getting married.

Weddings create opportunities for in-depth pastoral care, culminating in high moments of public worship. For me, these events highlight the specialness of public liturgies. I like to think that I as a pastor can help a couple getting married enter more deeply into that sacred space of God's love. But these moments of walking with others also change me – they push me at deep levels to deal with issues of joy, intimacy, and sometimes pain. They push me to prayer.

It may be that being asked to officiate at a wedding sparks in me that edge of my personality that thrives on trying to create something unique and personal for that moment. It was in getting to know a couple, with their personalities and values and dreams and struggles, that ideas emerged for crafting a wedding service that reflected both who they were and how God wanted to bless them and their community. I share some of my reflections on weddings as an example of public ceremonies I have thrived on.

Gary Harder

Our Wedding

I begin with reflections on Lydia's and my wedding in 1964. We so much wanted our wedding to reflect our love, our values, and our faith.

We decided to open the service with the congregational hymn "Praise to the Lord, the Almighty," a hymn beloved in our tradition. With it we would begin our wedding service with praise to God, which was important to us, and would do so with a strong, well-loved hymn, which was also important to us.

Lydia's father, a lay minister in the Niagara Mennonite Church who would officiate our wedding, was troubled by our choice of hymn. "People will just think that you, Lydia, are praising God for finally finding a man to marry." Unspoken was the assumption that since his daughter was twenty-five years old, really already an "old maid" in that context, people would smirk behind our backs about her choice to sing a praise song. Maybe the congregation would even think that we were praising God that we could now start having sex together. (We were of the old school, where full sexual expression waited till after the wedding.) We persisted, and the congregation sang a rousing, full-throated, full-harmony praise song to begin our nuptials.

Our culture is changing rapidly. The age of twenty-five is no longer considered the outer age limit for women to get married before it is "too late." Singleness, even for those older, is now more of a choice and more widely accepted. What has not changed, in my mind, is the appropriateness of beginning a marriage with praise to God. Praise is central to all worship, and particularly appropriate for a wedding service. With praise, we name our conviction that God created our world out of love and for love. In praise, we name our conviction that God created humans to relate intimately with God and with each other. We name that God is the source of all love, and now particularly the love that the couple wants to commit to each other. A wedding

172

is a time to celebrate our deepest relationships, our opportunity for intimacy, our sexuality, our gift of family and community.

But there was another, rather sobering reality affecting me and my family at our wedding. My father had died only three and a half months earlier. I, along with my family, especially my mother, were still in deep grief. My mother was happy for our wedding and wanted to celebrate it with joy, and she did put on a brave face. But grief still intruded for all of us. I missed my father terribly at that moment, a deep sense of loss. My mother bravely entered the festivities, but in the end her joy couldn't help but be restrained – and interrupted – by her loss.

Lydia's and my wedding carried poignant contradictions – but so perhaps does every wedding. The family of origin is no longer the primary family. A new family bond is created. There is both a letting go of an earlier primary bond, and the creating of a new one. Most of us long for deep intimacy but are also a bit afraid of the rawness of it, the exposure of our true selves.

Balancing Tradition and Creativity: Our Uncle John

We were both enjoying the conversation, though we differed sharply from each other. I was young and brash and full of new visions for doing weddings. He was, well, a seasoned, wise *Ältester*, a bishop-like figure in the Mennonite church in the Niagara area. He also happened to be Lydia's uncle. Lydia's uncle John represented the best of the traditional way of thinking about weddings.

Somehow, I had launched into my enthusiasm for (and surely, my expertise in) preparing couples for their marriage and their wedding service. After all, I had officiated at all of three by that time. "Couples need to be involved in planning their own wedding," I said with excitement. "It has to become their own. It must reflect who they are. They are invited to choose their

Scriptures and hymns, and even to write their own vows. The wedding service needs to be personalized, because that is when it is most meaningful to them. I will guide them, and perhaps constrain them when they go outside of the bounds of what I think is appropriate for a worship service, but the couple has to be deeply involved in planning their own service."

Uncle John smiled, paused for a while (after all, he probably had some hundreds of weddings at which he had officiated to reflect upon), and said, "Gary, you are very young and very eager. Let me tell you how I think about weddings. I believe that the wedding service is a gift of the church to the couple. It is a gift that the church has developed thoughtfully and carefully over a long time. The whole service, with the Scripture texts and the vows and the sermon, are the gift I offer the couple on behalf of the church. The recipient of a gift doesn't choose what is in it. The couple cannot create the gift. The wedding service, created by the church, is much bigger than any one couple. They need to receive this holy gift with joy and not try to improve on it to satisfy their own likes and dislikes. It is a good thing when wedding services don't change much from one time to another. Yes, the sermon may have some changes in it."

And there you have it: two sharply different visions for planning wedding services. I've often reflected on that conversation and on the "wisdom of the tradition" that Uncle John represented. And yet I also still invite couples to be involved in helping to plan their own wedding service, and I still envision a service that feels personal to them.

By now I have officiated at significant number of weddings, though I suspect I will never catch up to the number Uncle John did, especially since I am now fully retired. I thoroughly enjoy meeting with couples to help them prepare for their marriage and for their wedding (five to seven meetings). Most people, perhaps after some hesitation, are amazingly open and eager to explore the issues in their relationship and to explore the transcendent possibilities in it. And I thrive on the public celebration of their vows and the opportunity, in the context of worship, to invite God and the congregation to bless their covenanting together.

In the end, I do feel that I am an instrument offering a gift (from the church and from God) to the couple and to their families and friends. It is a gift of blessing, of assurance of God's love for them, of my support and the church's support of their marriage through the long haul of married life. It felt rather satisfying to me that my very last duty before officially retiring from full-time pastoral ministry was to officiate at a wedding.

Not All My Colleagues Share My Enthusiasm

I know that not all my colleagues in ministry experience this enthusiasm toward weddings. Many say they feel burnt out by them. Some, especially those in more mainline denominations, are almost overwhelmed by the number of weddings they are called on to officiate, and they struggle to maintain an enthusiasm for the job, sometimes even resenting the fact that in this domain they are agents of the state as well as of the church. "Why can't couples who are not really committed to the church just go to a justice of the peace to get married? Only those who are really sincere about their faith should come to the church for its blessing."

There are many reasons to be cynical about the church wedding "business." There are reasons why many pastors and priests dread the coming of May, June, July, and August, the primary wedding months – reasons beyond the inordinate amount of time they consume. Most of us could make a long list of inappropriate and even bizarre requests that couples make for their wedding service: music more suited to a bar than a church (though choosing a favorite hymn doesn't necessarily work out better. I still chuckle at one couple's choice of a favourite hymn

— "Master, the tempest is raging"); theatrics more in keeping with a Hollywood movie; vows that are a long list of what each likes about the other but are not actually vows. And then there is the reception afterwards — especially when the bar is open, alcohol is flowing freely, and guests are treated to repetitious and dreadful speeches with a profusion of inappropriate and off-colour attempts at humour.

Preparing for a wedding also sometimes unleashes hurtful family dynamics. Whom does the couple invite when there have been parental divorces and remarriages, or when old tensions between mother and daughter resurface over who makes decisions and about what? And how do we pastors respond to a couple who comes to us only because "my grandparents got married here and it would be nice to get married in the same church"?

Perhaps the biggest struggle we pastors have is with the wedding industry itself. This immensely profitable industry has little to do with marriage or with covenants. Rather, it flourishes on creating and fulfilling dreams — dreams that are a fantasy and that are exorbitantly expensive. Ah, the perfect wedding. The bride as Queen for a Day. Perfect (and expensive) clothes. Perfect (and expensive) pictures. Perfect reception (with a very expensive meal and free-flowing liquor). A mythically perfect wedding launching a mythically perfect marriage. A flamboyant and excessive spectacle that may leave the couple (and even their parents) financially and emotionally bankrupt. Apparently, an average Canadian wedding costs close to $30,000.

And many clergy simply resent the enormous amount of time and energy that is taken up with conducting weddings — time and energy not always appreciated, and which certainly could have been well spent on more urgent ministries.

An Instrument of God's Blessing

Despite all these reasons for cynicism, I confess that I love my pastoral involvement in preparing a couple for their wedding, in officiating at weddings, and ideally, in walking with a couple in their marriage journey. Perhaps I am just naive and sentimental and foolish. No doubt we clergy are sometimes merely "used" by a couple to facilitate their "beautiful dream wedding."

And yet, I believe that there is a new, God-given opportunity for significant ministry waiting for us each time. I believe that there is a "gift of blessing" that God truly wants the church to extend to the couple and their families and communities. What if pastors saw "God's opportunity" rather than a "resented duty" facing us with each new couple? What if we assumed the following three things each time a couple asked us to officiate their wedding?

First, the pair has come to the church, and to me as the pastor, because deep down they genuinely want to grow a deep and permanent marriage, and have some sense that a religious ceremony might help them toward that end. They may sound superficial in their wedding "wants"; they may have relational issues to work at. They may not be fully ready for marriage. Many couples come with some fear and anxiety, because they know the statistics about failed marriages and have likely experienced some of these casualties in their own friendship and even family circles. They might have had personal experience of their own where a relationship they thought would be permanent ended, perhaps in painful ways. And yet they have made the momentous decision now to get married anyway. And they have come to the church to do it, hoping that this will help them forge an intimate and lasting relationship.

Let's assume, in the second place, that they have come to a pastor or priest to officiate at their wedding because deep down they do want their lives and their relationship to be touched and blessed by God. They may not be churchgoers. They may have reacted against or even rejected the church. They may resist the thought of too much religious language in their wedding service. But if they have come to the pastor, can we not assume that they are somewhat open to the spiritual and transcendent ministry of the church?

And in the third place, let's assume that the guests coming to the wedding are also expecting something special. In recent years, most weddings that I have been involved with have an amazingly diverse guest list. The guests come from a relatives list, a work-place list, a community and friends list, and perhaps a church list. Often the gathering is an inter-racial, inter-cultural, inter-denominational, inter-religious, and perhaps agnostic mix of people all wanting to genuinely celebrate with the couple. And maybe because of – or in spite of – their own marriage or family experience, these guests genuinely want the couple's marriage to succeed. They do want it to be blessed. The wedding may be an opportunity for them to reflect more deeply again about marriage, perhaps their own and certainly the couple's. This may make them more open to hearing something about God's love and God's blessing of these kinds of covenant relationships.

If these assumptions are even partially valid, then a huge opportunity awaits the church and the pastor. I'm sure I have officiated weddings that Uncle John would probably have refused to do. I have married people from outside the church and people who claim no faith. I have married people who are divorced. I have married people with a troubled history. I have married alcoholics. I have married couples who were living together (as a large percentage of couples now are). I have married couples when the baby is on its way. I have married couples whose parents have objected so strongly to the union that they refused to attend the wedding. Perhaps Uncle John would question not only how I plan and conduct weddings, but also whose weddings I agree to officiate. Am I moving too far outside of my tradition in doing these weddings?

I still reflect on what Uncle John said: "The wedding service is the gift of the church to the couple getting married." But what is that gift? Is a fixed and unchanging order of service, or liturgy, the best way to express that gift?

My Basic Thesis

My basic thesis is that God is in the blessing business. God wants to bless people. God wants to bless families. God wants to bless marriages. This is the gift that God has entrusted to the church. Not only the church, of course – God will never be limited by the church. We in the church have often been poor stewards of God's love and blessing, often not knowing whom to bless and whom to curse. In Canada, we only need to look at the recent exposure of the churches' horrible complicity in the disaster of the residential school system for Indigenous children. We are inclined to hoard God's blessing for ourselves and for our people. But I believe that God has entrusted to the church a large outpouring of blessing that goes far beyond the church and which a needy world is longing for.

God, it seems, is so full of blessing that even the whole created universe gets a large dose of it. After creating every living creature in the seas and in the air, the storyteller of Genesis adds, "God blessed them, saying, 'Be fruitful and multiply and fill the waters and the seas, and let birds multiply on the earth'" (Genesis 1:22).

The storyteller repeats this effusive blessing after we humans were created. "So God created humankind in his own image, in the image of God he created them; male and female he created them. God *blessed* them, and God said to them, 'Be fruitful and multiply, and fill the earth and subdue it.'" (Genesis 1:27–28; italics added)

This blessing becomes focused in a powerful way in the story of Abraham. It was the reason Abraham was chosen by God in the first place.

> Now the Lord said to Abraham, "Go from your country and your kindred and your father's house to the land that I will show you. I will make of you a great nation, and I will *bless you* and make your name great *so that you will be a blessing … in you all the families of the earth shall be blessed.*" (Genesis 12:1–3; italics added)

Clearly Abraham is not to keep God's blessing for himself and for his family and for his tribe. God wants to pour out blessing "on all the families of the earth." Choosing Abraham is God's way of doing this. Abraham will carry this gift from God. It will be an awesome privilege and responsibility. Abraham's people will be tempted to claim this gift for themselves only and reject any sense that God could love and bless "outsiders."

I believe that God has chosen the church (and the synagogue and the mosque) for the same purpose: to be an agent for releasing blessing "on all the families of the earth." And maybe we can release some of this blessing on couples wanting to get married.

My own Mennonite tradition has often thought more about boundary issues when it comes to marriage than about blessing opportunities. But do we think that God is interested only in blessing "Mennonite marriages," or even "Christian marriages"? Does God want to bless only perfect (or almost perfect) and mature and pure Christian couples and families? What does it mean that God chose Abraham to be the source of blessing for all families on earth – which I assume would surely extend beyond only Jewish families and Christian families? After all, Abraham's story itself is filled with some very human and very un-godlike adventures, even though he was called to be the source of spreading God's blessing. He it was who passed off his own wife as his sister to save his own skin when he was in Egypt land (Genesis 12:10ff.). And he basically disowned his slave mistress Hagar and his son Ishmael by her (Genesis 21:8ff.). God seems to be ready to use very flawed humans to disburse blessing.

If God is in the blessing business and delights in blessing couples and families, then this gift is held in sacred trust by the church (and the synagogue and the mosque). It is not really the gift of the church as much as it is the gift of God, held in trust by the church. If it were the church's gift, then the church would be too tempted to try to control it and to apportion it out to its own advantage. Then we would be tempted to give or withhold this gift, based on our own assumptions of whom God wants to bless and whom God would choose not to bless. But do we always know this with certainty? It is God's gift of blessing that we are called to release into the lives of a couple getting married.

I do want to make a distinction between giving the church's blessing and giving our approval. These are not necessarily the same thing. I have officiated at a few weddings where I was uneasy and not fully approving. In a few of these cases I have later been pleasantly surprised by how healthy a marriage the couple has grown. And conversely, some very solid Christian couples have in the end not been able to make their marriage work. I have refused to do some weddings because there seemed to be no way to negotiate how each party – that is, couple and pastor – could maintain its integrity by doing it, especially when the couple refused to participate in any marriage or even wedding preparation. I refused to do a wedding where the young woman very clearly wanted to use a marriage certificate only because it was her ticket to staying in Canada as an immigrant. Several couples made their own decision to go elsewhere when they realized the preparation that would be involved.

Strangely enough, I am not aware of a single couple who turned away after learning that I would frame the wedding as a worship service that would include prayers and a homily. After hearing me out, every couple, including those who did not name themselves as Christian, welcomed invoking God's presence and blessing for their ceremony. They did long for this blessing.

Our approval or disapproval is based on our fallible insights, understandings, and perhaps prejudices. Our blessing is based on God's lavish outpouring of grace and love.

Wedding Stories

Many pastors will have a whole repertoire of delightful wedding stores to tell. Funny things happen at weddings, quite apart from attempted humour at the reception. But beautiful and holy things happen at weddings, too. I included some wedding stories, mostly of the holy kind, in my earlier book (*Dancing through Thistles in Bare Feet*), so I will limit myself here to some wedding memories that still make me smile.

The Impatient Groom

One impatient groom, long before we had come to that point, asked in a big voice heard by everyone, "Isn't it time for the kiss yet?" My pronouncement that they were husband and wife probably wasn't heard over the loud laughter of the congregation.

The Bride Swept off Her Feet

At one wedding, I felt a bit like a hero. The bride fainted as she was finishing her vows, and I managed to catch her before she crashed to the floor. She recovered, finished her vows, and as far as I know is still married.

The Embarrassed Clergyman

One wedding was particularly casual. There were maybe a dozen of us gathered in a backyard. The bride's dog stretched out comfortably on her feet. I too got caught up in this casual, informal atmosphere. I got her name wrong. I knew her quite well. The couple wanted to repeat their vows after me. I started out, "Will you, … " and said the wrong name. Good thing we were in a backyard. She roared with laughter. Sheepishly I corrected myself, and became the butt of many jokes at the reception.

The Alcoholics

One wedding stands out for all the right reasons. A middle-aged couple, whom I had never seen before, came into my office to ask if I would officiate at their wedding. The first thing they told me, after stating the reason for their coming, was that they were both alcoholics, were both divorced, had both rejected the Catholic church of their upbringing, and weren't sure whether they had any faith at all. They had been totally turned off by the church. They had heard from a relative who had been present at an earlier wedding where I had officiated that she had liked the way I did it. "We know that you will want to ponder your answer to us," they acknowledged, "but we are ready to share our story with you if you seriously want to hear it."

How could I say no before I heard their story? And yet the warning bells rang loud in my head. They carried a huge amount of baggage.

"I am ready to listen," I said. "Tell me your story, and then we will decide together whether you want me to officiate at your wedding, and whether I am ready to do it."

They told me their ongoing story. They both were "dry" alcoholics who faithfully attended AA meetings, both were in therapy, and both had done an amazing amount of soul-searching. They were far more aware of who they were, their issues, and the dynamics of their relationship with each other than are most couples who come to my office. They were eager to meet with me for a number of sessions to process ongoing issues in their relationship, and, if I agreed, to plan their wedding together. And they wanted to engage me in conversation about faith. They said they were sceptics. But it seemed to me that there was a kind of hunger within them, and openness, to see if faith could still be a part of their lives and their marriage. Why else would they come to a pastor of a denomination unknown to them?

I said yes. And after I explained how I would make the wedding a "worship service," they too said yes. And we embarked on an amazing wedding and marriage preparation journey together.

The wedding took place in a club, not a church. The gathered families and friends, I was told, were mostly disillusioned former churchgoers, just like they were. And they listened intensely. No alcohol was served at the reception. At the meal, Lydia and I were seated at a table with the couple's children and their spouses. And spent almost three hours deeply engaged in conversations about faith and about relationships and about marriage. We left exhausted and exhilarated. Seldom do our more traditional church weddings lead to this depth of conversation.

I don't know the couple's ongoing story. But I was convinced that God wanted to pour out a blessing on them and their families. I was convinced God wanted me to say yes to them.

The Wedding Where Everything – Well, Almost Everything – Went Wrong

It is always more complex to conduct an out-of-province wedding. My official licence to do weddings is an Ontario one. It is a rather complicated process to get a licence from another province. But I had started in time, and now had the licence in hand. That wasn't the problem. I had even encouraged the couple to get their marriage licence well in advance.

I tend to prepare rather carefully, both for a trip and for a wedding. This time I had even gotten my suit dry-cleaned. And Lydia had arranged for our bed-and-breakfast place online in the city where the wedding was to be held.

We arrived in the city in plenty of time, found the right address, knocked on the door, and encountered our first surprise. The bed-and-breakfast had no record of our booking. The online booking agent hadn't informed the host. We couldn't stay there, said the manager. Well, after seeing our consternation he relented and said that with some switching around we might be able to stay for that night, but we would have to find someplace else for the next night.

Feeling both relieved and still anxious, I went to the car to bring in our suitcase and my newly dry-cleaned suit. And couldn't find it. I had forgotten it at home. No suit for the wedding. Off to Moore's to buy a new off-the-rack suit, which they promised would be fitted by noon the next day – I hoped in time for the wedding. I don't handle this kind of crisis very well. And then to find overnight accommodation yet. Thankfully that was resolved when the manager said there had just been a cancelation and we could stay the next night after all.

Somewhat relieved but still stressed, we went to the restaurant dinner where the parents and a few uncles and aunts of the couple were meeting to get acquainted. In the middle of that meal came the next hurdle. The couple phoned. They *hadn't* gotten their marriage licence after all. They had assumed it was possible to obtain it online rather than go into an office. It wasn't. And the office where they could get the licence was, of course, closed. Thus, no marriage licence.

Time to do damage control. I actually relaxed. Nothing could be done now about the licence. I proposed that we go ahead with the wedding as planned, and later the couple would go to a justice of the peace to legalize their marriage. Not having that piece of paper at hand should not dampen the joy of the ceremony the next afternoon. And it didn't. I even got my new suit with minutes to spare.

The wedding service itself went off beautifully. Memorable to me was the full use of three languages in the service: French, German, and English. This reflected so well the family heritages of the couple. Maybe everything went right after all.

Saying a Reluctant Yes

Sometimes I agonized over whether I could, with integrity, officiate at a wedding.

The couple came to my office to ask me to officiate at their wedding. I had come to know each of them in different contexts before they became a couple and knew that each had significant personal issues to deal with. I felt uneasy about their relationship. After meeting with them several times, it was clear to me that they weren't ready for marriage. I encouraged them to wait a year, gave suggestions for how they might work at their personal issues and their relationship. Somewhat reluctantly, and a bit angry, they left my office and said they would be back.

A year later they returned, claiming that they had made good progress on working through their issues. In the meantime, the potential groom's parents, members of our church, urged me to go ahead with the wedding. After meeting with the couple several times, I was still uneasy and feeling ambivalent. But are intuitive feelings enough to deny a request to officiate at a wedding? Several times previously I had been pleasantly surprised when other couples, also not ready for marriage (perhaps just immature), formed very strong marriages. Is it the pastor's responsibility to say no to a couple's request because of some uneasiness with their relationship? Besides, the groom's parents were pressuring me to say yes.

I did say yes (a reluctant yes). It was a fine wedding. A year later they separated, and then divorced.

Saying a Reluctant No

The letter came via email from England. A gay couple wrote that they wanted to come to Canada to get married and asked if I would officiate at their marriage. One of the men came from Canada, and had been given my name by a relative in Ontario. Our church had just come through its long, conflictual process around the issue of homosexuality. Both I and the church were still feeling wounded by the outcome.

Personally, I have come to an "open" position on this matter. I welcome LGTBQ people in the church. And I believe that a covenanted marriage relationship is healthy for both heterosexuals and homosexuals. On a personal level, I was open to officiating at a gay marriage. But my ordination credentials and my credentials to officiate at weddings are held in trust by our denominational body. And this body was not ready at that time to bless my blessing of a gay marriage.

Very reluctantly, and with a heavy heart, I wrote back to the couple saying that I could not officiate their wedding. I would be glad to meet with them, and to bless their marriage, but not to sign a document on their behalf. I didn't hear back from them. No doubt they were again angry at "the church," and surely also at me, for again denying them the privilege open to all other Christians. As I write this I too feel angry – and disappointed in myself. Was there a better answer?

The Story of the Wedding at Cana (John 2)

Jesus was invited to a wedding at Cana. Every indication is that this wedding started out as a rather ordinary one – at least until the wine ran out. The storyline offered by John (and only John) is very sparse, so it leaves room for a lot of speculation.

Jesus, his disciples, and his mother were invited. Why is not noted. Were they relatives, or simply friends? Or were they included in a general invitation to the larger community to come celebrate a wedding? These guests were not from the village of Cana, located some nine miles from Jesus's hometown of Nazareth. A bit of a walk it was.

Nothing is said in the story about the wedding ceremony itself. Perhaps that was just assumed. In fact, we have no accounts anywhere in the Bible about an actual wedding ceremony. What is mentioned in this story is that the wine ran out, no doubt a huge embarrassment to the family in whose home (not synagogue or church) the wedding took place. Why did the wine run out? No explanation is given. Was it inexcusably bad planning, or bad management? Was the family on the poor side and unable to afford to stock up on enough wine for the large number of guests they felt obligated to invite? Or did some of the guests (including Jesus and his disciples) drink too much, taking advantage of the free wine? And since the celebration perhaps went on for seven days, the cultural norm, there would be a lot of opportunity for overindulgence. Or, as some commentators suggest, perhaps the fault lay with some of the invited guests who were expected to bring along wine of their own and didn't do so. Perhaps the words of the mother of Jesus to her son – "They have no wine" – was a gentle rebuke that he and his friends hadn't brought along enough wine themselves.

For some reason Mary, the mother of Jesus, is concerned about the empty wine barrels. Was she a close relative of the family who would assume some of the shame herself? She registers her concern with her son. "They have no wine." Did she expect Jesus to fix the problem, or was this just information, or even gossip, to pass on?

Jesus at first indicates that this was not of concern to either his mother or to him. "Woman, what concern is that to you and to me? My hour has not yet come." She responds by telling the servants, "Do whatever he tells you." Perhaps she is just washing her own hands of the matter and lodging it with her son, the real head of the family. Or does she really expect Jesus to do something about it?

It seems that Jesus then changes his mind about how concerned he should be about this absence of wine. He tells the servants to fill six stone water jars with water, each of which holds "twenty to thirty gallons." And Jesus promptly turns the water into wine, the first recorded "sign" or "miracle" of his ministry. It is a whopping amount of wine. And this wine is so good that the chief steward remonstrates with the bridegroom for now offering the best wine at the end of the celebrations when the guests may be too drunk to really appreciate it, rather than at the beginning when everyone could still be impressed with its quality.

One hundred and twenty gallons of wine? That would be enough for ... well ... maybe too much. But then, so often in Scripture the gifts of God are described in terms of extravagant abundance. Abundant wine is often the symbol of God's extravagance. The vision of Amos for God's wonderful future, for example, will include mountains that "drip sweet wine" (Amos 9:13). Jeremiah reports that "my people shall be satisfied with my bounty, says the Lord," a bounty that centres on "grain and wine and oil" (Jeremiah 31:12–14).

An ordinary wedding at Cana, turned extraordinary. It was not the careful planning that ensured a smooth, uneventful wedding. The invitation list included the one person who would make this wedding memorable, a never-to-be-forgotten celebration that would be talked about for years – in fact, for twenty centuries.

I tell this story because it gives me some pause in my enthusiasm for engaging in marriage preparation and officiating at weddings – and in my discomfort with an open bar at the reception. It is strange that there isn't a single record of a marriage ceremony in our Scriptures. Perhaps the closest we get is the story of Isaac marrying Rebekah. They are complete strangers to each other. The text simply says, "Then Isaac brought her into his mother Sarah's tent. He took Rebekah, and she became his wife; and he loved her" (Genesis 24:67). No ceremony is mentioned. It seems that with intercourse they become husband and wife.

One More Wedding

And now, as I am writing about weddings, Lydia and I have been invited to participate in another one. The groom is a relative. The bride is a granddaughter of a dear friend. Since the wedding will be held in Toronto United Mennonite Church and I am no longer a pastor there, we cannot quickly say yes. Protocol needs to be followed. The couple needs to process this with the present pastors. That conversation has happened, and now we can say yes. We look forward to those nuptials. We think they will be rich with God's blessings.

I love being involved with weddings.

INTERLUDE
Rooted and Grounded in Love

March 12, 2005

*A wedding sermon for the wedding of our son
Kendall and his bride, Charleen.*

Metaphors and images are leaping out all over the place from the Scripture texts you have chosen for your wedding, Charleen and Kendall. Watch them jump like trout in a brook. "A watered garden." "A spring of water." "Waters that never fail." "Rooted and grounded in love." "The breadth, and length and height and depth of love, a love that surpasses knowledge." I love each of these images, and I have taken great delight in hearing your enthusiastic and imaginative reflections on them. But I just can't get them together into any coherent pattern or message. My brain is delighted but overstimulated. I will simply try to offer you a series of reflections on the metaphors and images that flow rather independently into this thing called marriage. I suppose if Isaiah can mix his metaphors, so can I.

But then marriage too, even at the best of times, never goes in a straight line, resists any comprehensive blueprint for under-standing it, and rejects any easy formula for living it out. I don't know if a *pastor* should be telling his parishioners on the verge of getting married that he doesn't have full answers for how to grow a marriage. But perhaps a *father* can confess that when he got married he knew very little about marriage, learned an awful lot in forty-some years, but doesn't really know how he got from then till now. Enough mystery remains in this intimacy thing to continually drive me to my knees in both thanksgiving and petition. And in confession.

But here you are in front of me, my son and my daughter-in-law (well, almost daughter-in-law), both of whom I love from the bottom of my heart, waiting to hear a word that will help you get married and stay married, and then to know intimacy as a part of it. It's even riskier than usual to say a word to a couple getting married when one of them is your son who can immediately see through any words of idealism that don't connect with the reality he experienced living in the home of that preacher.

I suppose this whole preaching thing at a wedding would be more of a cinch if the Bible had only one model for a good marriage and only one plan to follow to find it. But it doesn't. The Bible reflects the diversity, and even chaos, of cultural norms in these things. But the Bible also testifies to the Spirit of God acting to bring people into the sphere of God's love and God's will. So we are left with some wonderful texts and some absorbing metaphors, but no single plan or formula. I appreciate deeply how you two have looked for biblical texts to guide you, and how you are already living with the metaphors that leap from those pages like trout from a brook.

Water (Isaiah 58:11)

The Lord will guide you continually, and satisfy your needs in parched places, and make your bones strong; and you shall be like a watered garden, like a spring of water, whose waters never fail.

Why am I not surprised that a woman who brings into her marriage the primary material asset of a canoe and a man who was once part of a crew of cousins called "the singing canoeists" would somehow find a text about water for their wedding and their marriage. Your wedding invitation, beautifully painted, suggests two streams or creeks merging into one, and I suppose that symbolizes the two of you finally getting into one canoe together. I know I need to be careful here. It would be wiser not to try to exegete a painting, and instead stay with trying to exegete a text. But I can't resist one observation and one story.

The observation is that the place where two rivers join tends to be somewhat turbulent. It often takes several kilometres before the waters merge into calmer integration. There are more undercurrents where waters merge, more waves and less visibility. The water can get quite murky there. But that is also where there is the best fishing, because it is a place teeming with life and energy and nutrients. This is just an observation. Make of it what you will.

The story is about a canoe mishap. It was your uncle and aunt, Kendall, who got us into it. Hugo and Doreen took us canoeing down the Bow River through Calgary. Trouble is, neither your mother nor I had ever canoed on a river before. We were veteran lake canoers but inexperienced on a river.

"Watch those rocks," advised Hugo helpfully as we got into the canoe. The river flowed faster than we realized. Still trying to find our balance and feel out the rushing water, we both tried to steer at the same time to avoid a rock that suddenly loomed before us. But not in the same direction. Mom steered left and I steered right. Within three minutes of launching our canoe, we capsized in the middle of the Bow River. We easily got ourselves and the canoe back to shore, wetter and more embarrassed than in any real danger, but we were soon blaming each other for the dunking.

Again, it's just a story. Make of it what you will. But I will add this addendum. Despite being wet and embarrassed, and after you get the hang of it, and after you have laughed at each other and forgiven each other, it is very enjoyable to canoe down a fast river observing the scenery, conversing about life, and navigating *around* the rocks. Marriage is mostly very enjoyable, even while you are learning to paddle in sync with each other – exhilarating, even. Marriage is a wonderful journey. But sometimes you get dunked.

Let's get back to Isaiah. Isaiah 58 is directed to exiles returning to Jerusalem. They have had a particularly hard life in exile in Babylon but now are anticipating recreating their community back home in Jerusalem. Isaiah is going to have a big word to say to them about what kind of community God wants them to create there. In Isaiah 56 his theme is to become a much more inclusive community, to include people in the community whom tradition, and even Moses, had till then excluded. Here in chapter 58 Isaiah challenges his people to become a much more "just" community.

Isaiah names true worship as loosing the bonds of injustice, undoing the thongs of the yoke, letting the oppressed go free, breaking every yoke, sharing bread with the hungry, bringing the homeless poor into your house, and covering the naked (58:6–7). In verse 11 comes this marvelous, hope-filled imagery of what the people of Israel will be as they begin life anew in their own homeland. Then, says Isaiah,

> the Lord will guide you continually, and satisfy your needs in parched places, and make your bones strong; and you shall be like a watered garden, like a spring of water, whose waters never fail.

But this comes after Isaiah challenges his people to look beyond self-serving self-interest. Look to the interests of the community, especially the marginalized folk in it. Care for the poor neighbour. Life cannot be reduced to technological consumerism. People cannot be reduced to a commodity. A marriage cannot be reduced to a contract. If your real worship moves beyond good liturgy to include living justly, then, in the words of Isaiah, "you shall take delight in the Lord, and I will make you ride upon the heights of the earth."

A Prayer (Ephesians 3:14–21)

We switch from Isaiah to Paul, from metaphors of water to images of trees and roots. These images grow out of a prayer, a prayer of blessing Paul prays for the Christians in Ephesus. I think it is also a wonderful blessing prayer for a couple getting married. It invites you, Kendall and Charleen, to sink your marriage roots into the artesian well of God's love.

This prayer invites all of us, but now particularly you two getting married, to be "rooted and grounded in love" – not first of all in your own love for each other, but in Christ's love. That is a bit of a sobering reality check. Of course, your marriage is grounded in your love for each other. But that isn't going to be enough. I'm not sure if we humans have the capacity to continually grow love on our own, to have a well of intimacy that never stops flowing in marriage. So many relationships start with such a passionate and sincere profession of love, and then eventually grow cold. And even an emergency pump can't always turn that love back on again. I think there is something too small, too limited, to anchor our deepest relationships only in our own capacity to love, or in another's capacity to return that love. We need to be connected to something bigger than we are, some bigger purpose, some bigger meaning, some bigger love to make a go of this thing called marriage.

The Ephesians prayer grows its conviction out of the faith that the all-powerful and never-ending source of love is the love of God shown us in Jesus, the Christ. And if we are rooted and grounded in that love, if our marriages are rooted and grounded in that love, it will fill every part of our being – we will be filled with the fullness of God, says Paul. And then our love for God and our love for each other will grow broader and longer and higher and deeper. I love that imagery. It staggers the imagination. Begin to grasp, to know, to experience, to hope for, to anticipate the breadth and length and height and depth of the love of Christ. And then you will begin to see the potential of our own human capacity to love each other – a love that keeps growing, a love that is limitless, a love that stretches in every direction and to every dimension. Then we can experience an intimacy that is inexhaustible.

The Launch

Well, Kendall and Charleen, your two rivers are merging today as you are getting into one marriage canoe together (please make sure you alternate who is sitting in the stern). I hope there is going to be at least some disturbance, but not enough to tip your canoe. Continue to live out Isaiah's challenge to put justice at the centre of your worship, and then you will hear this blessing on your marriage: "The Lord will guide you continually … you shall be like a watered garden, like a spring of waters that never fail." Above all, root and ground your marriage and your love for each other in the love of Christ, which surpasses knowledge, for then your own loving can keep on growing broader and longer and higher and deeper too, an intimacy that is watered lifelong by God's blessing.

And know also that your parents, your families, and this whole congregation gathered here blesses you and loves you – and will come running if ever you do get dunked.

10

A Funeral's Sombre Cadence

Somewhat reluctantly, with the encouragement of my wider family, I agreed to preach the sermon at my mother's funeral. In one sense, this was an easy funeral to do. Mom died at ninety-seven years of age, died a good death, and was deeply loved by her extended family and by her community. Her funeral would be a wonderful opportunity to celebrate her life and to reflect on the faith and relational legacy she left us.

Mom was fifty years old when my dad died. She spent a year grieving, isolated, and lonely on our farm in Rosemary, Alberta, and then made the momentous decision to sell the farm and relocate to Clearbrook, British Columbia, to start life all over again. And what a life, and what a community she created for herself there. She took nurse's aid training and was hired by the Mennonite nursing home there. She joined a new church. She developed close ties with her many relatives living in the area. She created a wide friendship circle. And she formed amazingly close bonds with a whole host of her grandchildren, both those living close to her and those farther away. I have a deep appreciation and respect for the way my mother created a significant and fulfilling life for herself after the tragedy of her husband's death.

I smile even now as I remember one particular conversation with her. We were in a teasing mode, and I asked her whether she had ever considered getting married again. Her answer? "Oh, I have had quite a few suiters. But, you know, they only really wanted someone to take care of them, cook for them, look after them. That is not the kind of marriage I want. After what your dad and I had together I would never be satisfied with anything less. I always said no." Bravo, Mom.

A funeral sermon celebrating her life and her faith should have been one of the easy ones. But I was quite reluctant to preach it. I felt I needed to grieve, and I needed to have another preacher comfort me in my grief. It usually was not wise, I thought, for a son, though a preacher, to do the homily. And yet there were both family reasons and church context reasons for my siblings to encourage me to do it. It probably says something about my family that we couldn't really agree with each other on who of the many Mennonite pastors in the area to invite to preach at the funeral.

We are a diverse lot indeed. We four brothers alone are spread out across an entire spectrum of faith and theology and church involvement. And then there were Mom's grandchildren. All of them loved their grandma dearly. She had an amazingly personal and special relationship with each of them. But some of them have no church connection at all, while others of them are pastors. And then there was the larger circle of relatives, a circle that included Mom as a beloved member, but a circle that spanned the whole range of theological conviction and church and non-church practice. Not an easy funeral congregation to reach into with words meant to celebrate a life and comfort those who were mourning.

How does one find words that ring with truth and honesty and love, and faith and hope, in a context and for a congregation with totally divergent world views and faith understandings? These words would need to reflect who Mom was, be integral to who I was, and speak to the grief and loss – and hope – of everyone there.

A similar scenario and dynamic is present at many funerals these days. But it is a unique challenge to find words when it is your mother whom you are remembering and celebrating, and your diverse family you are trying to comfort. I realized that I did a lot of my own grieving hunched over my computer. There were tears aplenty on the pages I was producing.

Tears were nothing new to me as a pastor officiating at funerals of people I cared deeply about. I have had a very deep emotional investment in many of the people I have accompanied to their grave. Hopefully this is true for all pastors. The challenge is that it is not helpful to lose emotional control during the funeral service, though no one wants the pastor to be a stoic either. Becoming over-emotional during the service puts the attention back on the pastor, away from the liturgy. I have become aware over the years that I sometimes store up some of my pastor's grief. I do grieve when people I have learned to love die. But when I am busy helping the family process the death of a loved one, I don't always pay enough attention to my own sense of loss.

And then, unexpectedly, I am surprised when attending a funeral without any leadership obligations, even if it is a person I did not feel particularly close to, that I shed many tears. Somehow, it then feels safe to release accumulated grief and tears that I needed to contain professionally.

There is a rather delicate balance at play between being a professional and being a friend, especially poignant at the time of the death and funeral of someone you feel close to.

Our Life's Story and God's Story

A few years ago, I attended a "high church" Anglican sung funeral liturgy. Our Pax Christi Chorale organist and pianist, the husband of our choir conductor, had died at a young age. I found this sung liturgy to be both powerful and comforting. Particularly striking to me was that we were into the second half hour of the service before the deceased person's name was even mentioned. The first half hour was totally focused on worshipping God. Later the priest would offer a remarkably insightful tribute to Bruce, but this was placed within the larger context of God's story.

And that is the challenge. More and more, it seems, funeral services are full of tributes and stories and remembrances and making the deceased into a saint – a status not always warranted. This veneration of the deceased does not yet make for a complete funeral liturgy.

I like to imagine an inner circle, surrounded by a second circle that is encompassed by a still larger circle. The smaller inner circle is the story of the person who has died. That story does need to be told – but told with integrity. An honest picture helps the grieving process much more than does a distorted and whitewashed picture. As a pastor conducting the funeral, I try to reflect who the person was. It was always a challenge to do this when I didn't know the person, as happened from time to time when asked to do a funeral from outside of my circle of acquaintances. Then it was especially important to meet with the family to let them explain to me how they saw and described the person who had died.

The second circle is the person's family and community – and church, if they belong to one. Who is grieving? What would help them in their grieving? What would offer them comfort and hope? What language and what stories would they be open to? What were the relationship dynamics like? This is important to me because in our faith tradition, the funeral service is not focused on the deceased getting into heaven, though that is affirmed, but on helping the family and other loved ones grieve, and inviting them to live into their own future.

The biggest circle, surrounding the two smaller circles, is the circle of God's story. It is the big-picture story, the only story big enough to make sense of the smaller stories of our living and our dying. That is why that sung Anglican liturgy was so meaningful to me. It embraced me/us in worship. We were invited into God's story, and then we could place Bruce's story, our personal stories, and our grieving into it. I like that movement. A funeral service begins with God's story, moves to the stories of the one who has died and of that person's family and community, and then places these into the big story of God's love and grace.

The Congregation

In my growing up years in Rosemary, Alberta, the entire church, including children, attended most funerals. From a young age, we children were made aware that death was both natural and very real. We saw the dead body lying in the coffin. We saw the grieving family crying. And we knew there would be sweets coming at the reception after the funeral service.

Mostly the gathered congregation at these funerals consisted of fellow Mennonites, though occasionally there were Mormon or Buddhist neighbours who also came. But usually it was a rather homogeneous group where common faith and common values and common rituals were assumed. What strikes me in our contemporary (and urban) context is both the diversity of the congregation at a funeral, and the absence of children (apart from immediate or extended family).

Why do we not bring our children to a funeral? Are we afraid it will traumatize them? Do we not want them to face the reality of death? I recall, as I write this, of standing at a graveside as a young lad and witnessing a friend of mine crying as the pall-bearers lowered the body of his older brother, who had died of polio, into the grave. I walked over to him and said something to him – I don't recall what – but I know he appreciated it. It was a natural thing to do. Maybe the experience of attending many funerals as a youngster helped prepare me for my role of presiding over funerals.

I look over the congregation at most funerals these days and see an incredibly diverse group of people – diverse in terms of people claiming or not claiming faith, diverse in terms of which faith, if any, they claim, and certainly diverse in terms of what they are expecting or looking for in a funeral.

But I do make this basic assumption. I think that most people attending a funeral come out of a deep need and longing to both express their grief and to hear some words of hope. When we face the reality of a death we are pushed to ask ultimate questions. Whether we claim a faith or not, death pushes us to ponder whether our dying is a final ending or a new beginning. I like to think that the gathered congregation is more open to hearing some big-picture Good News about God at a funeral than in almost any other setting. The challenge is to find the kind of language about God and about life after death that will connect with such a diverse assembly.

But here is a bit of a warning. People who are emotionally invested in grieving may be very open to hearing Good News about God, but they will also be sensitive to what may feel to them like spiritual manipulation. What we preachers dare not do is take advantage of this emotional openness and sensitivity to try to push people to make faith claims they are not ready to make. God's Spirit will do any inviting to faith.

A Hard, Hard Learning

My first two funerals as a pastor were for people who took their own lives. I was not at all prepared for this. I could hardly comprehend the reality of suicide itself, let alone know how to respond to the families involved and lead a service that had any hope in it at all.

In my very first funeral, I responded very poorly to the needs of the family, especially of the mother of the young adult who took his own life. And she was quite upset with me. She lived in another province, having remarried after the death of her first husband. Her anger at me was that she heard of the death of her son through the police and not from me, the pastor. She needed to hear this terrible, shocking news from a pastor rather than from an officer of the law. She had needed me to call her. And I hadn't.

It probably was true that I learned of this death only after she, the mother, had been notified, and so I wouldn't have been able to beat the officers in telling this tragic news. But it was also probably true that even if I had known about it in time I still may not have called her. I was in shock. I was discombobulated. I didn't know how to respond or what to do. It took me some time to drum up the courage to call her – and this was to start making funeral arrangements, a concrete task rather than being the bearer of horrible news.

The next time I faced a suicide death, I was a bit more grounded and ready to be a pastor. The challenge this time was that the widow of the man who had taken his own life wasn't ready to acknowledge the cause of death. She told her relatives he had died of a heart attack. I pleaded with her to name the reality. She refused. "But how can the funeral have any integrity if we are not honest about the story? For your sake and the families' sake, the true story has to be told." She wouldn't budge. Was it my responsibility to be honest with the congregation even if this violated my relationship with her? I was in turmoil.

The congregation was already gathered for the funeral, a full house. The extended family was meeting in the basement awaiting the beginning of the service. Ten minutes before the service was to start she came to me. "I think you are right, Gary. I will give you permission to tell the true story of his death." With this huge burden lifted, I informed the relatives in the basement, and then the congregation. It was still a very difficult service, and there were huge shock waves, but the funeral had its integrity and the long healing journey could begin.

Stories

Many of my colleagues say that they much prefer doing funerals to weddings. On the surface that sounds very strange. After all, weddings are very happy events and funerals are full of grief and pain. Why prefer to be involved in an event that pulls at the rawest emotions of our being rather than one that is supposedly so joyous?

But that is the point, they say. Most people who are grieving are amazingly open to a sensitive listening ear – and to the Spirit of God. It is a sacred privilege to accompany a family through the journey to and through death.

Most of us pastors have also experienced very difficult and troubling funerals. Sometimes a death and a funeral bring out the worst of family conflicts and resentments and bickering. There are stories to tell. But in my experience, more often it is the deeper side of coming together to deal with grief and saying a good good-bye that wins the day.

The Four Brothers

This happened when "Anne" died. Hers was a funeral that caused me some concern and anxiety. Most of her family relationships were in a mess, though she had been in a long healing journey to straighten out the problems in her own life.

Anne came to our church in a wheelchair as soon as our newly built church opened. "It's accessible," she said, "so I thought I would try it out." Anne came to us from the community with both physical and emotional struggles, and with a history of abuse at the hands of her father. But she was already on a fine healing journey. "I know I need help from the church," she said, "but I also want to be able to contribute to the church." And she did. She developed good friendships. She wrote fine poetry and shared it with us. She had a special sensitivity.

Then she quit smoking. But her apartment still reeked of smoke, always a temptation to indulge again. And the walls were yellowed from the smoking. Our youth group decided to scrub her walls down and repaint her entire apartment. She glowed with her thanks.

Now her biggest struggle was with her alienated family, with four brothers who refused to have anything to do with her. They rejected her for insisting that her father had abused her. They just didn't believe her. Or they just didn't want to believe her. She was able to mend fences with one brother, whom she had rejected for being gay. After our process at TUMC around homosexuality, she apologized to him for her homophobic attitude, and they were reconciled.

And then in her mid-fifties she died. Her brothers, three of them from out of town, gathered most reluctantly to say farewell. At the visitation, I talked with them and tried to invite them to help plan the funeral service. They wanted nothing to do with funeral planning for their sister. "We don't even really want to be here," they said. "We have come out of duty. Only duty. We will attend the funeral but nothing more."

I planned the funeral with the help of a few of Anne's church friends. Several of these friends would offer tributes. We selected some of her favourite Scriptures to be read. The evening before her funeral, Al called. Al is a wonderful saxophone player. He offered to play at the funeral. He said he felt "called" to do it. Was this the nudging of God? I said yes.

The funeral service begins. Three of the four brothers are looking glum and grim and uncomfortable there in the church. There are opening hymns and Scriptures and prayers and tributes. Their faces are wooden, closed, frozen with discomfort and denial. But then Al starts to play. He plays Anne's favourite hymns. As he is playing "Amazing Grace" something else amazing is happening. I see it as I watch the brothers' faces. They unfreeze. They soften. They melt. Soon there are tears. God is working a miracle through a saxophone I had not planned for or requested.

Right after the service one of the brothers rushes outside to grab a cigarette and try to compose himself. At the reception in the church basement after the service there is an open mic for sharing stories. A niece gets up and says, "I did not want to be here today. My mother made me come, out of family duty. Our entire family is kind of messed up, alienated. I think today is the beginning of some kind of reconciliation, the beginning of us as a larger family trying to get together again."

And then one of those brothers, face now very soft, takes the mic. "The service today gave us a picture of a sister we never knew. Thank you for that. It was so honest and yet so loving. I'm sorry I didn't believe my sister."

A Very Difficult Funeral

"Tim" took his own life. His was a long, painful journey of trying to come to terms with his gayness. He fought with his identity. His family fought with his identity. The church didn't know how to struggle with his identity. Then came the news that he had ended his fight by ending his life.

Several years earlier Tim had requested baptism – baptism by immersion. Our church practised baptism by "pouring or sprinkling," not by immersion. Tim requested baptism by immersion. I was open to this request, so I dunked him. It was a rather powerful experience. Some months later Tim asked me, "Did you dunk me all the way under?" I was puzzled by his question. Surely the efficacy of baptism didn't depend on the amount water over someone's head.

I assured Tim that yes, I had submerged him all the way. Only much later did that question make sense to me. I was slow to catch on. He had not come to terms with his gayness. He fought it. He believed that if he was fully immersed in baptism, God would relieve him of his homosexuality. He would be healed, set free. That didn't happen, and now he was disillusioned. And he took his own life. I had tried to reassure him that God accepted him in his gay identity. But I felt like I had failed in my pastoral ministry to him.

It was a very difficult funeral.

I have presided over three funerals of young men who took their own lives. Each of them was gay, and each of them struggled with being accepted and/or acceptable. I have agonized over what message we as a church were giving them. The church, and we as pastors, have much to ask forgiveness for.

Death at the Beginning of Life

A pastor from out of province called me to let me know that a young couple from his church was now at the Hospital for Sick Children in Toronto. They were there because their unborn child was in medical emergency. Would I offer pastoral care to them?

I hurried to the hospital but arrived just after the child was stillborn. The parents were devastated. The mother was holding their lifeless baby. I heard their story and their anguish. The mother asked, "Would you hold him and pray with us? We need to be reassured that God is holding our baby and us." I prayed with them, adding my tears to theirs.

Some years later I was in their province for a church conference. A couple with three children in tow saw me, greeted me by name with huge smiles on their faces. I vaguely recognized their faces but couldn't bring to memory their names or the context of our acquaintance. "You prayed with us and our stillborn child in Toronto. That was so important to us. That helped us face the future. We want you to meet our three wonderful children."

There is something particularly painful and poignant about the promise of new life that is not fulfilled, whether because there has been a later-term miscarriage, a stillbirth, or an infant that couldn't survive out of the womb. Whether the prayer service is in a hospital room, a living room, a graveside, a crematorium, or church, the experience is profound.

INTERLUDE
A Life Too Brief: A Memorial Meditation
for Adam Daniel Shantz

This funeral sermon was previously published in Vision: A Journal for Church and Theology *4, no. 1 (Spring 2003).*

> Neither death, nor life, … nor anything else in all creation, will be able to separate us from the love of God in Christ Jesus our Lord. (Romans 8:38–39)

Right now, that is hard to stomach, Lord.

> God will wipe away every tear from their eyes. Death will be no more. (Revelation 21:4)

Right now, that is hard to believe, Lord. Right now, Lord, the words that resonate in us are those of the psalmist:

> You have broken us in the haunt of jackals, and covered us with deep darkness. (Psalm 44:19)

Today we know sorrow of a particular sort. We grieve a baby who will not grow up among us, whose personality will not develop in our midst. We grieve a child who will not become an adult. For we have laid to rest today what might have been, a potential that will not be realized.

Dreams. Plans. Expectations. Hopes. The first birthday? Will never be celebrated. The terrible twos? Won't be endured. First day of school? No tears shed. First date? Nothing to be anxious about. Graduation? No party. Marriage? No grandchildren.

All dreams dashed. This has been a particularly wrenching time for you, Lisa and Marcus, and for your families and friends, for all of us. High hopes. Then anxiety over a traumatic birth. Adam rushed to Mount Sinai Hospital. Waiting. Worst fears confirmed. No significant brain activity. And then waiting again, waiting and praying that Adam might die. And a long time he took in the dying. He had spunk, resilience, stubbornness – stuff to be proud of.

And there was much, much more than agonizing waiting. So much more. Deep loving. Bonding. Holding. Tender caring. A family and a community holding vigil. Praying. Being cared for and held in the love and prayers of others when your own prayers failed to form.

No Words

Adam's life was like a book that is too short. The book has a beautifully crafted cover. Physically, Adam looks perfect. The title is boldly written: Adam Daniel Shantz. Proud authors: Marcus and Lisa Shantz. But when the book is opened, no words are written inside. For Adam's brain has ceased to function. And without a brain there can be no thoughts, no reasoning, no words, nothing that makes sense. To him or to us. None of our questions make sense. None of our nice theological answers make sense. None of our groping for meaning leads anywhere.

The book is too short. Period. Adam Daniel Shantz. A cover and no words inside. We don't know how to deal with life without words.

Except that this too-brief life, this too-short book, has had a powerful effect. Many people have read it and are stunned by its visceral impact. Despite no words. No words in the book, no words to describe and explain its impact on us, and no words to offer comfort to the authors who had envisioned so many words, so many sentences, so many chapters. How can such a thin book draw us in so completely and take us to such depths?

Life will never be the same for you, Lisa and Marcus, nor for your families, nor for the rest of us. We have all been profoundly touched. And in that deep touching we have been grounded again in what is basic, ultimate. Our lives and our faith have been tested and deepened.

And through that experience, we find the beginnings of hope and the beginnings of healing. Adam has touched us to the core, and so, I believe, has God, though we may not know how. It is all beyond words.

You have loved and wept and held and nurtured and fallen exhausted to sleep. And in utter weariness and weakness you have grown, become stronger, expanded your capacity for loving and for praying, even as words have failed you.

The Word

Life is so much more than words, or the lack of them. And the Word runs deeper than words.

> In the beginning was the Word, and the Word was with God, and the Word was God. He was in the beginning with God. All things came into being through him ... What has come into being in him was life ... And the Word became flesh and lived among us, and we have seen his glory, the glory of

a father's only son, full of grace and truth. (John 1:1–4, 14)

John claims that Jesus was the Word, who became flesh and lived among us, identified with hurting humanity, loved people with God's kind of love, suffered terribly, and was killed. But God raised him up because such love cannot finally be killed. It cannot die. It rises triumphant, so we believe in resurrection and have a hope deep within us that cannot be snuffed out, no matter how much we cry out in pain and no matter how much doubt and anger we throw at this Word. This Word cried with Mary and Martha in their grief, and cries with us in our grief, too.

Paul, too, points us beyond words:

> We know that the whole creation has been groaning in labour pains until now; and not only the creation, but we ourselves, who have the first fruits of the Spirit, groan inwardly while we wait for adoption, the redemption of our bodies. For in hope we were saved … Likewise the Spirit helps us in our weakness; for we do not know how to pray as we ought, but that very Spirit intercedes with sighs too deep for words. And God, who searches the heart, knows what is the mind of the Spirit, because the Spirit intercedes for the saints according to the will of God. (Romans 8:22–24, 26–27)

Even our praying isn't limited or defined or encompassed by our words, because when our words fail, the Spirit of the Word prays for us. Thanks be to God.

> Who will separate us from the love of Christ? Will hardship, or distress, or persecution, or famine, or nakedness, or peril, or sword – or oxygen deprivation?

… No, in all these things we are more than conquerors through him who loved us. For I am convinced that neither height, nor depth, nor anything else in all creation – not a tangled umbilical cord, or grief, or unanswered questions, or wordlessness – will be able to separate us from the love of God in Christ Jesus our Lord. (Romans 8:35, 37–39)

The life of Adam Daniel Shantz was far too brief. The words we desperately wished to read will never be written. But the life story is not ended. We will take as promise Paul's affirmation that nothing can separate us from the love of God in Christ Jesus, and John's claim that God will wipe every tear from our eyes (Revelation 21:4). Promise. And hope. And maybe even praise. Praise for Adam's brief life and its profound impact on us. He was a gift from God. He was a gift of life. He was a gift of love.

And you, Lisa and Marcus and the rest of your families, held this gift gently, lovingly, tenderly, compassionately, prayerfully, until he could die and return to God, from whom he came. Know that in death Adam is not separated from God's love but is fully embraced by it. And know that in grief, you are not separated from God's love but are fully embraced by it. And know that even praise will come again to your hearts and to your lips, like a welcome dawn after a dark night. Praise will come.

You requested that we end this service by singing "Praise God from whom all blessings flow." You said you would probably not be able to sing it. But you needed your community to sing it to you and on your behalf. Praise is the direction of your lives. Praise of God's faithfulness is the direction of a life of faith even in a time of intense grief.

"Praise God from whom all blessings flow"

Dear, compassionate God, from whom we come, to whom we return, in whom we live and move and have our being, we are here today with a particular grief, for the brief life and tragic death of a baby. And in our grief, we give thanks for Adam Daniel Shantz, a gift that was precious and is now returned to you. For Lisa and Marcus, their families and community, we pray. Sustain them and renew them with strength and comfort, love and praise.

> See, the home of God is among mortals. He will dwell with them; they will be his peoples, and God himself will be with them; he will wipe every tear from their eyes. Death will be no more; mourning and crying and pain will be no more. (Revelation 21:3–4)

Praise God from whom all blessings flow, praise him all creatures here below, praise him above, ye heavenly host, praise Father, Son, and Holy Ghost. Amen.

PART FOUR
WHEN THE MUSIC IS DISCORDANT

Every pastor will experience conflict. That is a given. In every human community and in any personal relationship there will be differences: differences of opinion, of personal conviction, of temperament. Conflict is normal, and perhaps even healthy. The challenge is to not let conflict break relationships and endanger one's ministry and the integrity of the church. The opportunity is to let difference – and even anger – be a catalyst for growth and deeper engagement. I say this even as I acknowledge that at times in my own ministry, I have been tempted to avoid conflict. I have not always had the courage to respond in healthy ways to issues, or to people who were upset with me.

In this section, I first write about the more ordinary discordant notes struck in routine ministry. Then I will share my story of a major crisis in my ministry that left me feeling broken by conflict.

11

Dissonance in Ordinary Time

The beginnings of my ministry were characterized by what I later learned were passive-aggressive tendencies. I could be very forthright – and I thought courageous – in preaching, but was quite passive in responding personally to people who disagreed with me, or had expectations of me that I was unwilling or unable to fulfill.

A story comes to mind from that beginning time of ministry. Several of the key leaders in the church where I began my pastoral ministry had a much more conservative theology than did I. They had an evangelical "witnessing" style that I was uncomfortable with. At one point, without consulting me, they invited a guest evangelist to an evening crusade-like rally in our church. As the pastor, I was expected to lead the service and, of course, thank the evangelist at the end.

I was conflicted. I had a hard time with both the way this evening came about and the evening itself. The invited evangelist had a syrupy style that turned me off, and a theology that was anything but Anabaptist. And yet I remained passive. I didn't challenge our leaders for inviting him. I didn't register my disagreement with the evangelist. I even thanked him nicely, if insincerely, at the end.

It would take a long journey of self-discovery to begin dealing with a passive reluctance to engage appropriately with people when I was upset with them, or they with me, or even when I just disagreed with them. Even in committee meetings – a huge part of ministry – I was inclined to withhold my voice when I was uncomfortable with a strongly stated point of view. That meant committee members didn't really know where I stood on a given issue, though they might have suspected that I wasn't openly stating what I thought. My reluctance prevented healthy dialogue.

And yet in preaching I was more courageous. I didn't hesitate to name my convictions, my theology, and my biblical interpretations. If people challenged me for what I said, I found it relatively easy to engage them in response.

There were times when members of the congregation got very angry with me. Once I went to visit a middle-aged woman in the hospital. Things weren't going well for her. She had alienated people in some of her relationships, including some family members. She was harbouring some bitterness in her spirit. She was in the hall outside of her room when she saw me coming to visit her. Her bitterness came pouring out. She yelled at me in high volume. She called me names. Nurses and other patients were listening. She let them all know in no uncertain terms how awful I was as a pastor, how I had neglected her, how angry she was at me. After a five-minute rant she lost steam, but not her audience.

Strangely enough, I remained calm during her outburst, and with all the ears listening in. She needed to vent, and I could be a safe outlet for her. I was surprised at my calmness, because I had not always responded well to other people's anger at me. I told her I heard her anger and would visit another time. I did, and that time we actually engaged in conversation.

An Anabaptist Theology of Church:
Implications for Pastoral Leadership

An Anabaptist-Mennonite understanding of church insists on "the priesthood of all believers," where every voice is respected and welcomed. There is no hierarchical structure where the pastor has unlimited power to control the agenda and determine outcomes. And yet by virtue of being named "pastor," there is power vested in that office. The challenge is always to sort out a healthy use of the pastor's power while respecting the fuller power of the congregation. A pastor is hired to lead but not to control. Inevitably there will be tensions in this sorting out.

A major part of a pastor's work is to be on many church committees. How strongly should the pastor exert leadership in committee work? My personal decision was not to be the chairperson on church committees, though I did give stronger leadership to our caring team and preaching team than to other committees. And yet I became aware that I sometimes displayed my passive-aggressive tendency in committee meetings, sometimes saying too little and sometimes saying things too strongly. In that way, I probably acted out an unhealthy pattern of leadership that caused confusion about what I thought was important.

It is in committee work that many important decisions in the life of the church are made. Committee work at its best can be very satisfying and fulfilling – if each member's voice is encouraged and respected, and if disagreements and challenges are openly invited. I needed to learn to become a catalyst for healthy dialogue in committee work.

Committees are often the setting where power dynamics between members are played out. In one church, "Tim," a member of a particular committee, had accumulated a significant amount of power in the congregation from a long history of mostly good leadership. The date for an event this committee was planning conflicted with a private event a friend of Tim's was considering. Without advising the committee, he assured his friend that the church would reschedule its event. At the next meeting, he informed the committee of this change. I could sense that the other members were uneasy and unhappy with this announcement, but they remained silent. They were afraid of Tim's power, and perhaps of conflict itself.

I responded to Tim: "I sense that you feel quite strongly about changing the date of our event for the sake of your friend. But I would like to hear how the rest of the committee feels about this." That seemed to free the others around the table to express their opinions. A very simple question empowered a committee to function in a healthy way. In the end, they decided not to change the date of their event, and Tim acknowledged his agreement.

Pastors need to come to terms with the fact that committee meetings are a major factor in church ministry. We can either resent their intrusion into our life, complain about the wasted time they take and how little they accomplish — or we can learn to make the best of them and see them as a continual opportunity for pastoral ministry. But how can we do this if we generally don't chair the meeting and don't want to impose our will on the outcomes?

Every meeting has three elements that are important to me. First is the relationship among committee members. Every meeting needs to include some way of helping members connect with each other. They are a team, not just a collection of individuals. They need to function as a team. Checking in with each other personally is important. (As an example, at TUMC each caring team meeting began with about a half-hour period where each member, including me as the pastor, shared what was happening in our personal lives.) The second important element is keeping in mind the bigger picture of the committee's work. Each meeting offers the opportunity to reflect on how the decisions of the last meeting have worked out and on what inspires the vision and purpose of their work. The committee needs to see its work as God's work. A quick prayer at the beginning may not be enough. Finally, it is important that the committee make good decisions on the agenda before them and assign responsibility for carrying forward those decisions.

Making good decisions and communicating them well to the congregation empowers a committee. As the pastor, I want to encourage and help facilitate this process. It is not "my" church. My voice is one of many, though I need to be aware of how strongly this voice is heard by others. The committee takes responsibility for the decisions made. This may also create opportunities for all to take responsibility when things don't go as planned. The responsibility does not belong only to the pastor.

I saw my pastoral role as helping a committee fulfill these purposes. My role was not usually to lead the meeting or to dictate decisions. I wanted to participate in the discussion and add my voice, but I especially wanted to encourage each member to offer his or her voice. I saw this as an opportunity to be a pastor to each member. I could hear and affirm each voice. And sometimes I would hear much more than what was said, and would later in private offer to make a pastoral visit.

I also wanted to pay attention to power issues between members. It is no surprise that even very well-meaning people exert inappropriate power. I saw two common roots for this misuse of power. First, very good-hearted, faithful, long-term church members are often totally unaware of how much power they convey, and how this can intimidate newer members. When I sensed this, I would ask them in private if they were aware of the unintentional power they exerted. Most were surprised, and even confused, by the question. But they reflected on it and made a point to listen more carefully to quieter voices. Second, some people speak loudly and exercise their power in intimidating ways because they carry a low self-image. The poorer they feel about themselves, the louder they speak. Hearing this, a pastor has the opportunity not only to intervene during the meeting but also to offer pastoral care to help people like this to get at the roots of that need to exert power.

I met periodically with church or committee chairpersons to encourage them and to help them think in these broad terms.

A Healthy Self-Image: Key to a Healthy Relationship

Dissonance and conflict are normal in the church, as they are in any human relationship. The key to being able to respond in a healthy way to conflict, and to deal with the issues that arise from it, is to pay attention to our own self-image and self-worth. When we feel positively about ourselves and when we value the other, conflict can be more easily worked at, and hopefully resolved.

One important ministry that is essential for a pastor to fulfill is to find many ways of assuring the congregation, and everyone in the congregation, that they are beloved of God. If congregation members know this and believe this, and feel that they are valued, then they will be open to hearing hard challenges and prophetic words from that pastor. Likewise, the congregation needs to find ways to affirm the pastor, offering support and love while holding the pastor accountable.

And yet in most churches some of the time, and in some churches most of the time, there are people who are unhappy with the pastor. A few of these people are bold enough to bring their unhappiness directly to that pastor, making possible an opportunity for dialogue. Others insist on being anonymous and shoot darts at the pastor from behind the scenes. They undermine ministry from the shadows.

How can a pastor respond to those who are unhappy with her or his ministry?

There could be many roots for this unhappiness. There will always be members for whom the pastor does not meet expectations. They are not on the same page when it comes to theology, or how to read the Bible, or to think politically.

They have expectations of the pastor in theological outlook, in preaching, teaching, community activism, or pastoral care that the pastor cannot, or will not, fulfill. They feel they haven't been visited enough. They feel too challenged by a sermon. And some churchgoers just carry a huge chip on their shoulders, usually from some pain they have experienced or from a low self-image.

The reality is that most congregations today have a wide diversity of people with a wide diversity of theological understandings, personal needs, political views, church experience, expectations of what they want from a pastor, and readiness to engage differences in a healthy way.

A Context of Shifting World Views

The Western church is part of the picture of a larger shift in world views. The church, like our society, has gradually moved through rather distinctive mindsets, sometimes identified as pre-modernity, modernity, and post-modernity. Each of these mindsets has a very distinctive expectation of what people want and need from a pastor. Each of these mindsets designates authority to the pastor in very different ways. A given congregation will probably contain folks representing each of these three mindsets. It is a huge challenge for a pastor to meet the varying expectations of a normal congregation.

I find it helpful to imagine a river into which three streams flow – a pre-modern mindset, a modern mindset, and a post-modern mindset. Where these three streams converge there is turbulence – but also a lot of energy and life. The challenge for the church, and for pastors, is that both turmoil and opportunity are part of the turbulence. Each of these mindsets understands the involvement of the congregation and the role of pastoral leader in different ways.

I offer an oversimplified picture. The pre-modern world view granted significant authority and power to pastors. They were viewed with a very high sense of "office." They had the power to make significant decisions. They were listened to respectfully and were seldom challenged.

The modernity mindset changed church life dramatically. The high sense of "office" that came with the pre-modern world view mostly disappeared. The congregation demanded a much bigger role and power in decision making. The expectation was that the pastor be professionally trained and demonstrate a high sense of competence in fulfilling the tasks of ministry. The pastor was now an employee of the church, expected to fill a management role, and subject to evaluations – and to criticism.

A younger, post-modern generation once again changed the expectations placed on the pastor. Now there was more focus on personal identity, on relationships, even on vulnerability. These individuals wanted more from a pastor than simply doing tasks professionally, and more than articulating beliefs and doctrine. They were looking for a pastor who was relational, vulnerable, inclusive, and able to engage them personally.

The pre-modern world view I grew up with was giving way to modernity's claims in some urban Mennonite congregations in the late 1960s and '70s. But there would continue to be overlaps between them. (there are still vestiges of pre-modernity in my own soul). A younger generation's embrace of post-modernity at the end of the twentieth century added another dimension to expectations of church and of pastoral leadership, but did not end the impact of modernity. The challenge for pastors is to try to have some understanding of what this mix of mindsets means for congregational life.

These shifting world views affect the expectations inherent in the relationship between congregation and pastor. They also come to the fore when the church is dealing with contentious issues and experiencing conflict.

Local Tension

Back to the small picture of the local congregation and local tensions between pastor and congregants. How might we pastors respond when someone is upset with us, unhappy with what we offer, or is just critical?

I learned, over time, that being direct and personal with the person unhappy with me worked best. This of course is easier to do if the offended person comes to me directly. My hope is that my relationship with the congregation is such that someone who is upset with me can feel free to speak to me directly.

After I preached a sermon in which I said some rather strong words that were political in nature, an angry member accosted me and told me how upset he was. I replied that I could see his point of view, though I wasn't ready yet to change mine. I offered to meet with him in his office the following week to explore our differences more fully. He agreed. We met for close to two hours. At the end, we still didn't agree, but we deepened our respect for each other and agreed to further conversations.

Not everyone has the courage or the self-confidence to come directly to the pastor with complaints or challenges. Some are too timid. But there are sometimes people who are just devious. They would rather undermine the pastor's authority from behind the scenes, sending anonymous notes or registering discontent with others, but not directly with the pastor. (I write this more from painful stories I have heard from other pastors than from personal experience.)

What worked best for me was that when I sensed unhappiness, I went directly to the person. I saw this as a pastoral opportunity. I would acknowledge our differences and invite a meeting where we could explore these feelings and issues more fully. This way the person knew that the complaint was taken seriously and not glossed over. Often these more pastoral ways of responding to criticism opened up a sharing of other pain or loss or unmet needs from this person's past.

The Pastor-Congregation Relations Committee

Most often the direct feedback to a pastor comes in the context of the various committees that the pastor attends. The committees share responsibility with the pastor for the programs of the church. Yet direct feedback on the pastor's role is also sometimes needed.

It is always a challenge for pastors to respond in a healthy way to feedback – whether positive or negative – and not to let it have too great an impact on their sense of self and self-worth. Feedback there will always be, sometimes in the form of healthy dialogue and other times in the form of complaints and critique.

Many churches have tried to address the issue of feedback by establishing a pastor-congregation relations committee (PCRC), sometimes called a personnel committee. I did not have access to such a committee during my regular ministry, but experienced one in Lydia's and my interim ministry work. I have, though, heard many stories from colleagues – some inspiring and some very painful. For me the PCRC has become a metaphor for both healthy and unhealthy ways of engaging with feedback.

An assumption I make is that it is in the candidating phase of the pastor-congregation relationship that the pastor names what she or he brings by way of strengths, gifts, calling, vision, and so on, while also acknowledging inadequacies and naming ministries they might not be able to fulfill. The congregation identifies its own ministry needs and visions and hopes. If there seems to be a good fit, a call is extended, the potential pastor accepts the call, and a covenant-like relationship is formed between pastor and congregation.

It is the task of a PCRC to nurture this relationship. At its best, a good PCRC facilitates a healthy relationship between pastor and congregation. The committee pays attention to the dynamics of that relationship, provides feedback mechanisms, and encourages healthy dialogue. It listens to the voices of the congregation and the voice of the pastor. It encourages direct, not anonymous, feedback.

But I also have observed and heard stories of dysfunctional PCRCs. They too easily become a "complaints committee," where disgruntled members lodge criticisms of the pastor – usually anonymously. Unhappy members, under the guise of confidentiality, insist that the committee bring their complaints to the pastor, pressuring the pastor to improve performance, or stop addressing controversial issues, or ... A healthy PCRC will not allow anonymity, secrecy, or unwarranted confidentiality. These tend to undermine both the pastor and the congregation. Rather, that committee will help facilitate direct, considerate engagement between the one giving feedback and the pastor.

I do offer one caveat to the principle of anonymity. If the pastor has been abusive in a hurtful way, taking advantage of the power imbalance inherent in a relationship with a parishioner, anonymity may be necessary, at least for a period of time, to provide safety for the complainant. At this point the pastor cannot be in control of the conversation.

There certainly are shy members who may need help in giving their feedback and in having a helpful conversation with the pastor. There may also be more crafty members who want to unsettle the pastor and not be held personally accountable for that.

And there are, of course, situations where it becomes clear over a period of time that the fit between pastor and congregation is not a good one, and that it is healthier for both to part ways. However, this cannot be decided by a series of anonymous complaints. It comes only by healthy and full dialogue.

If it becomes clear to both pastor and congregation that the covenant between them is no longer a mutually fulfilling one, they need to find a way of disengaging in which each respects the other and does not wound the other. The PCRC can play a very important role here, first of all processing this transition with the pastor and then facilitating a healthy conversation between pastor and congregation.

My sole experience of a PCRC, during our intentional interim ministry work, was positive. I thought the committee worked very well, responding in helpful ways to feedback from the congregation and facilitating dialogue. The committee communicated often and openly with the congregation. It invited feedback and brought this to our meetings. I saw this as a model of sensitive listening and communication.

These PCRC meetings were both lively and enjoyable. As interim pastors Lydia and I named what we were experiencing, what our agenda was, and what our concerns were. Together we explored plans for the next phase of our ministry, and how these would be communicated to the congregation.

A PCRC can play an important role in facilitating healthy ministry.

12

When the Music Becomes Too Loud

One of the huge issues facing the church today is the inclusion of LGBTQ people. In the New Testament church, the issue was including Gentiles. Both issues are or were extremely contro-versial. I would argue that the inclusion of Gentiles in a church founded by Jewish followers of Jesus was a more extreme chal-lenge than our struggle with including people who identify as LGBTQ. In both cases, both religious and cultural barriers were or are at play.

I want to share some of my struggles in my journey toward inclusion of LGBTQ people. I will do so by interjecting reflec-tions from the stories of Acts 10 and 15, as well as referring to passages from Mark, Isaiah, Galatians, 1 Peter, and 1 Corinthians. It is not that I identify so much with Peter and Paul, leaders for the inclusion of Gentiles. Their stories are cosmic and mine is totally local. But I do identify with the immense religious and cultural shift it signified then, with its inevitable controversies.

I have always thought of myself as a somewhat reluctant leader. I have not sought leadership, though it has sometimes been thrust on me. I became leader of our youth group at my home church, of the 4-H calf club in our community, chair of the board of directors of Canadian Mennonite Bible College, chair of the Leadership Commission of Mennonite Church Canada – all reluctantly.

Being an introvert, I am inclined to be publicly cautious. I tend to think things through before acting, and sometimes don't act quickly enough or courageously enough. As a pastor, I have been quite comfortable helping other people deal with conflict – but not so comfortable being at the centre of it myself. I did not see myself as a strong leader who could rally people to a vision.

So how was it that I, a cautious, reluctant leader, became embroiled in the story of the church struggling to include gays who are Christian, a story that had national implications across Mennonite Church Canada? But first I offer reflections on Peter's story.

Peter's Journey to Including Gentiles

My hunch is that Peter would also have been reluctant – maybe extremely reluctant – to think of himself as a leader championing the welcoming of Gentiles into the church.

Yes, we start with Peter: erratic, impetuous Peter, the disciple filled with bravado – and failure. Mark tells the story this way:

> And Jesus said to them, "You will all become deserters; for it is written, 'I will strike the shepherd, and the sheep will be scattered.'"

> … Peter said to him, "Even though all become deserters, I will not." Jesus said to him, "Truly I tell you, this day, this very night, before the cock crows twice, you will deny me three times." But he said vehemently, "Even though I must die with you, I will not deny you." And all of them said the same. (Mark 14:27–31)

We know how that story ends. Peter does deny Jesus – three times, in fact. The story might have ended with the last verse of Mark 14: "And he broke down and wept."

But the story doesn't end there – John completes this story. The resurrected Jesus offers a breakfast of fish to Peter. Reprising the three denials, Jesus asks Peter three times if he loves him. Peter responds, "You know that I love you." Jesus gently says, "Then feed my sheep" (John 21:15–17). The very fallible Peter, the one who denies Jesus to save his own skin, becomes a key pillar in the newly forming church. In one way, he is a "new" Peter, forgiven and empowered to be a leader of those who follow Jesus. But he is still limited by his strict Jewish world view and by his impetuous personality.

Acts 10 tells the story of another of Peter's many conversions. Tired after a long journey, he goes to a rooftop to pray, falls into a trance, and has a bizarre vision that challenges the very core of his religious upbringing. Before him is spread food from creatures that he has known from childhood are totally unclean and would make him unclean. He is told to eat. He protests, "By no means, Lord; for I have never eaten anything that is profane or unclean." But the voice responds, "What God has made clean, you must not call profane." This scene is repeated three times.

Finally, Peter is ready for his encounter with the Gentile Cornelius, the supposedly unclean other. At the house of this Gentile, Peter makes some astounding claims. He tells those assembled there, "You yourselves know that it is unlawful for a Jew to associate with or to visit a Gentile; but God has shown me that I should not call anyone profane or unclean."

Peter's next statement is even more radical. "I truly understand that God shows no partiality, but in every nation anyone who fears him and does what is right is acceptable to him." The Holy Spirit "fell upon all who heard the word," and Peter baptized all those gathered there. Peter was the leader who brought Jewish and Gentile believers in Jesus together into the same "church." And stirred up a hornet's nest of criticism and mess.

My Journey toward Including Homosexuals

As a youth, I fully accepted the sexual ethos and mores of my church and home upbringing. We didn't talk about sex – except maybe for "dirty" sex on the schoolyard. It was assumed you remained a virgin until you were married. Any girl who "accidentally" became pregnant before marriage was taken before the church and disciplined. If there was a contrite confession, the couple could retain church membership, though that did not silence the gossip. I had not even heard the word "homosexuality" and wouldn't have known what it meant had I heard it. I knew nothing about sexual abuse, though there were rumours going around in my home community about a father who was not always nice to his daughter.

It was as a pastor that I was confronted by stories of sexual abuse and the enormous damage that abuse caused. I didn't know how to respond adequately, though I listened sympathetically. I began to read about the issue, attended some workshops, looked for referral resources – and sometimes preached about it, naming the damage it caused.

I was much slower in addressing the pain that homosexual people experienced from both society and the church. I hadn't met any gay people – or so I thought. Mennonite gays probably realized that it was not safe for them to be open about their orientation in the church, and wouldn't have trusted me as pastor because I had never indicated that I was open to hear from them.

But reality eventually intruded. Christian homosexuals were coming out, and doing so in the church. I was beginning to hear their painful stories of exclusion. They claimed they were both gay and followers of Christ, and wanted and needed a church. At one point, I led a funeral service for a young man who had taken his own life and suddenly realized that his suicide had something to do with being gay and not being accepted.

I knew that I had to come to terms with how I as a pastor would respond to those who were gay, and how I would lead the church in response to gay people who wanted to be part of the church.

A young lesbian woman who had grown up in the church met with me to tell her story – and to confront me about what stance I would take toward her coming out to me. She told me she was distancing herself from the church. As I heard her story, I sympathized with her. I felt I could accept both her being lesbian and being a Christian. But I also knew that I hadn't done the theological and biblical work necessary to convincingly advocate for her to the church. I tried to explain this to her. I said that I still needed more time for my own processing of the larger question of how the church should deal with homosexuality. I was being honest, even if not particularly helpful or encouraging to her.

We did stay in touch. And I did struggle with what the Bible says about same-sex sexual activity. What, in the end, helped shape my much more inclusive stance? Two things: First, being a pastor and hearing the painful stories of a number of gay people. I know a lot of Christian gays who exemplify the spirit of Christ in their relationships and in the church. And yet they don't feel accepted by the church. Second, reading the Scriptures. I did not see in the Bible a uniform condemnation of homosexuality. The far deeper thread is a trajectory of inclusion (exemplified by the stories of Acts 10 and Isaiah 56).

Perhaps my "slippery slope" re-reading of Scripture began with feminism. As a theologian and scholar who used Scripture extensively in her work, Lydia helped me look at biblical stories in a new way. Women could not be pastors? Jesus chose women to tell the news of his resurrection to the men. While Paul says that women should be silent in church (1 Timothy 2:12–15), he then affirms the two women who are leaders in Philippians (4:2–3). The issue is more complex than a simple reading allows.

Maybe the same thing held true for what the Bible says about same-sex relationships. Maybe the church had not looked deeply enough at what the Scriptures say about sexuality in general and homosexuality in particular. The biblical story is far too complex and nuanced for us to simply look at the laws of what is clean and unclean in Leviticus and determine from them that homosexuality is an abomination.

It seemed to me that there were huge challenges resulting from the way the church had read the few texts in the Bible that deal with same-sex activity and from them inferred a biblical denunciation of being homosexual. But there were also challenges arising from the way people on the pro-acceptance side of this issue sometimes took the Scriptures too lightly.

Particular Challenges to Both Sides of the Debate

I tried, with Lydia's help, to list the challenges and complications that each side of the debate faced in how they used Scripture on this issue.

Challenges for those who affirm the acceptance of homosexuals

- Where the Bible mentions sexual acts between men, it is always portrayed as negative and prohibitive. The language used, especially in Leviticus, is that of "abomination." As far as I know sexual acts between women are not mentioned in the Bible.

- Nowhere in the Bible are same-sex covenants affirmed.

- The majority of Christians throughout history have read the Bible as condemning homosexual sex.

- It is difficult for us who are affirmative to be self-critical of our culture and to be aware of cultural influences that may predispose our stance and impact our understandings of sexuality.

Challenges facing those who have a more traditional understanding of homosexuality

- There are very few texts about same-sex activity in the Bible, so it may not have been an important theme for biblical writers to struggle with. The importance of any theme in the Bible can be traced by how often it is mentioned. For example, responding to the needs of the poor is mentioned countless times; homosexual acts only rarely.

- The traditional view is also culturally shaped (as is the biblical view). Our emotional investment in this question shows us that the traditional position is also influenced by our culture and upbringing.

- The texts that speak about men having sex with men do not seem to be speaking about committed covenantal relationships, but about abuse and lust and violence and control.

- Jesus is silent on the matter. We claim that Jesus is the centre of our faith and of our ethical understandings. It should give us some pause to make something Jesus doesn't mention into a defining criterion of acceptance in the church. Jesus seemed to have more important concerns – poverty, justice, peace, welcoming the stranger and the outsider, loving enemies ... Surely as followers of Jesus, we should take his Sermon on the Mount (Matthew 5–7) as a more important text than Leviticus 20, along with his heart-felt prayer for unity among all his follower (John 17).

- It is a challenge for the traditional view to offer Good News for homosexual people if they are excluded from the church and are not a part of the conversation and debate.

- What is it that can be named as sinful in a covenanted same-sex relationship?

What became clear to me was that both sides in the debate around this hot issue claimed to be biblical. Both sides referenced biblical texts and stories. Sometimes they interpreted the same texts differently. Sometimes they chose different texts to focus on. *But both sides were committed to following Scripture.*

I have a deep respect for all who base their convictions on Scripture, even if their interpretation is very different than is mine. I have less respect for those who are only parroting biases not based on thorough biblical work.

The Trajectory of Inclusion in the Bible

In the end, the "trajectory of inclusion" in the Bible (Isaiah 56, the example of Jesus, Acts 10, Galatians 3:28) was the tipping point for my "conversion" to a more affirming view. Isaiah offers a prime example in the Old Testament and Acts 15 in the New Testament.

Isaiah

Isaiah dares to include people in the community of faith whom Moses had specifically excluded. In Deuteronomy 23, Moses names categories of people who should be excluded from "the assembly of the Lord." These include those whose testicles are crushed or whose penis is cut off (eunuchs), those born of an illicit union, and, very specifically, Ammonites and Moabites.

Isaiah challenges these exclusions. He specifically names foreigners and eunuchs as people he will "bring to my holy mountain, and make them joyful in my house of prayer; ... Thus says the Lord God, who gathers the outcasts of Israel." The only stipulation for inclusion is that they keep the Sabbath and hold fast to God's covenant (Isaiah 56:1–8). And then Isaiah states what Jesus himself will later quote: "For my house shall be called a house of prayer for all peoples."

The story of Ruth is another example: a Moabite – a foreigner – who is excluded by Moses but later welcomed into our salvation story and is, astonishingly, named in the lineage of Jesus.

Jesus

All four Gospels tell story after story of Jesus inviting conversation with people the community shunned: Samaritan, foreigner, sinner, woman, tax collector, leper – you name it. Surely that is a huge message for those of us who are often tempted to limit our community.

All of these Scriptures and stories were part of my own conversion toward inclusion of Christian gays. Now the question for me was how I as a pastor would try to lead the church into inclusion. Our local story is small indeed. I want to look, first of all, at the far more momentous story of the Jerusalem conference. How did Peter and Paul try to lead the early Christians through conflict?

The Jerusalem Conference

Acts 15 tells the story of the conflict-ridden meeting of the early leaders struggling with the challenge of fully accepting Gentiles into the fellowship of the church. Luke, the writer of Acts, sets the stage for this conference.

> Then certain individuals came down from Judea and were teaching the brothers, "Unless you are circumcised according to the custom of Moses, you cannot be saved." And after Paul and Barnabas had no small dissension and debate with them, Paul and Barnabas and some of the others were appointed to go up to Jerusalem to discuss this question with the apostles and the elders. (Acts 15:1–2)

I chuckle over the language used: "no small dissension and debate." That meeting must have been very intense. Certainly, it was a huge turning point in the story of the church. Was the conflict resolved? Yes and no. They did come to a conclusion: The apostles and the elders, with the consent of the whole church, then sent leaders to Gentile converts with this message. "For it has seemed good to the Holy Spirit and to us to impose on you no further burden than these essentials: that you abstain from what has been sacrificed to idols and from blood and from what is strangled and from fornication" (28–29).

The trajectory of inclusion of Gentiles has been launched. There will be ongoing challenges to this inclusion, but it cannot be stopped. We are all one in Christ.

My Own Fallible Leadership

Unlike Peter's successful move to include Gentiles in the community of Jesus followers, my own attempt at leading TUMC toward inclusion seemed to end in failure.

The years 2002 and 2003 were very difficult for the congregation, for my associate pastor, and for me as pastor. My associate pastor told me that she had fallen in love with another woman. We knew that we had to process this development fully. Many in the congregation had traditional convictions about homosexuality, while many others were much more open to this new development. Given who our congregation was, we knew that we needed to develop a thorough process of discernment to help us find our way forward.

What should be my role as pastor in this process? I personally had come to a more inclusive position, and I had a deep appreciation and respect for my associate. But I was pastor to the whole congregation, including those who had a deep conviction that homosexual activity is condemned by the Bible. I could not use my pastoral power to silence those voices. Part of my challenge was to know when to explain my own convictions to the congregation. I was afraid that if I did so too soon, I would silence and perhaps alienate those who held a traditional view. If I waited too long, I could be accused of withholding pastoral insights that the debate needed – perhaps because I was a coward who feared conflict.

For the most part, our congregational leaders did an excellent job in planning and carrying out a study and discernment process that lasted well over a year. People chosen for committees to lead various aspects of the process came from all perspectives. As a congregation, we did very thorough biblical, theological, sociological, and psychological work. We planned to wrap up our process in a series of congregational decision-making meetings that June.

In April, I released a pastoral letter stating my personal convictions gained from my understanding of what the Bible says about sexuality.[14] All other voices had by then been heard. It was time to bring in my voice.

As expected, response to my pastoral letter was quite mixed, though generally there were expressions of appreciation for the fact that I had publicly stated my convictions. My stance did not really surprise anyone. Some thought I should have expressed my opinions much earlier. Some, of course, challenged my reading of the Bible and were angry that the pastor's words might "sway the vote."

And yet it seemed to me that the whole congregation was still accepting me as its pastor. My pastoral covenant with the congregation was not being questioned or challenged. Yes, some thought I had been too careful and too timid for too long in stating my convictions, and others totally disagreed with my way of reading the Scriptures on this issue, but somehow my covenant with the congregation was holding. I was still respected as pastor. Our long-term, mutual relationship of trust and accountability and love was still holding.

But this relationship would be tested once more as our congregation gathered in June to make a decision about my associate pastor's covenant with the church.

Decision-Making, Brokenness, and Healing

The congregation's final decision-making meeting that Saturday in June ended badly — and I'm not only referring to the decision we reached to release my associate pastor, a decision I disagreed with. We had wounded each other deeply. I felt that we had abandoned the Holy Spirit in our battle with each other — or

---

14 This statement is available from Toronto United Mennonite Church.

perhaps the Holy Spirit had abandoned us as we fought an unholy war with each other. We were very angry with each other. Harsh words were shouted on all sides. In all my years of ministry I had never felt as broken as I did that afternoon.

And then I was asked to close the meeting with prayer. And I couldn't. I confessed that I felt too broken inside to pray. The pastor couldn't even pray.

What I – and the congregation – realized in hindsight, I think, is that God was at work in our mess and our brokenness, even if we didn't recognize it at that time. But there was no quick fix, neither for me nor for the congregation. A few of the people I held dear decided to leave the congregation and did not come back for worship, though they stayed connected in other ways. Essentially, we held together as a congregation. In a rather deep sense it seemed that we knew that our worship of God through Jesus was a deeper value than was our agreement or disagreement about what we thought the Bible said about sexuality.

Some voices wondered whether I would, could, or should stay on as pastor. We were a broken congregation. I had failed in leading our church to a healthy outcome. We were divided, wounded, and feeling that we had failed God and each other. And yet I wasn't hearing God telling me to leave. Maybe a wounded congregation and a wounded pastor still needed each other.

Three public events each contributed to healing my wounds. The first of these was the opportunity to attend Mennonite World Conference in Bulawayo, Zimbabwe, in August 2003. This event, happening once every six years, was exactly what I needed: seven thousand people from around the world meeting together, worshipping together, and lifting the roof of our huge assembly hall in full-throated singing. Lydia and I had many wonderful opportunities to be together with people from Zimbabwe and from around the world. Over and over we sang together and shared stories. Many of the Zimbabwean stories were far more heartbreaking than our stories. We heard countless tellings of food shortages, of family members dying of AIDS, of political violence. And yet the Zimbabwean people sang with so much joy and so much power. We were hosted by a family in a small village a forty-five-minute bus ride from the conference site. The bus, packed with conference goers, we two the only whites, rocked with music, with leader-response singing the whole way. My spirit responded with joy.

A second public event that played a part in my healing journey was a lament service at our church that August. TUMC had established a healing and reconciliation team to help facilitate our communal healing journey. That team wisely initiated plans for a service of lament. The team heard from almost everyone in the congregation, gathered their expressions of pain and anger and disappointment, and created from that a litany of lament that became the centre of that morning's worship.

I dreaded that morning but knew that it was necessary for healing to happen. We needed to publicly express what was on our hearts – in worship. It was a huge release, both for the congregation and for me as pastor. One church member said after the service, "That was the worst worship service I have ever attended." There was a truth to that outburst. But I think that lament Sunday marked the beginning of a remarkable healing journey.

Earlier that morning, in my dread and in my prayer time, I wistfully prayed that God would spare us any visitors that morning. Why impose such a hard service on guests? Wouldn't it be a total turn-off? God answered my despairing prayer in another way. Two guests from the community came that morning. Later, both decided to become members of the church. They said a church that could be so open and honest and transparent was exactly the kind of community they needed and wanted to be a part of.

The third healing, public event was my retirement in 2007, four years later. Sunday afternoon was the last event of a full weekend of celebrations for me. I was officially retiring as pastor. The final moment of that final service was a prayer of blessing for Lydia and me, led by the conference pastor for Mennonite

Church of Eastern Canada, Muriel Bechtel. She invited everyone who wanted to come forward to lay hands on us. One of
the first to come forward was the person who had been most
angry with me during our process four years earlier. As he put
his hands on my shoulder I shed tears. Here was a public expression of reconciliation and forgiveness between us, expressed not
in words but in powerful symbol.

I also felt that forgiveness and reconciliation had happened
more broadly within the congregation. Relationships within
the congregation were in a totally different space than they had
been four years earlier. Our engagement with each other was so
much healthier now. Our crisis had made us look deeply within
ourselves. We were becoming a healthier congregation.

In reflecting on my own pastoral journey with the congregation through our crisis time, I think that the pastor-congregation relationship, built up over the years, helped see us through.
Despite everything – despite the anger and the disappointment,
and maybe even disillusionment – I think that the relationship
of trust and respect and love that had developed over the years
between pastor and congregation helped carry us through the
crisis. Nobody suggested I resign. Even those who were angry
with me wanted me to visit them when they were ill. My relationship with the congregation was never really threatened.

A covenantal relationship of trust between congregation and
pastor is a powerful thing.

A Local Story in the Context of the Wider Church

A local church story, when it includes something the wider
church considers controversial, does not stay local. During the
year that our church was wrestling with the issue of homosexuality, our story was drawing national attention. We had kept our
provincial body, Mennonite Church Eastern Canada (MCEC),

informed and involved in our process. MCEC had walked with us through it, offering both challenge and support. We wanted to be accountable to the wider church.

Some people in another provincial-area Mennonite conference were more deeply troubled by our story, by our open processing of the issue of homosexuality, and by my public stance of inclusion. They sent a small delegation to have conversations with us and to attend a worship service at TUMC. Following that, leaders of this area conference invited a return visit, asking me, along with two others from our church, to meet with their pastors and church leaders to "explain" ourselves.

Three of us, representing the diversity of opinion on this issue at TUMC, went. That weekend was both difficult and memorable for me. The day-long Saturday meeting with pastors and leaders was intense. The three of us tried to explain our process, our decision, our disagreements with each other, but also our respect for each other. Most of the questions and challenges were directed at me as the pastor. These leaders were at a very different place than I was in accepting gays in church. They could not understand how I could read the Bible in any other way than as a condemnation of homosexuality.

When the meeting ended – I think we were all exhausted – the woman on our team who represented the traditional side of the debate – the side these area leaders also embraced – came to me and gave me a big hug. We differ on this issue, but we respect each other deeply. Those leaders seemed stunned. How could we disagree with each other so openly, and still embrace each other with such respect?

There was also a very personal side to this visit. The meetings took place in the community where my mother lived, and she hosted me for that weekend. Of course, she knew why I was there and what the reception might be like in her much more conservative community and church. She was eager to hear our story from me personally. And she wanted to hear how I read the Bible on this issue and how I had come to my position. We had a wonderful evening together. And then my mother, in her late eighties, burst out – "Gary, I so wish that our pastors could really hear you explain these things. They need to be open to how you read the Bible."

Mennonite Church Eastern Canada

The provincial conference body, MCEC, was also processing the question of gay inclusion in the church. TUMC's story was only one of a number of stories that needed attention. It was a church-wide issue.

MCEC organized a weekend pastors' retreat devoted to studying what the Bible says about same-sex activity, and how the church could respond to gay people wanting to be accepted by the church. Two of us pastors were asked to be resource people. It happened that both of us had "Gary" as our first name. The other Gary read a paper representing a traditional reading of the Bible. This Gary then read a paper outlining a more inclusive reading of the Bible.[15]

Several things remain important to me about that retreat. One was the very respectful and attentive listening, and then engagement, with each other. We were all wrestling deeply with Scripture. Perhaps it made a difference that the other Gary and I respect each other personally and can each affirm the other. This may have helped set the stage for the discussion.

When the official part of the retreat was over, three older, retired pastors sought me out. They told me how much they appreciated the whole discussion, including my paper. They told me they were holding to the traditional view but that they now could see, and respect, another way of reading the Bible on this

---

15 Both papers (dated Fall 2003) are available from Mennonite Church Eastern Canada.

issue. They said that they were so grateful for this dialogue. We shook hands with tears in our eyes. It may be that retreats like this (and other, much more public events with other resource people) have helped MCEC congregations process the question of inclusion in generally more respectful and less hostile ways.

And yet, the church will probably never be free of conflict.

Conflict in the Early Church

It shouldn't surprise us that church conflict has been a reality throughout the history of the church – including in the New Testament period. The Jew-Gentile issue will resurface in the early church, as conflict is inclined to do. And soon the leaders themselves will be in conflict. By the end of Acts 15, Paul and Barnabas will part ways because they are angry with each other.

> Barnabas wanted to take with them John called Mark. But Paul decided not to take with them one who had deserted them in Pamphylia [Acts 13:13] and had not accompanied them in the work. The disagreement became so sharp that they parted company; Barnabas took Mark with him and sailed away to Cyprus. But Paul chose Silas and set out, the believers commending him to the grace of the Lord. (Acts 15:37–40)

Was Paul perhaps a bit hasty in his dismissal of a young John Mark, who still had some maturing to do? These leaders of the church are still very human, very fallible, and still find themselves in conflict. Even Peter and Paul will get angry with each other. In Galatians 2, Paul tears a strip off Peter:

> But when Cephas [Peter] came to Antioch, I [Paul]
> opposed him to his face, because he stood self-con-
> demned; for until certain people came from James,
> he used to eat with the Gentiles. But after they came,
> he drew back and kept himself separate for fear of
> the circumcision faction. And the other Jews joined
> him in this hypocrisy, so that even Barnabas was led
> astray by their hypocrisy. (Galatians 2:11–13)

Perhaps Peter was pulling back a bit from his amazing inclu-
sionary vision and speech of Acts 10. The pressures on him
would have been enormous, and he, like all of us leaders, was
undoubtedly susceptible to such pressure. But is Paul's hugely
confrontational stance the best way for leaders in the wider
church to work out their differences?

The stories of the early church and its first leaders remind
us that God calls very human and fallible leaders to lead a
very human and fallible church. The leaders break out of their
restrictive world views and religious upbringing to forge a new
peoplehood of God following Jesus. Surely God uses them and
blesses their work in astounding ways. But they are still bound
by, and limited by, their personalities and their biases.

In 1 Peter, the writer offers an inspiring affirmation to the
church: "But you are a chosen race, a royal priesthood, a holy
nation, God's own people, in order that you may proclaim the
mighty acts of him who called you out of darkness into his marvelous light" (1 Peter 2:9). But from our perspective and world
view today, we may be troubled by the acceptance of societal
norms that Peter goes on to advocate. Accept the authority of
every human institution? Honour the emperor? Slaves accept
the authority of their masters with all deference? Wives accept
the authority of their husbands? (1 Peter 2:13–21).

We are never fully free from the world views we live in, no
matter how committed we are to God's world view as revealed
in Jesus.

Other Leadership Conflicts

The church in Corinth is a prime example of leadership disagreements that probably contributed to more substantive conflict. It is clear from chapter one of 1 Corinthians that the major leaders of the church are in conflict with each other and are creating factions to get support. Paul writes,

> It has been reported to me by Chloe's people that there are quarrels among you, my brothers and sisters. What I mean is that each of you says, "I belong to Paul," or "I belong to Apollos," or "I belong to Cephas," or "I belong to Christ." Has Christ been divided? (1 Corinthians 1:11–13)

Later in this first letter to the Corinthian church, Paul will spend a number of chapters addressing disagreements regarding worship, what we might compare to the "worship wars" going on today in the church. First of all, Paul addresses the issue of the divisions created by how the Corinthians observed communion. Apparently, their practice accentuated the social divisions between rich and poor (1 Corinthians 11:17–33).

The other division created by worship likes and dislikes was between those who were more "charismatic" and those who were more "rational." Paul spends three whole chapters (1 Corinthians 12–14) trying to help the Corinthian church sort this out. In the end, he says that they urgently need each other in the "body" of Christ (chap. 12), that the most important gift of all is love (chap. 13), and that both "spirit and the mind" are important in worship (chap. 14).

The New Testament stories of church divisions and friction among leaders remind us that conflict is normal – even in the body of Christ. The stories also remind us that church leaders sometimes help resolve conflict in healthy ways, and sometimes contribute to the conflict. It is part of being human.

Like Peter and Paul, we too are products of our time and culture. We try to follow Jesus, to be faithful to his teachings and his example. But like the early church leaders, we too are limited by our own world views and our own cultural accommodation. And yet God works in us and through us – or in spite of us.

We hear a lot of comments about a "messy" church today, as if the church's being in a "mess" is a contemporary issue or insight. From its very beginnings, the story of the church has been messy. And the church's leaders, including heroes of faith like Peter and Paul, have sometimes contributed to the messiness.

The church and its leaders are always, first of all, human. The church, from its very beginnings and throughout its history, has always been in a mess. There is no such a thing as an ideal church. Some of its leaders have made an enormous contribution to the growth of the body of Christ. But all of them seemed to also have a dark side.

And yet – and yet it is Christ's church. And yet it is a place of Good News. And yet we leaders try to be faithful to Christ, and mostly are. And yet we have the awesome privilege of helping people pay attention to God's love for them.

I conclude with a quote from Eugene Peterson:

> The Biblical fact is that there are no successful churches. There are, instead, communities of sinners, gathered before God each week in towns and villages all over the world. The Holy Spirit gathers them and does [her] work in them. In these communities of sinners, one of them is called pastor and given responsibility in the community. The pastor's responsibility is to keep the community attentive to God.[16]

We all need continuous conversion to God's way and God's love.

---

16 Eugene Peterson, *Working the Angles: The Shape of Pastoral Integrity* (Grand Rapids, MI: Wm. B. Eerdmans, 1989), p. 2.

INTERLUDE
Through the Disorientation

August 24, 2003

A sermon preached on our "lament" Sunday at
Toronto United Mennonite Church.

The Psalms are so honest, so real. All human emotions are named. The Psalms cut through all the layers of anesthetized greyness. They cut through the shallowness and the denial and the trivialization and the self-deception that we humans throw up as shields for self-protection. They cut to the core of our life's experience, and do so without the benefit of anesthesia. In them we feel pain at the depths. In them we feel exultation at the heights of celebration.

The Psalms go deep, and they go high. In them the poets express great candour and pain and passion and joy. In them God meets the community and the individual in the middle of untamed darkness and despair. In them God is present in surprising moments of celebration.

Walter Brueggemann writes about three kinds of psalms, reflecting on three stages of our human experience.[17]

---

17 Walter Brueggemann, *The Message of the Psalms: A Theological Commentary* (Minneapolis: Augsburg Publishing House, 1984).

1. Psalms of Orientation

These are psalms with a satisfied sense of well-being. These psalms articulate the simple joy and delight in the goodness and reliability of God. Life is good. God's creation is wonderful. Many of these psalms are in fact hymns to creation. They express a confident, serene settlement of faith issues. Doubt is far away. God is known to be trustworthy and generous. Life is well-ordered. Fear is absent. Thanksgiving is the normal expression of gratefulness for the good life.

"The Lord is my shepherd, I shall not want ... even though I walk through the shadow of death I fear no evil" (Psalm 23). It is a wonderful psalm of a satisfied confidence and faith in God.

2. Psalms of Disorientation

Life does not stay in that satisfied state of well-being. At some point for each of us life gets disoriented, gets thrown off the nice track. We are faced with crisis. There are many psalms of disorientation: psalms of life in crisis, in pain, in doubt, psalms where the poet is struggling with the absence of God. There is in them a language of entering the darkness. They are psalms for a season of anguished hurt.

Human life does enter seasons of hurt, alienation, suffering, and death. Then language of rage, resentment, self-pity, even hatred, is blurted out. These psalms offer abrasive speeches of lament. The old, the familiar, the safe, the secure way is threatened or even dismantled. It is so "biblical" to challenge God then. And so Christian. A lost job. A broken relationship. A medical diagnosis. The death of a loved one. A marriage runs into a rough patch, as all marriages do. A congregation comes into crisis.

Psalm 13 is a personal psalm of lament. Blame is fixed firmly on God:

How long, O Lord? Will you forget me forever?
How long will you hide your face from me? How
long must I bear pain in my soul, and have sorrow in
my heart all day long? How long shall my enemy be
exalted over me?

Consider and answer me, O Lord my God! Give
light to my eyes, or I will sleep the sleep of death,
and my enemy will say, "I have prevailed"; my foes
will rejoice because I am shaken.

But I trusted in your steadfast love; my heart shall
rejoice in your salvation. I will sing to the Lord,
because he has dealt bountifully with me.

This psalm ends with a hint of praise. Memory of the past
gives some hope that the psalmist will be able to rejoice – in the
future, if not now. But not now. Now it is time for lament, for
accusation, for blaming God.

Psalm 13 is one of the tamer psalms of disorientation. Some
of them become almost scandalous and offensive in their anger.
Some lash out in fury against God and against their enemies,
wishing them awful deaths.

3. Psalms of New Orientation – A Surprising Breakthrough of Joy

Deep loss. And then amazing gift. God is surprisingly present. A
new thing happens. Joy breaks through the despair. Where there
has been only darkness, there is now light. God has intervened.
Life is again full of delight, amazement, wonder, awe, gratitude,
and thanksgiving. A rescue, a deliverance, a saving, a healing,
a reconciliation. There is again a joyous assertion that God is
indeed present and active, just when we had lost hope.

You have turned my mourning into dancing; you
have taken off my sackcloth and clothed me with
joy, so that my soul may praise you and not be silent.
O Lord my God, I will give thanks to you forever.
(Psalm 30:11–12).

There is a whole new orientation. It is not a return to the
old, stable one. It is not a return to the way things were. This
is no going back. Rather, God brings a newness that can't be
explained, or predicted, or programmed – it can only be confessed and testified to.

A depression suddenly lifts. Grief and mourning do turn to
a new gladness. A relationship is restored. A pain-filled healing
journey from abuse brings an awareness of wholeness that
feels miraculous.

Our Present Disorientation Here at TUMC

On this, our lament Sunday, I want to adapt this framework to
our story as a congregation, and to my story as your pastor. I
want to speak here for myself – both for myself personally and
as a pastor. This may also be your experience.

I have publicly expressed my "broken pastor's heart" over our
decision making on June 21. I acknowledged, while trying to
make a closing to that meeting, that my heart was broken and
that I felt immobilized as a pastor, so immobilized that I couldn't
even pray publicly to end the meeting. The next day, Sunday,
during my pastoral prayer, I felt the same heaviness, and prayed
for our broken congregation. The congregational meeting on
June 21 was the most difficult and painful of my entire life. I was
more disoriented as a pastor then I have ever been before. I will
try to explain my brokenness and my disorientation.

Disorientation always comes as a rude interruption of a previous orientation. For me it was a disruption of my belief that we had engaged in a very good and healthy process till our last two congregational meetings. We had, in my opinion, deepened enormously our understanding of some of the issues around human sexuality, including homosexuality. We had wrestled seriously and deeply with the Scriptures. We had explored our understanding of sexual ethics for all Christians. And we had struggled with what it means to be the church of Jesus Christ when we disagree fundamentally with each other about deeply held convictions of faith. We have, in my opinion, developed a very helpful Statement of Beliefs around human sexuality.

In the face of that, there were for me two particular sources of disorientation. The first was the decision to discontinue our covenant with my associate pastor. I do accept that decision. I do accept the will of the congregation. But I am aware of a lot of grief within me about that decision.

For most of my professional life I have been a solo pastor. When my associate joined me four years ago I was thrilled with this colleague-ship. I have immensely valued having a co-pastor. Our weekly staff meetings, always including a time of prayer together, were a very important part of my work week. I have experienced her as a deeply spiritual person who has a very rich and profound prayer life. I grieve deeply the lost of a trusted, loved colleague and co-pastor.

The second disorientation for me was the breakdown of what I feel had been a very dialogical and respectful congregational process until then. When it came to decision making time for our congregation, we couldn't maintain our open engagement with each other. In the end, we hurt each other in the way we processed the final decision. I personally felt despondent and depressed by mid-morning of June 21, long before any decisions were made. The tone of that day had early on become that of a win-lose battle rather than a common search for possible solutions, including the need for compromise on all sides. We started battling politically and were no longer searching for the Spirit of God to guide us.

I feel I failed you, the congregation, as pastoral leader. I was not able to advise our leaders wisely about how to interrupt our suddenly dysfunctional process. I did not give adequate pastoral care to those leaders who also were, and are, hurting. I did not give enough personal support to my associate pastor.

I continue to have full respect for deeply held personal convictions, especially when they are grounded in a personal understanding of Scripture. On this issue, it is clear that we are polarized. We hold very deep convictions on both sides of acceptance and non-acceptance of same-sex covenants. For both sides, these convictions are rooted in our reading of, and understanding of, the Bible. They are rooted in how we understand the Gospel of Jesus Christ. I have a deep respect for these convictions. I have a full respect for both a "no" vote and a "yes" vote.

But I was deeply disappointed in the way we exercised our franchise. When it came to crunch time, it seemed to me we began to fight in hurtful ways.

Additional Issues for Me

My general orientation is to trust people easily and expect to be trusted in turn. I am inclined to see the best in people sooner than the worst. I tend to take people at face value and believe what people say. I am inclined to optimism. My disorientation is that some people have lost trust in me as a pastor. There has been some suspicion of me as a pastor – comments about "a fixed outcome," for example. I struggle with the mistrust that some people have of me as a pastor. It feels as if the open, honest, free, face-to-face easy acceptance between me and some people has been broken.

My general orientation as a pastor is not to be afraid of differences of opinion and differences of conviction. It is to welcome them and name them and bring them into the open so that we can search together for deeper truth as these are shared, respected, and debated. My disorientation is that in the end our dialogue broke down, and we weren't able to respect each other's convictions. In my disorientation, I felt angry and dispirited and depressed; empty of energy and enthusiasm.

Reorientation

What then about reorientation? Will the psalms of reorientation ring true for us? Probably it is still too early for us as a church to know a full reorientation. We will need to trust that it will yet come.

Psalm 13 helps me to have this hope: "But I trusted in your steadfast love; my heart shall rejoice in your salvation. I will sing to the Lord, because he has dealt bountifully with me." The Psalmist is looking into the future with confidence and hope. So will I. So will you.

The church is not my church. It is not our church. It is Christ's church. Like every church of Christ, TUMC is very human, and now quite broken. It is also now less arrogant, quite deflated and humbled – along with its pastor.

But God has not left us. Some of us may be angry with each other, and perhaps also with God, but that doesn't cause God to leave.

For me personally, my experience at the Mennonite World Conference held in Zimbabwe started me on a journey of reorientation. There were some seven thousand people, more or less, four out of five of us black in colour, who gathered from around the world. We shared an amazing diversity – in colour, race, and culture; in how we worship – in music, in praying, in expressing our faith; in how we deal with ethical issues. When have we in North America had to deal with whether the second or third wife in a polygamous relationship could become a church member?

There are so many reasons why Mennonite World Conference should not work. But there we were, an incredibly unified, happy gathering of brothers and sisters in Christ. There was an amazing acceptance and closeness – an embracing of each other. The worship was powerful and wonderful. Energy and life flowed everywhere. The Spirit of God was much in evidence.

In the "assembly scattered," held two days after arriving in Zimbabwe, and before the formal assembly sessions began, we stayed at the Matopo Brethren in Christ mission station. There they have a large Christian high school. A wonderful girls' choir had stayed behind during school break to both guide us for a few days and to sing for us and with us, over and over again. One time, during our worship, we were asked why we had come to their country to experience Mennonite World Conference. Many answers came pouring out. At one point I said, "I have had a very difficult year. I have come to have my soul filled." And filled it was – to overflowing.

Maybe in the end, reorientation has to do with letting God fill our souls in a new way. May this lament Sunday help open our lives to God's healing.

POSTLUDE
WHEN THE MUSIC STOPS

Does retirement end one's calling? Am I still a pastor now that I am fully retired from pastoral work? Is being a pastor still a part of my identity, or is it fully severed from who I now am? I was a pastor who loved his calling. I keep on getting introduced as a "former pastor," mostly, I like to think, with respect. Who am I now?

At this point I feel comfortable with my status as "former pastor." I am quite happily retired. I feel no urge to fix things in my home congregation. I enjoy the sense of being cared for by my church community rather than being responsible for that church community.

But my present pastor asked me an important question as she offered me pastoral care: "What gifts do you as a retired pastor have to offer our church and the wider church?" The question assumes that I still have some gifts that could be useful, and that God's calling in my life didn't end the moment I stopped getting paid for what I did. I am still a child of God who has some purpose in life besides just passing time until I die. My pastor's question assumes that callings and gifts don't die on the vine when not nurtured by a salary.

But what is that purpose now, and what gifts can I still offer without interfering where I shouldn't interfere?

I find it a bit easier to think of an ongoing calling from God and using what gifts I might still have in serving the wider church. I occasionally get invited to preach in area churches. I mentor some other pastors, either through a formal mentoring structure or, more frequently, informally when pastors seek my advice. There have been a number of occasions when I, and sometimes Lydia and I together, have been invited into intensive and extensive conversations with pastors and other leaders around difficult congregational discernment issues. We enjoy this and feel that our experience – and our gifts – may have some value here.

I am not as afraid of conflict in the church as I once was. I am not as afraid of listening to counter-voices, or of naming as honestly as I know how what my convictions and perspectives are, even when there is resistance to them. I have experienced the resolutions and the healing that comes when you create a safe atmosphere for deep engagement. I can encourage pastors and other leaders to be both sensitive and courageous in inviting needed conversations around contentious issues.

I am still convinced that the key to effective pastoral ministry is the quality of the relationship between pastor and congregation. I like to think of this relationship in covenantal terms. I am aware that the Bible uses covenant language primarily in describing the relationship between God and God's people, and surely in that relationship there is a power imbalance. We humans are not on an equal footing with God. But covenant language speaks of a loving, reciprocal relationship. It speaks of mutual expectations and of regularly reviewing and renewing that relationship and that commitment to each other, especially when we humans have failed to live up to it.

I like to think that the relationship between congregation and pastor is, at best, a mutually supportive, mutually enriching one. It seems to me that the process in the Mennonite church of calling a pastor, and of ordaining, licensing, and blessing a pastor are done within an understanding of a covenant-like relationship. There is a mutuality and respect and relational understanding built into our polity. The expectation is that there will be a mutual and accountable relationship that includes the wider church, the local congregation, and the pastor.

A healthy relationship between congregation and pastor is much more than simply being nice to each other. It includes, and doesn't preclude, truth telling, challenging each other, holding each other accountable, and being ready to work through conflict. These things are most possible when negotiated within the framework of an honest, respectful, and love-filled relationship.

Perhaps one of the gifts I can still offer the church is to encourage this kind of relationship. My hope is that this book will offer such encouragement – and challenge. My hope is that the testimony shared here – a testimony of how much I have valued my calling, and have embraced the churches that invited me to live out this calling among them – will encourage younger pastors to join me in metaphorically singing the life-giving ministry duet with the congregations that call them. I hope it will encourage lay people to pay attention to the relationship between pastor and congregation. The church too needs to reflect on what gifts it can offer the pastor, both from individual members and as a congregation.

What gift(s) can I offer my home congregation, where I used to be the pastor? I am still trying to sort that through. I feel very comfortable, at this point, in being a lay member of the church and being nurtured by our worship and our fellowship. I preach very occasionally but am not ready to be involved in any official way. I am presently serving on our summer student support committee, which I thoroughly enjoy doing. With full retirement I have switched from leadership to followership, from being on the front lines to being behind the scenes. When invited, I may sometimes have some wisdom, gained from experience, to offer. I hope to always be a supporter, an encourager, a cheerleader for the leaders, and an enthusiastic lay person who visibly shows that he loves the church.

Lydia and I no longer spend much time in public ministry. But we really enjoy inviting people into our home. Recently we have hosted dinners for friends and for newcomers to the church. In each case, it seemed that the conversation went into deep places. Lydia is particularly good at initiating these conversations. It may be that one of the biggest contributions we can make in our continuing retirement is to offer hospitality – unofficial hospitality.

The reality is that the official music does stop, and the employment duet does end. All formal ministries do. Hopefully these end with a healthy transfer of pastoral leadership – healthy for both pastor and congregation. And hopefully retirement will also feel like a blessing from God, a new stage for living as a child of God.

God's music will never end.

ABOUT THE AUTHOR

 In a time of shifting worldviews and chang-
ing expectations of the church, how does a
pastor navigate the challenges, joys, and pains
of ministry? How does a church support, love,
and hold accountable its pastoral leaders? The
key lies in the relationship between pastor and
congregation – in the duet they are singing,
in the rhythms of their life together.

In this book, Gary Harder reflects on the difficulties and
rewards, the missteps and humour that are part of learning that
ministry duet. Here he celebrates the mysterious ways God
works through, and sometimes in spite of, the people singing
God's songs together. We reach for harmony. We hear dissonant
notes. We catch only a glimpse of God's beautiful music. And
that is enough.

CPSIA information can be obtained
at www.ICGtesting.com
Printed in the USA
LVHW11s0114141018
593454LV00001B/1/P